falling up

Hay House Titles of Related Interest

falling up

my wild ride
from victim to
kick-ass victory

DANA LIESEGANG
with Natasha Stoynoff

HAY
HOUSE

HAY HOUSE, INC.

Carlsbad, California • New York City
London • Sydney • Johannesburg
Vancouver • Hong Kong • New Delhi

Published and distributed in the United States by: Hay House, Inc.: www.hay house.com® • *Published and distributed in Australia by:* Hay House Australia Pty. Ltd.: www.hayhouse.com.au • *Published and distributed in the United Kingdom by:* Hay House UK, Ltd.: www.hayhouse.co.uk • *Published and distributed in the Republic of South Africa by:* Hay House SA (Pty), Ltd.: www .hayhouse.co.za • *Distributed in Canada by:* Raincoast Books: www.raincoast .com • *Published in India by:* Hay House Publishers India: www.hayhouse.co.in

Cover design: Tricia Breidenthal • *Interior design:* Pamela Homan
Interior photos: Courtesy of the author, except where noted

Library of Congress Cataloging-in-Publication Data

Liesegang, Dana, date.
  Falling up : my wild ride from victim to kick-ass victory / Dana Liesegang with Natasha Stoynoff.
     pages cm
  ISBN 978-1-4019-4634-0 (hardback)
  1. Self-actualization (Psychology) I. Stoynoff, Natasha. II. Title.
  BF637.S4L534 2015
  973.928092--dc23
  [B]
                                          2015016567

Hardcover ISBN: 978-1-4019-4634-0

10 9 8 7 6 5 4 3 2 1
1st edition, November 2015

Printed in the United States of America

To all the women and men
who have been sexually assaulted,
silenced, and blamed,
it is not your fault.

And to Jack, the love of my life.

CONTENTS

FOREWORD

I know that the seemingly impossible in life is, in fact, very possible. I've had miracle upon miracle happen for me personally, and have observed them showing up for others many times.

I was introduced to Dana Liesegang on a cruise to Australia a few years ago. My daughter Serena and I met her in the gym, and then Serena saw Dana later on, dancing and really enjoying herself. My daughter was struck by the fact that Dana was in a wheelchair and seemed to be having such a great time. She invited Dana to have dinner with us, and thus began a beautiful friendship between us. I learned all about what had happened to put Dana in that wheelchair, as well as the journey of self-improvement that had led her first to my books and then to seeing me in person. As you will read in these pages, it is an absolutely phenomenal, amazing story of courage and survival and sheer determination.

Although doctors had given her no chance for a life beyond that of a wheelchair-bound quadriplegic, Dana gave herself the goal of walking again. She set the intention, and repeated the affirmation: *I am walking.* She worked incredibly hard on her physical training, but when we first met, there was one piece missing: forgiveness.

I have spoken many times over the years about the power of forgiveness, particularly with respect to what happened on August 30, 1974, at the grave site of my father. For years, I had been filled with rage at this man who had abandoned my mother, my two older brothers, and me (I was just an infant at the time). I had been so resentful of him for so long that my first impulse was to urinate on his grave. But then in one Divine moment, I was able to send love where hatred and bitterness had previously resided. That forgiveness changed my life, and ultimately caused me to call my father "my greatest teacher."

Similarly, Dana learned to forgive the person and circumstances that had put her in that wheelchair. She learned the truth of what I often say: *When you change the way you look at things, the things you look at change.* That that's not just a clever play on words; it's really a quantum truth. At a quantum level, we know that the nature of the universe is that whatever we're observing changes depending on how we observe it. Dana found that there is a correlation between forgiveness and healing, and her life improved immeasurably.

Dana Liesegang reached that goal she had set for herself: In front of an astonished crowd at one of my lectures, she made her way to the stage from the back of the room—using a walker, not a wheelchair. As I watched this true inspiration experience the power of her intention, I just had to sing what I thought was a most appropriate song: "The Impossible Dream," from *The Man of La Mancha.* Dana had shown everyone in that audience that there really is no such thing as the impossible.

As Dana then took several unaided steps into my arms, I told her, "You said that you would do it, and indeed you did . . . you are one of my heroes." As time passes, she is getting even stronger physically— but she's also learning to recapture the light within herself that had remained darkened for so many years. It has been a tremendous joy to witness.

I absolutely love this girl, and I love this book. I know you will, too.

I AM,
Dr. Wayne W. Dyer

PREFACE

I write this memoir with much love in my heart for all of the people—family, friends, and strangers—who have crossed my path in the past, who are with me now in the present, and who will appear or continue to be by my side into the future.

My memories are based upon actual people, conversations, impressions, and events in my life to the very best of my recollection. Although they are my truth, they may not be the same truth as someone else's. I share them here to further my own emotional healing and, hopefully, to help others embark on their own healing paths.

Many names have been changed, and certain characters are composites. Some dates are my best guesses, as chronology is not always easy for someone who has suffered a head injury. And while I discuss medical diagnoses, symptoms, and remedies in this book, please be mindful that I am not a medical doctor.

To face the truth of one's past can be difficult, but to stay in a state of fear and denial keeps a person from moving forward and truly living. To me, sharing truth is the ultimate expression of love and hope for a better today and tomorrow.

PART I

Before the Fall

CHAPTER 1

A River Runs Through It

From the moment I could walk, I didn't stop moving.

Growing up in the tiny, remote community of Three Lynx, Oregon, I was running out the back door of our red house by age three. I wanted to see the world as far and as fast as my strong little legs would take me.

We lived 50 miles southeast of Portland in Clackamas County, in what people might have called a one-horse town, except all we had was one school and one paved road. Although there were several houses, the town didn't have a grocery store, a coffee shop, or even a stoplight.

Local folklore has it that our town got its name when early settlers were building a hydro pipeline. One day, the story goes, some loggers were clearing trees at dusk and saw three jet-black lynx sprint past and disappear, their bright eyes flashing. I never knew if the story was true or not, but I believed it as a kid. Even so, I wasn't afraid of a wildcat jumping out at me from the forest—it took a lot to make me afraid. The sign someone had put up on the back roads warning to Beware of Bigfoot did the trick, though.

Our home was on top of a hill, the first of 19 clapboard houses dotting the mountainside and tinted the colors of freshly dipped Easter eggs. Ours was red and the Walts' was orange and the Lincolns' was cream like the inside of a Cadbury Creme Egg. The Bootons four doors away had a gray house, like my dad's silver 1979 Dodge pickup truck.

The nearest grocery store was 21 miles away in Estacada (they had a stoplight, too). As a kid growing up in Three Lynx, you had to be resourceful when you needed a junk-food fix. You had to use your wits. If you showed up at the Lincolns' back door with a quarter, Mrs. Lincoln would be willing to sell you some of her surplus "black market" candy that she kept on a shelf in the basement. As you waited by the door, down the stairs she'd go to her stash of Kit Kats, Big Hunks, and Baby Ruths.

One winter the snow was so heavy and the roads so icy that no one could drive, and the snow came up to my chest. For a week, Portland General Electric—for whom most of the adults in our community worked—helicoptered food in to us. Yet however inconvenient Three Lynx was location-wise, it made up for it in its splendor.

Our enclave was surrounded by miles of wild, dense forest in every direction—a wonderland of overgrown pine trees that were part of Mt. Hood National Forest. Clackamas Creek snaked its way from the top of the mountain to the bottom, reaching the Clackamas River, where Native Americans had fished and settled some 10,000 years earlier.

If you looked down at us from up above, and you were the kind who believed in a curious Creator with a sense of humor, you'd think that God had pressed a cookie cutter into the green wilderness, lifted out a chunk of greenery from the mountainside, and thought, *Hey, let's put some people in here and see what happens.*

In the summer of 1974, when I was an equally curious three-year-old looking for adventure, my universe consisted of the 300 feet surrounding our home—a soft playground of backyards and laid-back, hippie adults and their barefoot kids.

Every morning right after *Sesame Street,* I'd scoop up my ragged bear, Teddy, and call out to my orange cat, Gabriel. "C'mon, Gabe!"

With my thumb in my mouth, the three of us would hit the dirt path. My mother, Melodie, knew my itinerary, and would be watching from the window as I went on my rounds. She wasn't worried, since she knew exactly where I was going and that I'd be okay. Our little community was the last gasp of it-takes-a-village "commune" living in the days of peace and love, and the residents of Three Lynx looked out for each other like one big family. Mom was also very big on teaching my two siblings and me to be independent and unafraid. Under her free-spirited philosophy, I felt that the world was a welcoming place with loving people and that I could take care of myself.

My rounds began at the Bifords' baby-blue house. Gabe would wait on the porch as I opened their front door. "Hi, Miss Dana," Mrs. Biford would say. "Come right in."

On the kitchen table, milk and cookies would be waiting. I'd hop up on a chair, put Teddy on my lap, and have a gab session with Mrs. Biford while dunking my cookies. From a very young age, I loved to talk to people, and when I got older, my mom nicknamed me "Chatterbox." I'd tell Mrs. Biford about what adventures Gabe and I had been on and what I'd seen on *Sesame Street* that morning. Fifteen minutes later, I'd be out her back door and on to the next stop—the Lincoln house, where I'd dunk, chat, and repeat.

I would make my way down the road—our street had no name— and wind my way back, hitting almost every home along the way. My social rounds netted me at least a dozen cookies, a food group that was a rarity in our home. Anything with that evil processed white sugar, like Kool-Aid, was contraband. When we kids wanted a snack, Mom told us to pick an apple off a tree or grab a handful of blackberries from a neighbor's bush. Most yards overflowed with fruit, and we all shared.

During my rounds, the neighbors would telephone Mom with a running commentary from each location: "Melodie, Dana's here having her cookies," or, "She's on her way to so-and-so's house now . . ."

By the time I circled back and reached Mrs. Booton's gray house, I'd need a bathroom break. I'd sit on the Booton toilet and try to sing a song I heard on the car radio—Donovan's "Mellow Yellow," which I was sure was about peeing.

Da da da da da . . . Mellow Yellow . . . that's right . . .

Using her rotary phone with the extra-long extension cord, Mrs. Booton would stretch the receiver from the kitchen and hold it up to the bathroom door so Mom could hear.

My social adventures would take over an hour. When I'd get home, I'd knock on our front door and pretend I wasn't me. Mom always played along.

"Hello there! How are you today?" she'd ask.

"Hi. I'm Jack," I'd say, "and this here's my dog, Crackers." I'd point to an empty spot on the ground, in between Gabe and me. "I'm a trucker!"

"Well, come on in, Jack and Crackers!"

I got my sunny disposition and imagination from my mother, who had cultivated both for survival purposes while growing up with five brothers in a God-fearing family in Estacada. In 1974 Mom was only 24 but already had three kids and one divorce, and was on to her second husband, Ken. He was a laid-back guy, and the major dad influence in my life for my first several years.

Mom looked like she'd stepped off the cover of a folk-music record—she was a petite beauty with long, Cher-like hair to her waist, doe eyes, beaded headbands, and flowing skirts. At bedtime, she'd read us tales about dragons and dwarves, and heroes and warriors, using stories like J.R.R. Tolkien's *The Hobbit* to teach us important life lessons.

ACROSS A FIELD BESIDE OUR HOUSE STOOD Three Lynx School, a white building with three classrooms for three dozen kids. The adults in our community worked at one of two places: either up at the school or down the hill at Portland General Electric. That's where Ken worked—he was a hydroelectric operator, and it was also his job to check the pH levels of the water and make sure it was safe to drink. He used to say we had the best drinking water in the world, as it was pure snowmelt from Mt. Hood.

Every afternoon at 4 P.M., a loud whistle blew from the megaphones near town. It was the signal for the men to come up the river or from the plant and gather at their crew quarters, get debriefed, and have a beer. For the kids playing outside, it meant that it was time to head home before your dad got there and dinner was ready.

When I started kindergarten in September '76, my brother, Gary, who's five years older than me, was going into fourth grade. Even though he wasn't the oldest at school, he was the coolest, the one everyone looked up to—Gary was what we called "Top Dog." He was born with confidence, charisma, and a swagger that said he was the leader of any pack. He was our school's version of Fonzie from *Happy Days* or Vinnie Barbarino from *Welcome Back, Kotter.*

Gary was my best buddy, my hero, and my role model; I wanted to be just like him. Although I was his baby sister, and we looked like a pair of mismatched socks together—he was tall, dark, and cool, while I was tiny, blonde, and bubbly—we were like-minded and twins in spirit.

We'd spend Saturday afternoons in the summer building forts using shag carpeting and dirty plywood from the dump. When my cousin "Little Jim" (who was my best friend after Gary) came over, we'd make bows and arrows from sticks and string, and play cowboys and Indians. Gary always got to be the gunslinging cowboy or the sheriff, and Little Jim and I always had to be the Indians who died in the end with an invisible bullet to the heart.

On rainy days we'd stay in and play with our electric race cars, or ride our bikes outside in the mud and get dirty. In the winter, we'd catch frogs in the icy creek and take them over to the community pool, which was closed for the season. We'd race them along the side of the pool to see whose frog would jump into the slimy water first.

But my favorite thing of all time to do with Gary was to go to our special place: the falls.

We'd walk up the back roads lined with thick trees, cross a dam over the creek by walking across some boards, then hike a deer trail until we reached the 90-foot waterfall. The sound of the water hitting the rocks was so loud, we could barely hear each other talk. That was okay, though, as Gary and I had an unspoken bond. We understood that this was a magical place and didn't need any words. We'd catch frogs and throw sticks and laugh—that said it all.

I was like a little brother to Gary, one of the boys. And that's how I liked it, because I wasn't girly in the least. My very pretty and delicate sister, Chrissy—who's two years older than me—was a sweet and classic girly girl who liked to wear dresses and pretend to be a princess and play with dolls. I'd rather pretend I was G.I. Joe, playing in the woods with Little Jim, who years later would join the Army. (My nickname for him then was "G.I. Jim.")

Considering that my favorite outfit was my brother's hand-me-down T-shirts and patched-up Levi's and I loved to get muddy, playing princess was like a punishment to me. My mother got away with putting me in dresses my first few years, but by the time I was about five and following Gary around, I saw no use for them. How was I supposed to climb a tree and catch frogs wearing a dress?

I loved my sister, though, so we found "neutral" games to play that didn't require her to get messed up or me to get prettied up. We had fun unless Gary came into the room, and then my allegiance went to him. He taunted our sister mercilessly, calling her "Chrissy-Pissy," until she'd scream, "Gaaaaarrrrryyyyyyy!"

"Shhh!" he'd say, trying to shush her up. "My God, you are such a tattletale!"

Invariably, Mom or Ken would come running and Gary would get in trouble—which only made him taunt her more the next time. That's when I first learned that a good sport never, ever, snitched. No matter how much you got hurt.

One time my brother and two of his friends climbed up a tall pine tree by the nearby dump. Gary hung from a branch ten feet up like a daredevil and, as I watched from below, dropped to the ground like a gymnast with a perfect dismount. His friends followed, and then it was my turn.

"C'mon, Dane! If you want to be in the club, you have to do it, too. Do you want to be in the club?"

Of course I wanted to be in Gary's club. Even though I was at least one foot shorter and several years younger than the others, I scrambled up the tree, crawled out onto the branch, and lowered myself until I was hanging.

"Okay, let go!" Gary called out from below.

They all watched and waited, but I froze. It wasn't something I'd normally admit to Gary, but I yelled, "I'm scared!"

"Nah, you can do it, Dane! Just let go!"

I didn't have a chance to choose bravery. I had waffled so long that my aching fingers slipped from the branch and I plummeted to the ground, spraining my ankle. I tried not to cry, but I couldn't help it.

Gary ran over, picked me up, and wrapped his arms around me. "Don't cry, Dane. You're tough, you're going to be okay," he assured me, as I limped home leaning on him. "You're in the club, you're good," he said. "But don't tell Mom about this. Okay?"

Naturally. Unlike my sister, I was no tattletale.

I WAS SHOCKED TO DISCOVER THAT even though I was a good sport and "in the club," the boys at school didn't like me.

I'd begged my mother to chop off all my golden hair so I could look more like Gary. On my first day of kindergarten, Gabe followed me across the field to the front door of the school and then, with a meow that said, "I'll be back later to get you," moseyed on home. Gabe wasn't like other cats—he was more like a dog in the way he followed me and was in tune with me.

My classroom was for kids in kindergarten, first grade, and second grade. I was the only girl in kindergarten, and one of only two girls in the entire classroom. Great! I knew how to be one of the boys and was excited.

But when Gabe met me out front a few hours later, I was in tears. "The boys didn't like me," I cried, burying my face in his copper-colored fur as we walked across the field.

When we got home, I told my mom what had happened. "They didn't want to p-play with me," I sputtered, "b-because I'm a *girl*." They had said the word *girl* to me like it was a bad word, like I had cooties.

My mother smiled and knelt down in front of me, drying my tears with the edge of one of her groovy peasant blouses. She put her hands on my shoulders and looked me squarely in the eye.

"Dana Leigh, listen to me," she said. (She always used my middle name when we were talking seriously.) "Don't worry about those boys. The next time they tease you, just look at them and laugh, and then walk away. They don't know yet how special you are. There is

CHAPTER 2

Heroes, Fighters, and Top Dogs

I soon became Gary's unofficial protégée, his Top Dog in training, simply by hanging out with him. We'd pretend to be explorers and hike along the Clackamas River until we got far enough away from the sign that said: WARNING! UNDERTOW! Gary's logic was that if we went to calm water a little bit above the rapids, there'd be no undertow—just a really strong current, that was all.

Across the river, Gary would spot a mound of sand. "We're going to swim across to Gilligan's Island!" he'd say.

Not only was Gary cool, but he was also the town jock. He could do anything with awesome ease, from soccer to track and field (not to mention baseball—when he was 16 he had a 92-mph fastball). He was fast, he was strong, and in my eyes he was invincible

"Watch how I do it," he instructed. "Then when I tell you to go, you swim where I swim, okay?"

"Okay."

He threw his shoes and T-shirt onto the riverbank, so I immediately did the same. At that age, I had six-pack abs from climbing trees and hiking hills with him.

Gary stepped into the water until he was up to his knees and dove in. He sliced through the water, swimming a little upstream, until he reached the other side and called out to me. "Okay, Dane! Do it!"

I waded into the freezing water and then tried to swim slightly upstream like I'd seen him do. Since I was only three-and-a-half-feet tall, though, the current pulled me downstream toward the loud rapids.

Gary ran downriver as I swam, coaching me. "You can do it! Swim hard! You're almost there!"

He'd tell me I was close, even if I wasn't. When I got near him, he grabbed hold of me in the water and yanked me to my feet. By that time, I was dangerously close to being swept away by the current.

"Good job, Dane," he always said, patting me on the back. We rested on Gilligan's Island for a while in the sun and skipped rocks— he excelled at that, too. Once we caught our breath, we swam back.

It didn't occur to me to be afraid or give up or think I couldn't do it. Because Gary saw no physical limitations for me, neither did I. He thought I was tough, so I was. There was never any doubt in his mind that I could do everything he could do and that I'd be safe.

Out of the water, on dry land, my brother taught me how to be another kind of fighter—with my fists. Whenever my buddy Davey and I got into a spat, Gary would say, "Let's take this to the dump."

The dump was east of the houses and our formal fighting ground. Through the 20-foot-high piles of garbage and old kitchen appliances, Gary would lead us to a boxed-in pit stacked high with gravel. "Okay, you two, get in there," he'd direct, as he sat on the edge of the pit. "I'm the ringmaster."

Davey was two years older than me and much taller, but he was a skinny kid and I had fearlessness on my side—and technique. Ken had taught me how to spit, but Gary and our father, Chuck, had taught me how to throw a punch—not like a girly-girl slap with an open hand and a limp wrist, but like a boxer.

Dad, whom Mom divorced when I was one, lived two hours away in the town of Hillsboro with his second wife, Debbie (Mom #2). He'd been a radioman in the Navy, stationed aboard the USS *Rankin*. He'd also grown up on the sketchy side of the railroad tracks and was a scrapper.

Some of my earliest memories of Dad are of him picking up Gary, Chrissy, and me in his pickup to go to the sand dunes or mud races— that's where the adults would race their Jeeps and trucks in the thick mud, and the kids would race each other in bare feet. Sometimes when he picked us up, Dad would have a six-pack of Miller Genuine Draft with him and give us each a beer. Nothing mellows out three kids on a two-hour road trip like a beer. Dad's father was straight off the boat from Germany, so I imagine he grew up with beer around and didn't see anything wrong with giving some to us.

Every Christmas, my brother and sister and I would spend the morning with Mom. Then Dad and Debbie would pick us up to spend the afternoon at their house, and then we'd spend the evening at a giant Liesegang get-together with dozens of kids running around. They were a big, close-knit bunch, and fiercely loyal to each other. Dad had four brothers and three sisters, and if you messed with one of them, you got the entire gang on you.

"Don't ever throw the first punch," my father would instruct. "If you get into a fistfight at school, I'll stand by you if you didn't swing first. But once someone hits you, hit them back—*hard.*"

It was something I kept in mind as I got into position with Davey in the gravel pit.

"Okay . . . go!" Gary would yell out.

Davey and I always started out horsing around, but Gary knew that as soon as one of us threw a "real" punch, the fight was on for real. It was usually Davey who struck first, and then I'd slug away per my father's instruction. The fight tended to end with my brother breaking us up, but one time Davey ran away humiliated that a girl was beating him up. Either way, I'd sometimes come home with bruises. Mom took my minor scrape-ups in stride.

My mother could be a fighter herself when the situation called for it. In her youth she had excelled at the graceful, ladylike sports of volleyball, baton twirling, and cheerleading. But as the only girl among five brothers, she was bound to learn how to throw a punch, too. As Ken used to say in his Buffalo, Nu Yawk, accent: "She's one tough broad, my little hot *tomaytuh.*"

I first saw the fighter underneath my mother's flower-child exterior when I was seven years old, during a family trip to the Timber Festival in Estacada. While Gary and Chrissy rode the Ferris wheel, I was in line with Mom and Ken to get hot dogs. A woman was behind us in line, and standing near her were a girl and boy about my age. The woman seemed tipsy, and when the children accidentally bumped into her, she grabbed them both and shook them, screaming, "What do you think you're doing, you stupid little shits?!"

The woman was clearly not the mother, but it wouldn't have mattered to my mom if she were. "Leave those kids alone," Mom warned her.

The woman murmured something under her breath, then slapped one of the terrified children.

"Stop it!" Mom yelled, stepping in front of the children and shielding them with her arms. The woman slapped my mother in the face, hard. A hundred feet above us, Gary and Chrissy were practically standing up in their Ferris-wheel seats watching the spectacle unfolding below.

My mother, apparently, also knew my father's rule for fighting: Never throw the first punch. But once you'd been hit, all civility was gone, gone, gone with the wind.

The woman's hand had barely left Mom's cheek when my five-feet-one, 105-pound dynamo of a mother was on her, knocking her to the ground and pummeling her nonstop. Ken swooped in and pulled my mom off—even as he held her suspended in midair, she kept swinging her fists like a cartoon character.

Both of my biological parents had a Jekyll-and-Hyde quality. On the turn of a dime—and you never knew what would cause the turn—Mom could go from fantasy-world flower child to child-having-a-tantrum, and Dad could go from funny, generous, and engaging to raging, seeing the world as a harsh place. As a child, I thankfully only experienced their good sides.

The women in my family tree had a bad habit of hooking up with rough, fighting men. From what I'd been told, Mom and Dad had some knockdown fights while they were married, sometimes fueled by too much liquor on Dad's end, and sometimes inspired by my mother's flirtatious nature. Dad didn't trust women very much, and Mom wasn't a saint during their marriage. In fact, for the first few years of my life, Dad apparently thought I was Ken's child since Mom had gotten together with him so soon after my parents had split.

Mom and Dad were opposites; she's the water sign of Pisces, and he's the fire sign of Leo. My father and I actually share the same birthday—July 25—and we're both lions who roar when provoked, but have big hearts.

With me, Dad could be a total softy, and this was the part of him I saw most as a kid. One summer when I broke my arm after speeding down a place called Walt's Hill on my bike and smashing into a cement staircase, the doctors put my arm in a fiberglass cast—a "snot cast," as Gary called it, because of its translucent gray-green color—so that I could still swim. I was like a mermaid who couldn't survive out of the water for too long.

"Make sure to dry it completely," the doctor warned me, "or you'll get gangrene and your arm will fall off." He was only joking, but I didn't know that.

The following weekend Dad and Debbie took us to Hagg Lake, and I jumped in and got that cast good and waterlogged. For the 30-minute drive back to Dad's, I hung my arm out the window to dry my cast, but it was still damp by bedtime and I was terrified.

"My arm will fall off!" I cried.

Dad attempted to comfort me as he tried not to laugh. He plugged in a blow-dryer and settled me on his lap in a big, comfy chair, aiming the heat at my cast for hours. We both fell asleep like that.

OVER THE NEXT FEW YEARS, my brother continued to toughen me up—physically and mentally.

"Dane, stick out your finger," Gary would say to me when we were playing outside. From behind his back, he'd produce a baby snake he'd found in the grass. They had red lines on them, so we named them "red racers."

"Let this red racer bite you," he'd say, "and you're in the club."

"Okay, Gare Bear."

We never knew if the snake was a biter or not; every so often I'd be lucky and it wasn't. When it was, I wouldn't flinch. And it was on to the next test.

"Dane, let this crawdad pinch you. If you do, you can be in my special club."

I'd nod and hold out my finger. If the claws were especially sharp, I'd let out an "ouch!"

"Here." He'd take one of my hands, close it into a fist, and place it above his heart. "Go ahead and hit me if you want—it'll make you feel better. You're in the club. "

I bet I belonged to more clubs that never existed than any other kid sister in Oregon.

Meanwhile, the females in the family tried to pull me back into their fold. At Christmas one year when I was about seven, for instance, I'd been hoping for a G.I. Joe action figure or a Tonka truck but got a Barbie doll instead. I cried my eyes out, thinking, *Don't they know the real me at all?* Gary and I chopped off the hair and pulled the heads off of Chrissy's Barbies in retaliation, and Dad took me to the nearest Toys "R" Us to exchange mine for a pinball game.

I didn't understand this whole gender thing. Why did being a girl mean I had to play with certain toys? Or wear dresses? Or have long hair? Or not be strong? I was short, but I was solid. I also had chubby cheeks that everyone liked to pinch.

When we were kids, if Gary poured himself a bowl of Raisin Bran before going to bed, I wasn't allowed to do the same. "Boys can have cereal at night, but not girls," Mom used to say, pulling the box away. "You'll get fat."

I was seven and didn't have an ounce of fat on me. But I'd earned the nicknames "Chubs" and "Porker" in the family, while Chrissy was called "Skinny-Minny Bird Legs." It was pretty clear that being skinny was better than the alternative.

IN THE NEXT FEW YEARS AFTER KINDERGARTEN, I had one more experience like my first day at school. I was staying at an after-school day care in Estacada and made a new friend whom I adored. With my short hair and eagerness to jump in mud puddles, he assumed that I was a boy, too. Two weeks into our brilliant friendship, he discovered I was a girl and refused to play with me anymore. It didn't make sense to me—I was the same me from two weeks earlier. Why did my gender make a difference?

On my own turf in Three Lynx, I had transcended the political gender wars. Once the boys got to know me at school, they looked up to me and followed me around like I did Gary. By the end of fourth grade, I was Top Dog of my class, and everyone knew it. Gary was now at a different school—Estacada Junior High—and he was proud of his protégée.

On weekends we'd ride our bikes, and I'd wear my favorite T-shirt: my brother's hand-me-down with a graphic of a motorcycle rider popping wheelies. We'd chew the Red Man or Copenhagen tobacco he kept in his dresser, and we'd speed down the hills together.

Gary would turn his head ever so slightly to one side and spit a wad of tobacco onto the road, so I'd spit, too.

We were cool as hell. We were unbeatable.

CHAPTER 3

Broken Hearts

In the summer of 1981, when I was ten years old, my enchanted life as Top Dog came to an end.

Mom called a family meeting with my brother, my sister, and me, and told us she was leaving Ken. We cried, begging her not to do it, but it had no effect. She gave Chrissy and Gary a choice of where they wanted to live: Gary chose to stay with Ken in Three Lynx so he could remain near his friends. Chrissy chose to live with Dad in Hillsboro—she got along better with him than with our mom.

"I want to stay in Three Lynx with Gary and Ken," I announced.

"You're too little to decide," Mom replied. "You're coming with me."

Leaving Three Lynx and my siblings was so traumatic for me that I only remember a glimpse of the good-bye—I sobbed as I saw most of what I loved disappear behind me as we drove away.

Mom and I moved into a duplex in Estacada, which seemed like a big city to me, with its 2,000 residents. Our landlord was a creep, and the man living next door to us beat his wife. Mom and I were watching TV one night when we heard her scream, followed by the sound of a body being hurled against the wall and falling to the floor with a thud. Men hurting women like that saddened me, and I hated the idea of anyone hurting me or Mom or Chrissy. I remember Mom talking to the wife in hushed tones the next day, but I don't think the beatings stopped.

That year, violence surrounded me; it sought me out. Or maybe I sought it out?

My status went from coolest kid in school to the most picked on. The change occurred before I even set foot in my new school, Estacada River Elementary. The September morning I boarded my first bus to start fifth grade, I was naive to the politics of gender segregation in school buses. The girls were sitting on one side and the boys on another; by habit (and personal preference), I gravitated toward the boys.

"Eww! You sat on the boy-eeees' side!" the entire bus taunted me. (On the bright side, at least they knew I was a girl!) I never rode that bus again—I walked the mile to and from school after that.

A few weeks later, I got my first bloody nose. My new friend, Becky, and I were walking to Big Jim's Corner Market after school when a sixth-grade boy came up and began teasing us. I didn't really like Becky that much, but she sat next to me in class and was tomboyish like me; plus, she was all I had. We were walking to Big Jim's so I could get some candy for Gary.

My only saving grace in our move to Estacada was that my new school was in walking distance to my brother's junior high. I'd collect glass pop bottles off the street and trade them in at Big Jim's so that I could buy Gary's favorite candy, Jolly Rancher sticks. Then I'd go to his school and knock on his classroom door.

"Hey, this is my kid sister!" my brother told his class, proudly. We were able to get away with my candy handoffs a few times before Gary's teacher put an end to it.

Anyway, the boy who approached Becky and me began horsing around, and she pulled my favorite baseball hat off my head and put it on the boy. I ripped it off his head and took it back. A few seconds later, the boy's fist was in my face, and I was gushing blood. Becky, the coward, ran away—but the accumulated pain I'd felt over the previous few weeks exploded within me, and I became a bulldog. I charged into the boy and knocked him over. I pinned his arms to the ground with my knees as he kicked with his legs, and I wound up to deliver the hardest punch I'd ever given. I was so angry and hurt, all I knew was that I wanted to hit him, that hitting him would make me feel better.

By this time, some other kids from school had circled us and were chanting, "Hit him! Hit him! *Hit him!*" I could feel the adrenaline pumping through my body. I wound up and then . . . I stopped, fist midair. It was like an invisible force was holding my arm back, like when you're in a dream and you can't move. I couldn't do it, and I didn't understand why.

In those few frozen seconds, the boy pushed me off and punched me again, even harder this time. I walked home bloody and humiliated. A lot of good it had done me, not wanting to hurt someone. It was the last time I ever showed mercy in a fight.

After that, I was in a string of them. A few weeks later I took on two neighborhood boys, ages seven and ten. The older boy threw the first punch and the younger one jumped in, so I took them both on, sending them running home to their mommy. A few weeks after that, a girl cut in front of Becky and me in line going into class, and I called her on it. She moved to slap me, so I punched her. I'd seen *Rocky* the night before and had picked up a few more pointers.

I'm not sure how or why I was getting into all these fistfights. I was a good kid and didn't really want to hurt anyone, but I had so much anger, pain, and sadness built up in me and didn't know how to express it. And being a fighter had brought me praise back home.

I cried a lot that year. To comfort me, Mom would sing her favorite Roberta Flack song, "Killing Me Softly"—although the lyrics were anything but uplifting. The song was about "dark despair" and men looking through women as if they were "not there."

THAT WINTER, OUR HEAT WAS TURNED OFF in the apartment, and I routinely ate SpaghettiOs out of a can for dinner. Mom had gotten a job at the supermarket across the street, but it wasn't enough money to make ends meet.

Years later, I had an epiphany about the lengths she went to in order to keep us surviving. I remembered the creepy landlord coming over and Mom ordering me to go get something for her at the grocery store. I didn't want to go and made a fuss, and she slapped me on the face. "Don't talk back to me! Go!"

I cried my eyes out and left, shocked that my mother would hit me. When I returned, the landlord was gone and Mom was upset, but we didn't talk about it. I figured she was upset because she'd hit me.

We left Estacada before the spring and bunked with Mom's childhood friend Chris, who lived in a single-wide trailer parked in a pasture 12 miles away in Colton. For the rest of fifth grade, I didn't have to worry about making new friends—I had Chris's cow, Ichabod, and her yellow Labrador retriever, Jasper.

I had always had an affinity with animals and grieved for my dear Gabe, who'd gone missing three years earlier and never come back. At Chris's, I played tag and hide-and-seek with Ichabod and Jasper, running into the hay barn and hiding until Ichabod found me and nudged his muzzle in my face while Jasper ran around us in circles. Yes, I actually played hide-and-seek with a cow—weird, but true.

Even though Jasper wasn't officially mine, I felt like he was, and he became my first dog love. With him, I discovered that no other creature loved so unconditionally and was as loyal as a dog—"God" spelled backward. Jasper and I grew so inseparable that one afternoon when Mom, Chris, and I left him in the trailer to go to a barbecue at a neighbor's, he suddenly showed up at my side at the backyard party. Had we left the door open? Mom and I took him back and found broken glass everywhere. Jasper had jumped through the trailer's side window, shattering it, to get to me.

Throughout my life, God would give me the gift of a dog when I most needed a friend—and, in turn, He would take them away from me when I most needed freedom.

I'D FOUND JASPER, AND MOM WASN'T LONELY for long, either—she never was. She met Ed on a blind date on the slopes at Mt. Hood Meadows ski resort. He looked like a short-haired Willie Nelson and wore Wrangler jeans and a cowboy hat, even when he skied. Ed owned his own business—a door-and-weather-stripping company. Much like Ken, he was funny, gentle, and kind. He also had a strong work ethic and rarely raised his voice to anyone, never mind a hand.

By the summer of '82 Mom, Jasper, and I had moved in with Ed in Troutdale, about 20 miles north of Estacada. We hadn't intended on taking Jasper, but after I left he became so depressed that he wouldn't eat, and Chris said that she couldn't bear to separate us and gave him to me. The following year when I was 12, Mom and Ed exchanged wedding vows on the slopes where they'd met. Gary gave Mom away, and Chrissy and I were bridesmaids, along with Ed's daughter, Susanne. We wore winter coats and skis, and celebrated with hot chocolate and melting marshmallows after the ceremony.

I now had a reassembled family unit and a new home. Chrissy moved in with us and we had Susanne as our new sister, and we even added a new dog to the family: Ed's collie–German shepherd mix, Willie.

From the get-go, Susanne and I took to each other like peanut butter and chocolate. On the surface, we were opposites in looks and personality. I was strong, bold, and bronzed by the sun. She lived on Cheetos and orange pop but was skinny as a rail, with strawberry-blonde hair and ivory skin. She was six months older than me, but we were in the same grade and actually had tons in common. We shared a room and both still slept with our baby blankets—hers was a white cotton one named "Bankie," and mine was pink with green stripes and a satin edge named "Nana" (short for "Banana blanket"). Mainly, we loved being silly together.

Amazingly, Susanne was able to accomplish something our first two years together that my mother, sister, and grandmothers hadn't been able to do—she pulled me a few inches closer to the girly side. Even at age 12, I hated taking showers or washing my hair, and I liked to go shirtless, whether I was swimming or walking around town on a hot summer's day. (A well-meaning neighbor of my father's once approached me with a shirt, urging me to put it on. I spat on her driveway in response.) Now I was blow-drying my hair and wearing a training bra, dipping my toe into womanhood. It was scary, but I was doing my best.

Nevertheless, puberty brought with it a whole new unexpected complication for me, beyond the usual challenges. Until my body began to change, there had never been tension between my father and me. But now we had a problem. Dad had never related to me as a "female" energy but rather had raised me like a son—sometimes

he even introduced me to people as "my youngest son" in jest. So as long as he could treat me this way, all was fine. Dad and I were both confused as to how I was supposed to act and be treated now.

To my father and brother, it was as if I *had* no gender. Gary used to come over to Mom and Ed's house, lie down on the floor, and bench-press me. I don't think my father noticed I was a girl until I was in sixth grade, and now that he had, all hell broke loose. It was a hard transition for both of us. I'd been playing on a boys' baseball team in fourth and fifth grade, and suddenly I was told "You can't play—you're a girl," and shipped off to girls' softball.

By the time I was in seventh grade, I had begun to notice how my father talked about and to women—including my mother and sister—and I didn't like it. He used words like *whore* and *bitch* too often, which hadn't registered with me before. Just because my sister wore makeup and had a pretty face and a beautiful body, that didn't mean she was a whore. Mom was married and in love with Ed—she wasn't a whore. I was a girl, but I wasn't what he described.

Puberty brought out another quality in me that he wasn't used to: I spoke out when I saw an injustice, and I spoke the truth.

One summer evening, Chrissy and I went roller-skating, and Dad came to pick us up at the rink. We were standing off to the side talking to some boys, when he spotted us. At age 14, my sister was turning into a beauty with her long glossy hair, olive complexion, and curves.

Dad had previously accused Chrissy of fooling around with boys (which she wasn't). So when he saw her at that moment, he lost it.

"You're acting like a whore," he yelled at her. Chrissy burst into tears.

"No, she isn't!" I yelled back at him. "She didn't do anything wrong!"

Dad turned to me. "You are a liar!"

"I'm not a liar!" I was such an honest kid that to be called a liar was the worst insult in the world to me. I stormed off and sat in the car. A few minutes later, I saw Dad and Chrissy exiting the building; he was pulling her by her beautiful hair.

In the car on the way back to Dad's place, he continued his yelling, Chrissy continued her crying, and I continued defending my sister, to which he responded: "Shut up, Dana Leigh!"

The next day we were all silent as Dad drove us to Mom's, and I jumped out of the car without a word. I hated him for what he had done to my sister. He was a bully, and I wanted nothing to do with him.

Inside, I sat at the kitchen table and told Mom what had happened. "I don't like him. I don't want to see him anymore. He's mean and he bad-mouths you and I'm tired of it. I'm tired of the way he treats women."

Mom of all people understood about my father's temper. "Dana Leigh," she said, "you don't have to do anything you don't want to do. I'll support whatever decision you need to make. But remember, he's your father and he loves you."

I loved him, too, but my decision was this: I was not going to talk to my father—ever again.

CHAPTER 4

Men of the House

Never lasted a year and a half—all through eighth grade and beyond—that's how long I didn't see or talk to my father.

In that time, I continued to build my physical and mental strength and discipline by swimming, cycling, and water and snow skiing. I also spent a lot of time with my uncle Kent and aunt Jeanne and her family, on camping trips by Lake Billy Chinook in the Cove Palisades State Park. Uncle Kent was Mom's youngest brother and a former photo interpreter for the Air Force. My funny, smart-ass, favorite uncle and his high-school sweetheart were the two most stabilizing forces (along with Mom's parents, Grandma Blanche and Grandpa Carl) in my seemingly ever-changing life.

We'd set up tents and water-ski and get so rowdy on our camping trips that the park rangers would come and tell us to quiet down. When Mom, Ed, Susanne, Chrissy, and Gary joined us, Mom made elaborate meals of seafood-stuffed pasta shells in creamy sauces—recipes she never had time to do at home—and we'd set a big table like a holiday feast. I'd share a tent with Susanne or sleep out by the fire, my favorite place.

Whenever my life was in chaos, I'd seek out Uncle Kent and Aunt Jeanne for a compassionate ear and sound advice about family matters.

"We know your father can be rough and your mom can be crazy, and they're not always easy to understand," they'd explain. "But they are your parents and they love you, and you need to love them as they are. And when you need us, we're right here for you. Always."

Most important, Uncle Kent made a deep and lasting impression on me regarding how women should be treated. He spoke to my aunt and me, and every other woman, with the utmost respect—he never said a mean word to or about any woman. As a couple, he and Jeanne were the rare example in my life of a healthy male-female relationship, and that early imprint was invaluable to me as a model of what to strive for and what was right and good.

Like Gary, Uncle Kent was and is a hero to me.

BECAUSE I'D STARTED SWIMMING MORE, my upper-body strength was fierce, which impressed the men in my family. At age 13, I'd reached my full height of five feet three inches—but I was 125 pounds of solid muscle. When I played football with my uncle and Aunt Jeanne's brothers, they could never wrench the ball from my iron grip.

"Jesus H. Christ," Uncle Kent would say, "she's strong, that girl."

He taught me how to slalom water-ski that year and was shocked by my perseverance. At the lake, even if it was a cold September morning, we'd get up early and put the boats in the water. The adults would do one pass of the lake on skis, but I'd go back and forth until my legs turned purple.

I'd arm wrestle whoever was willing—Gary, my mom, my sister's boyfriend *and* his four brothers. When I needed money, I'd work at Ed's company cleaning up, or I'd chop wood and stack it up in the basement until I'd chopped and split four truckloads full and Ed would give me 50 bucks.

Despite my estrangement from my father—or maybe because of it—I had a great year and was more independent than ever. The separation even enabled me to feel more comfortable with myself and with my blossoming womanhood. In eighth grade, I felt as if boys liked me for the first time . . . and I liked them back. I was even voted "Class Flirt" in the yearbook. I always did have that gift of gab.

At the end of the year, my report card had a mixture of A's, B's, and C's, with the same comments by each teacher: "Talks too much in class," but, "Dana has a positive attitude that reflects on others!"

Mom shook her curls as she scanned my report card. She'd gone from '70s Cher hair to an '80s *Flashdance* look—shorter and permed.

She even wore leg warmers because of her new night job as an aerobics instructor. "If you get 'talks too much in class' when you get to high school, you'll be grounded for a month."

"But how can I have a 'positive attitude that reflects on others' if I don't talk to them in class, Mom?"

"Don't be a smart-ass, Dana Leigh."

I couldn't sit still enough to pay attention all day in class or do homework for hours after school. I needed to *move!* I joined the swim team at the Vancouver Swim Club—20 miles away in Vancouver, Washington—when summer vacation started after eighth grade, riding my bike to practice. The route ran through winding, dusty, rural roads and along the highway, and took one to two hours. Once there, I'd swim fast for 90 minutes. My body was rock solid, and I had a 27-inch waist—I was a lean, mean, fighting machine.

At the family vacation that summer at a lake house in Seattle, I enlisted Mom and Ed to row the boat next to me as I swam across the lake. They followed me in the little white rowboat under the hot sun as I freestyled across for a mile. Ed rowed while Mom drank a glass of wine, watching me.

"Sweet Pea?" she'd call out. "Are you okay?"

"Yeah, Mom, yeah. I'm good!" I'd yell back, sputtering water. "Let's keep going. I can do anything I set my mind to!"

IN SEPTEMBER 1985, AS I STARTED ninth grade at Prairie High, I met the girl who would become my lifelong friend. Amy was from the rival high school, but we were both on the nearby swim team. Amy was a backstroker and butterflyer, and I was a freestyler and breaststroker. We used to joke that we could be our very own medley relay team.

At four feet eleven inches and 86 pounds, Amy was even tinier than me in stature. Our personalities were as diverse as our looks: As boisterous, rebellious, and "flirty" as I was, she was shy, introverted, and intellectual. I would egg Amy on to try new things, from kissing a boy to eating Mom's weird-tasting health food. Meanwhile, she'd be the practical, logical one of the team—the brains of our outfit, I'd call her. "You're *life* smart," she insisted. We made a good team; we appreciated each other's differences.

Amy was my main friend as I roamed in and out of cliques at my own school, where I felt alienated from most of the other students. I was too much of a nonconformist to fit with any one group (my favorite pair of socks had the slogan NORMAL IS BORING). Sometimes I felt like a dog begging for a bone. That's always been my dichotomy: I can be incredibly social, but also a loner who doesn't fit in.

I was still teased by both girls and boys because I was sturdy and strong—I was stronger than half the damn high school. I wasn't fat by any means, but thanks to my swimmer's build, I was a stout kraut. And I wanted people to love me and accept me for who I was—starting with my father.

That spring during ninth grade, I received a handwritten letter in the mail from him:

> Dear Dana,
> Please come and see me. I love you. I'm sad and I miss you.

I hadn't invited him to my eighth-grade graduation, and he'd been very hurt by that. But I wasn't ready to see him then. After I got his letter, I agreed to a meeting.

We had our first heart-to-heart, adult conversation. I brought up the reason I'd stopped talking to him: his boorish, sexist behavior. Then he brought up something that had pained him deeply and for a long time, which hadn't occurred to me before.

"I'm sorry," he said, "but I know you think of Ken as your dad, and it's very upsetting to me. *I'm* your father, not Ken."

I shrugged. He was right—I did see Ken as my dad.

We talked a bit about that for a while. We were both hurt, and I wanted to make things better between us.

"Okay, I'll see you again," I told him. "But these are the rules. If you want me to visit you, you can't bad-mouth my mom, and you can't say mean things to Chrissy."

"I promise."

If felt good to put boundaries in place with my father, allowing myself to say no when someone I loved hurt me. I was 14 years old and only beginning to figure out the male-female dynamic. As I've said, I'd heard that the women in my family had a history of picking men who could be hurtful. By telling my dad that I wouldn't put up with his angry outbursts, I felt I was breaking the unhealthy pattern set before me.

That was my hope, anyway. But that summer, those hopes were dashed.

TWO MONTHS AFTER MY EMPOWERING TALK with my father, and just before my 15th birthday, one of my uncles got hold of me.

Doug was one of Mom's brothers—he was fun but also troubled, and he drank too much. I was staying at Grandma Blanche's to attend the Estacada Timber Festival (the one where Mom slugged that woman several years earlier), a weekend of beer gardens, log-rolling contests, ax-throwing contests, and pole-climbing contests—you know, really exciting stuff. Since I knew I was going to be out late one night, I arranged to stay at Uncle Doug's, instead of waking up Grandma.

I slipped into his house after a great time with some old schoolmates and curled up on the living-room couch. I was almost asleep when my uncle appeared in front of me in his underwear, reeking of beer. He pulled the sheet off me and lay down on top of me, grabbing my boobs through my tank top and sticking his tongue down my throat. I froze in horror, shock, and disbelief, and then I found my voice.

"Stop it! *Stop!*" I pushed him away. *"What are you doing?"*

"What's wrong?" he asked. He was surprised, as if fooling around was expected of me—my duty, even.

What's wrong? Everything is wrong. You're my uncle, I'm scared, you're kissing me, you're sticking your hard-on against me, I don't know what to do or say. . . .

"I'm just tired," I mumbled.

That ridiculous answer placated him without hurting his ego, I guess. He shrugged and left the room.

The next morning, I felt disgusted, ashamed, angry, and completely violated but said nothing to him. I left the house quickly and walked back to Grandma's, punching the air as I walked.

I hate you, I was thinking.

When I got home two days later, I told Mom what happened.

"Honey, he must have just been drunk. You know your uncle," she replied. "We'll go have a talk with him and straighten this out."

I didn't want to go, but Mom made me. I know what she was trying to do—get it out in the open, clear the air, make him apologize so I'd feel better. Maybe a part of her was hoping that it was a misunderstanding on my part. I'm sure she didn't want to think that her brother would do something like this to her daughter.

We went to talk to Uncle Doug at his work, and he mumbled a vague apology. I just wanted to get away from him, and never set foot in his house again.

I didn't tell anyone else about what had happened at the time, not Dad or Gary or Uncle Kent. When Uncle Kent found out years later, he wanted to take a baseball bat to Doug. Somehow, *that* sentiment made me feel better.

"Why didn't you tell me?" Uncle Kent asked.

"Mom didn't protect me," I told him. "So why would I think you would?"

Soon after the incident with Uncle Doug, I started throwing up.

After gorging on too much food, I stuck my fingers down my throat to make myself vomit on purpose. It felt like such a relief, I began doing it once or twice a week after that. After dinner at Mom and Ed's, I would stroll out back among the five acres of field behind our house and stick my fingers down my throat. At Dad's, I'd binge on candy, potato chips, and cookies, and do the same.

I didn't connect my overeating and barfing my guts out to what my uncle had done; I'd never heard of bingeing and purging or bulimia, something many young women do when they feel overstressed or at war with their bodies. In a way, my body had indeed betrayed me. I was a strong fighter—why, then, had I not been able to keep myself safe during two fumbling minutes in the dark? I'd heard murmurings of this kind of thing happening in our family before. Maybe looking like a boy for so many years had protected me.

Now that I was becoming a young woman, was this my fate?

IN SEPTEMBER 1986, I WAS 15 AND BEGAN TENTH GRADE. I was weightlifting for phys ed, and the PE teacher, who was also the football coach, wanted to see if I could bench-press 125 pounds. He had an ongoing list on the weight-room wall that named the football players who could press that much, and so far, there were only two who could do it. That day in PE, I became the third name—and the only girl and non–football player—on the list. I even beat the quarterback!

I watched the coach put my name on the list with a little smile. I'm sure he wanted to show his team, "Look at this. A girl can do it —how about you?" It probably ended my high-school dating career on the spot.

Just as well. After the Uncle Doug thing, I fell off the map socially and athletically. I stopped swimming and saw less of Amy and Susanne, who had shifted into the cheerleader crowd. Instead, I began hanging around the stoners at school and drinking too much beer. I wasn't into pot, though—I was already laid-back and goofy enough, I didn't need anything to make me that way. But I *was* looking for a group where I could belong. I was a short-haired athlete who didn't smoke pot hoping to fit in with the stoners. It was ridiculous.

That year I punched the only black kid in school in the face. I'd had a scuffle with JB the year before when he'd picked me up and pushed me against the lockers, then dropped me. I'd fallen to the ground, my back stabbed by the jagged locker latch and lock. This time, JB snuck up on me when I was waiting in line at the student store. I didn't know who was behind me; all I knew was that a hand had gone up between my legs to my crotch. I swung around, doing a 180, and—*boom!*—JB's mouth was suddenly gushing blood. He was shocked and pissed off—apparently I'd embarrassed him in front of about 30 other students when he'd been trying to show off.

"Don't you ever, *ever* do that again," I told him, and walked away.

I kept bulking up. By the following summer of '87, when I turned 16 and was about to start 11th grade, I had ballooned up to 160 pounds—a gain of 35 pounds in one year. Dad and I celebrated our birthday with a big pizza, and he and Debbie gave me a diamond necklace and a two-liter bottle of wine cooler as a birthday present.

I spent the next two years trying to diet and exercise off those 35 pounds, going for weeks eating only melon. But I couldn't lose weight no matter what I did—even my throwing up didn't help. Years later, I would understand why. Thanks to the trauma of what my uncle had done at such a crucial time in my life—when I was beginning to embrace being a young woman—I was building a barrier around me, a thick armor of flesh to keep away enemies.

The last two years of high school, though, were punctuated with new traumas I didn't foresee. My beloved Jasper had died after being accidentally shot by a neighbor. I'd since inherited the neighbor's German shepherd, Runaway. His name was apt, as he kept running away from our neighbor's house to be with me. They ultimately decided to just give him to me ("He's clearly your dog," they said, handing me his leash before they moved away). As I've said, God has always given me a dog when I've most needed one, and Runaway became my best friend during a really tough time.

One day when I was being a smart-ass with Mom, she slapped my shoulder and Runaway growled at her. He'd seen Susanne and me play fight before and knew the difference between pretend and real anger; he thought she was hurting me.

A few days later, Mom called the vet. "I told him what happened," she said, "and he said Runaway could turn on you, so we have to put him down."

It was the first time in my life I thought my mother was lying to me. "He would never turn on me," I insisted. "He's loyal to me! He protects me when no one else does!"

Mom wouldn't listen, and the appointment was made for the following week. Chrissy, Susanne, and I tried to change her mind and fought for his life, but she wouldn't budge.

When the day came, Mom drove, and I got in the backseat with Runaway (he wouldn't get into a car unless I did first) and went into the vet's office with him. I was sobbing. He trusted me so completely; I was tricking someone I loved into a deadly trap. I didn't understand why we had to kill a completely healthy dog who had done nothing wrong, but I felt powerless to stop it.

I said good-bye to my best friend that day, and I hated my mother for what she'd made me do. I thought of one word to describe her, which I'd never used before. I'd heard my dad call her this many, many times, though: *bitch.*

THE FOLLOWING SUMMER OF '88, before my senior year, two of my cousins on Dad's side of the family were visiting from Germany. Dad had rented a condo in Sunriver, Oregon, for a bunch of us to stay in together. One night, we'd had a few too many beers and Gary and I started our usual roughhousing, as we always did. Gary walked by and punched me on the arm, and a minute later we were on the floor, taking swings at each other—two Top Dogs having a play fight.

I felt a steely grip on my arm, yanking me up.

"Dana, that is not ladylike!" said Dad, as he punched me hard on the shoulder himself.

Not ladylike? Once again, I was being told not to be myself. Wasn't this the man who taught me how to fight? And if I was now supposed to act like a "lady," what was he doing punching one? It was confusing —especially that word, *ladylike.* I wondered how many women didn't fight when someone grabbed them because they'd been taught it wasn't ladylike.

At the end of that year, I was grabbed again.

We'd finished a big Christmas Eve dinner at Grandma Blanche's, and I was saying good-bye to another uncle of mine, Mom's brother Roy. Uncle Doug had been there all night, and I'd spent the evening dodging him and keeping my distance. I couldn't bear to even make eye contact with him. Uncle Roy and I were in the kitchen and everyone else was in the living room. I leaned in for a hug, and he grabbed my face and stuck his tongue down my throat—just like that. I jumped back in disgust and shock. He gave me a look like, *I dare you to say something.*

All I could think was, *Why? Why have two of my uncles done this?*

I went home that night as the clock struck midnight and Christmas arrived, sick to my stomach. Clearly it didn't matter how I looked: I had one uncle pawing me when I was lean, and another when I was fat. None of it made sense to me. I didn't bother telling my mother what happened this time. Uncle Roy hadn't been drinking, so she wouldn't have an excuse for him like she had for Doug; she would've had to face a harsh truth about the men in the family, and I knew she wouldn't want to, or couldn't.

I couldn't think of anything worse that could happen after that. And then, something did. In the spring of 1989, Mom announced that she was leaving Ed. Why? I didn't know, and I don't think she did either. Once again, my family was to break into little pieces and scatter.

It was a cruel irony, then, to discover that as my senior year of high school came to a close, my class had voted me as "Most Spirited" in the yearbook.

What a joke. I didn't think any of them even knew my name.

CHAPTER 5

Rebel, with Cause

I said good-bye to high school and my childhood in classic Dana fashion.

With six of my parents—Mom and Ed; Dad and Debbie; and my former stepdad, Ken, and his wife, Bonnie—watching, along with Uncle Kent and Aunt Jeanne, I wore my fluffy puppy-paw slippers as I walked across the stage to accept my diploma. A few years earlier, Gary had flipped up his gown and shown his undies at his ceremony, so I had a certain family tradition to uphold. (Susanne represented the more serious side of the family, and as class rep she gave a thought-provoking speech to the grads.)

Mom left home right after graduation. Just like that time she left Ken, we all tried to convince her to stay. But once she'd made up her mind, it was over and there was no convincing to be done. She moved six hours away to Friday Harbor, Washington, to live with some asshole guy who owned a sea-kayaking company. Ed, Susanne, and I felt abandoned. Then when Susanne left for Washington State University, it was time for me to move on, too.

I never thought about college for myself. I didn't think I had the smarts, and there wasn't money to send both Susanne and me anyway. She was a straight-A student all through high school; meanwhile, I often stayed up late and stole her homework to copy after she'd gone to bed. I didn't want to do schoolwork—I'd rather be outside or talk to people instead of sitting still. So since I'd coasted with no particular focus in mind, it was assumed that she'd be the one to go to college.

I did have one idea in the back of my mind, though, but wasn't sure if I had the guts to go through with it. I'd taken the ASVAB (Armed Services Vocational Aptitude Battery) test a few times, thinking that maybe I'd join the military once I graduated. Yet now that the day had arrived, I chickened out.

Instead, I moved in with Gary and his girlfriend in Portland after I turned 18. I celebrated my adulthood by buying a pack of Marlboros and a *Playgirl* magazine, and huddling with Amy in a church parking lot, chain-smoking and giggling our asses off at the naked guys.

I worked at a local sandwich shop for a few weeks, then got fired for accidentally giving the boss a wrong social security number. I took that as a sign to muster up the courage to telephone an Air Force recruiter, since that's the branch of the service where Uncle Kent had gone. I had talked to Army recruiters when they came to our high school, but had crossed them off my list.

"You'll have to lose weight or you won't look good in a uniform," one of them had told me, giving me a critical once-over from head to toe.

The topic of my weight didn't come up with the Air Force recruiter, but he did ask, "Have you ever smoked pot?"

I thought about my one or two attempts in tenth grade that had left me nearly choking to death. "Yeah."

"Try the Navy." *Click.*

It was well known in military circles that the Navy was more lax and easier to get into than the Air Force, whose officers were considered the spoiled brats of the military. But after the brief and illuminating conversation I'd had with this recruiter, I wasn't in the mood to make any more calls, so I put the idea aside again.

Meanwhile, Dad and Debbie were trying to talk me into living with them in Hillsboro. Dad loved his kids and wanted us around him, even when he wasn't getting along with us. I was reluctant, worried that Dad's sexist attitude toward women would make me crazy and we'd end up having another big blowup. Plus, I adored living with Gary again. I loved being around him and felt so free and on my own, not having to answer to anyone.

The flip side was fewer bills to pay at Dad's and his full refrigerator, compared with Gary's, which typically only contained Coors Light and milk. Dad also lived closer to Amy and some of my cousins. I definitely didn't want to live with Mom and her new boyfriend—she was far away, and I was still angry with her for leaving Ed. I considered asking Ken and Bonnie, but by now they were busy with two little kids and had their hands full. Meanwhile, my sister, Chrissy, had moved to Hawaii to be with her boyfriend.

Finding a home had officially become a game of musical chairs. I decided to take a chance and go to my father's house. Maybe it would be a time for us to grow closer. And what was the worst that could happen?

I MOVED IN WITH DAD and got a job at Scottie's Auto Body shop in the fall of 1989, detailing cars and rotating tires. I liked that I could wear jeans and a sweatshirt and get grubby and use my physical strength, which surprised the rest of the grease monkeys. I'd walk across the shop with one tire balanced on my left shoulder and another hoisted under my right arm with ease.

The guys would jump up and say, "Hey, we'll help you with that!"

"Nah," I'd tell them. "I got it, I'm good. Thanks."

I felt at home at the garage. One of my co-workers, Gene, was the biggest jokester and prankster, and I loved the guy. He was in his early 50s with a big belly and his own special chair—a seat from an old car that he'd mounted on wheels. He never washed his coffee cup, and he had a laugh that climbed up from deep in his gut.

"Hey, dumbshit!" he'd call out to me, when I was at the other end of the garage. "Come here!" It was his pet name for me, a term of endearment in his vocabulary. He was the ultimate smart-ass, forever teasing and torturing me and telling off-color jokes.

Gene was the right type to take me under his wing. Once when I accidentally damaged a car that had just been painted, hitting the door against something as I backed it out of the shop, he stood up for me and then showed me photos of the car he once smashed up so I wouldn't feel bad.

While Gene was my buddy, another mechanic became my secret romance. Adam was 20 years my senior and very much married. He told me I was beautiful and took me on limo rides up in the hills of Portland. He bought me flowers and took me out to dinner, careful to choose places where no one would know us. He gave me attention I wasn't used to but clearly craved, so I thought I was in love with him.

A part of me genuinely believed he'd leave his wife to be with me, as women in love with married men usually think. The more realistic part of me knew that the relationship was a dead end. Things indeed ran their course, but being with Adam was just what I needed at the time—attention without strings attached. Plus, keeping it a secret from my father was to my benefit. He already thought women couldn't be trusted, and the last thing I needed was to hear him call me that other word besides *bitch* he used for Mom and Chrissy: *whore.*

The term Dad used for me at the time was *macho.* At five feet seven inches, my father was four inches taller than me, but we weighed the same—his Levi's fit me perfectly. My shoulders were wider than Dad's, and in my mind I was just as muscular and strong.

"You're too macho for your own good," he'd tell me, gruffly. "You walk and look like you play football for the Green Bay Packers."

An hour later, he'd come looking for me. "Dana, I need you to come help me carry this couch into the house."

And yet, I had a great time living with Dad for those few months. Beneath his sometimes crusty exterior, he was as gooey and mushy as they come. He was big on hugging and having good talks, and we spent long afternoons playing golf—he played and I caddied, and we hung out and drank beer all day, good father-daughter stuff. I knew he was trying hard to win my affection.

Dad worked as a foreman at Northwest Marine Ironworks in Portland. He was a "rigger," and one of his jobs was to remove asbestos from Navy ships. When we were kids, Dad used to let Gary, Chrissy, and me run around on the decks and take us up in the crane to look down at the ships and the river. I still loved going there and being on the ships.

There was one thing Dad would do every morning right after he woke up that used to break my heart a bit. I remember first hearing him when I was 15 and staying overnight at his place. I was in the hallway on the way to the bathroom when I heard him talking to himself in his bedroom.

"Tomorrow," he was saying to himself, out loud, "will be a better day."

I heard him say it many mornings after that, and I always meant to ask him: Why do you wait until tomorrow for a better day? Why can't the better day be right now, *today?*

INEVITABLY, MY FATHER AND I DID CLASH over my modern-day, "women's libber" attitude and his chauvinistic one. We loved each other but often argued; that was us in our true form. Our arguments about women, marriage, work, and the two sexes in general were ongoing and heated. I confused and irritated Dad because I defied everything he thought about women. I was strong, I was independent, and I wanted to work and earn my keep and never have to rely on a man. I wanted to do everything and anything a man could do, and more.

"Dana, you can't do that. You're a woman. The *man* is the man of the house."

"Yes, I can. You can't tell me that I can't."

"Women don't get promoted unless they sleep with someone." My father was trapped in a '50s time warp.

"Dad, that's not true."

"It's okay for a man to have sex, but if a woman does, she's a slut."

"Dad, *that's not true!* And it's not fair!" Thank goodness I hadn't told him about Adam.

I didn't understand why he viewed women the way he did, and although I fought his sexist bullshit as much as I could, it didn't do any good. By February 1990, after six months at Dad's, it was time for me to strike out on my own.

Amy and I talked about getting an apartment together, and my father was not happy about that idea. "Number one, you can't afford it," he said.

I knew what number two was, and I loved him for it. He'd just finally gotten me and didn't want to lose me again. But when I wanted something bad enough, I found a way to make it happen.

I didn't know what the word *manifest* meant back then, but looking back, that's what I did. I manifested my way right out of Dad's house by provoking a fight—a biggie.

One afternoon he and I were watching TV in the living room, and we both got up from the couch to go to the kitchen. Dad was walking behind me and for whatever reason, he leaned forward and bit me on the shoulder, in fun. That was Dad joking around. It was probably his way of showing love. But it hurt—more than he must have realized, I assume—and I was ticked off.

"Ouch, Dad! Don't!" I pushed him away and continued to the kitchen.

He chuckled, then caught up to me and bit me again.

"Dad! *I said don't!*"

He bit me a third time, and this Green Bay Packer saw red. Just like when I'd slugged JB back in tenth grade, I spun around and smashed my fist into Dad's face with a solid, roundhouse punch—a punch he had taught me, no doubt. And like with JB, my punch to the mouth dazed Dad for a second and knocked him off balance. He took a step back in shock.

I had broken the cardinal family rule: I'd thrown the first punch. (*And* I'd been "unladylike.") Whatever happened to me now was fair game; he himself had taught me that. I'm sure Dad's next reaction was totally automatic, a reflexive, knee-jerk move.

He threw me over the ottoman in the living room and onto the floor. "You will respect me!" he yelled, shaking my shoulders. "I am your father!"

It all happened so fast, in seconds. I was in shock, too, and I could see that he was now horrified. When he released me, I got up and stormed off to my room, crying. He hadn't hurt me, but he had scared and upset me. As a fellow Leo, I could be just as stubborn and temperamental as he was.

I took a sociology class later on in college and learned that the parent you're most like is the one you get along with least in your teen years. I'm more like my dad than I realized then. No one was going to be the boss of me but me, and it was about time I had the guts to take charge of my life. I went to my room and my decision was made: *I'm done. I'm outta here.*

The next day, without telling anyone, I called up a Navy recruiter and we talked. He arranged for someone to pick me up from the auto body shop after work to take the ASVAB test again. Two weeks later, I stripped down to my underwear and bra for my physical at the MEPS (Military Entrance Processing Station) in Portland and was sworn in and given orders for basic training at Naval Training Center Orlando.

Before I left the MEPS, I found a pay phone to call my father. I was elated and confident about my decision. I had the slogan from the Navy TV commercials in my head—"You are tomorrow!"—and it reminded me of Dad's own morning mantra: *Tomorrow will be a better day.*

When he picked up the phone, I said, "Dad! Guess what?! *I am tomorrow!*"

"Dana? What do you mean?"

"I joined the Navy! I just swore in! I am 'tomorrow'! I am the 'better day'! I go to Orlando for boot camp in two weeks!"

I was flushed with pride, and waiting for him to tell me I'd done good. He didn't hesitate at all with his response.

"You. Dumb. Shit."

CHAPTER 6

Tough Enough

Two weeks later I left my world behind—the first girl that I know of in the family to join the military. Everyone was proud of me . . . even Dad, I suspected, although he didn't come out and say it. He and I had made up after the living-room scuffle without mentioning a word about it.

Before I left for Orlando, he gave me some advice: "Boot camp is a game, Dana. Do what you're told and keep your mouth shut. When they tell you to jump, ask them 'How high, sir?' Once you're in the fleet, it's a regular job."

He knew I was tough enough; what he and everyone else was worried about was that my smart-ass mouth would get me into trouble.

I ARRIVED FOR EIGHT WEEKS OF BOOT CAMP at RTC (Recruit Training Command) Orlando on April 23, 1990, on a hot and muggy night, scared to death. As I got off the bus in single file with the other male and female recruits, we were immediately yelled at.

"You are trees, ladies!" a company commander shouted, as he separated the boys from the girls (we hadn't earned the right to be called men and women yet, we learned). "And the boys are rocks. Rocks and trees do not mix!"

He split the girls and boys into two separate lines, and divided us into companies—I was put into Company K069.

We woke up at five o'clock the next morning in temporary quarters to more yelling. "Get on line, recruits!"

I jumped out of bed. I had no idea what a "line" was, but I followed the other recruits who'd been there for a few days and seemed to know. When one recruit sleeping in the bunk above me didn't get up, Chief Barlow—tanned, handsome, 30-ish—went over and roughly yanked her out of bed. We had 15 minutes to "shit, shower, and shave" in a communal shower, and no doors on the toilets.

"After you use the toilets, you will salute the head!" Barlow instructed. "The head" is a Navy term for toilet, and "saluting the head" meant to put the toilet seat up, to prevent crabs. (How that prevented crabs, we had no idea.)

After 15 minutes of bathroom time, we were back on line. We were sent to the chow hall for breakfast, then back to the temporary barracks with important homework: Learn all the ranks and how to recognize who's who by the insignia on their uniforms.

After homework time, we were hustled outside that first morning for an unexpected splendor. At 8:33 A.M., all the companies gathered outside to watch the space shuttle *Discovery* launch into the sky. It was an awesome moment, and so symbolic of the unknown but thrilling adventure we were all embarking on.

Back inside we gave up our civilian clothes (except bras) to be mailed back home, in exchange for boot camp–issued sweatshirts, sweatpants, dungarees, or working uniforms that we'd wear for the rest of our military life. We spent the next two days stenciling it all with our names . . . my nine-letter last name usually meant that it took me longer than the others.

A few days later, we were taken to the barracks, our new home for the next two months, with the boys on one floor and girls on another. Each floor was one big room with rows of metal bunk beds, or "racks." This was where we learned what the military was about: sleep deprivation, learning their ways, and being broken down and built back up. We learned how to fold our clothes as small and neatly as we could so they'd fit in our racks once we got aboard ship and so our lockers in the barracks would be tidy and uniform. Uniformity and paying attention to detail was drummed into our heads day and night, for good reason—one wrong or unexpected move aboard ship could mean your life and everyone else's.

The first few weeks, I took my father's advice and kept my head down and my mouth shut—my family and friends would have been shocked by how quiet I was. I was nervous and felt alone so far away from home, so I needed to lie low and figure out the rules.

Mom sent me one of her favorite feel-good books from the hippie era, the mega-bestseller *Jonathan Livingston Seagull,* as a spiritual strengthener. It was about a seagull learning about life and taking flight.

Without knowing quite what I was doing or how to do it, I began to do my own "internal" work. Like Dad, I had devised my own mantra. Every morning I'd look in the mirror and say out loud, "I can do this. I can make it through boot camp. I am strong."

Gene back at Scottie's Auto Body sent me letters with dirty jokes to make me laugh and boost my morale. (He'd also include contraband bubblegum in the envelope, with notes like: *I hope you get in trouble for this—100 push-ups!*)

In week four, a little miracle happened.

Every night the new recruits were required to write down our "comment of the day" and hand them in to the commander. Our comments were anonymous, so you could write anything you wanted and he'd never know who wrote it. One night I was feeling a bit more like my goofy, bold self and I wrote down the teaser of one of Gene's off-color jokes:

Question: What lives in a dark hole and only comes out for ice cream and sex?

The next morning Chief Barlow and Petty Officer Mickler came in to put us through our drill making our racks. We had two minutes to make our beds and put our toes to the line in front of our beds.

"I want to know who wrote this, and I want to know right now!" Barlow yelled.

Oh, shit.

Everyone was quiet, especially me. And then one of my bunkmates, who'd heard me tell the joke earlier, yelled out, "Liesegang wrote it, sir!"

Traitor! I thought, and braced myself for punishment.

"Lyzz-gaang, you wrote this?" Barlow barked.

"Yes, sir. And it's pronounced *'Lee-see-gang,'* sir."

He refused to say it correctly my entire time in boot camp. Maybe it was part of my breaking-down/toughening-up process.

"Lyzz-gaang, get out here."

I appeared from behind my rack and toed the line.

"I want you to tell this joke to the company."

So much for flying under the radar! I cleared my throat. "What lives in a dark hole and only comes out for ice cream and sex?"

No one said anything. I paused, then stuck out my tongue out as far as I could, like a kid at the doctor's office. The room exploded with laughter—even Barlow laughed his ass off. In class later that afternoon, it happened again. The teacher asked if anyone knew any jokes.

"Liesegang does, sir!" It was the same girl who'd ratted me out in front of Barlow. Once again, I was ordered to deliver Gene's crowd-pleaser. This time, my audience was mixed—both rocks (the boys) and trees (girls)—and the guys roared.

"Liesegang, you're Company K069, is that right?" asked one of the red-badged inspectors, whom we called "Russians." "Your company is full of machinists' mates and enginemen—*snipes,* as we call them. Company K069, you will now be known as "the Guttersnipes.""

After that day, my reputation as boot-camp comedian took on a life of its own. I kept everyone laughing, from recruits to officers to commanders, repeating every one of Gene's jokes I could remember, and I went from quiet and scared to confident. My stand-up skills even gained me a nickname.

One day as we were being fitted for our dress uniforms, another recruit attempted to tell the "Chubby" joke. I have no idea where that joke originates but I knew it well, and this recruit could not pull it off to save her life, as she was skinny with hollow cheeks. To tell the Chubby joke, you have to be round-faced like me and, well, *chubby.*

Even though I'd lost a few pounds before arriving at boot camp, there was no hiding from my fellow recruits that I was still considered overweight by the Navy; I was required to wear a blue headband that signified I was over the ideal pound range and had to lose weight during boot. I was a natural for the Chubby joke.

"Nah, this is how ya do it," I said to the skinny recruit. I pushed my cheeks together with my hands and squished my face and took on a Southern drawl: "Hi. My name's Chubby. My mama's chubby, my daddy's chubby. Even my goldfish is chubby. One day my daddy says to me, 'Chubby, how'd you like to go for a motor-sickle ride?' I said, 'Sho', Daddy, sho' . . .'"

We'd been talking to Petty Officer Mickler at the time, and she was busting a gut. "C'mon, Chubby. Chief Barlow has to see this."

She escorted me straight to Chief Barlow and ordered me to repeat the Chubby joke. I squished my face with my hands.

"'Chubby, is this faaast enough for you?' 'No, Daddy, let's go faster . . . faster, faster, faster . . . slowwwwww down,'" I pulled the skin of my face tight to mimic the wind in my face. "One day, my mama says, 'Chubby! How do you smile through all that fat?' And I said, 'It's easy, Mama, it's easy—see?'"

From that day forward, my nickname was "Chubby" and I was an official hit. No matter where I was, I'd be asked to do the Chubby joke. Chief Barlow had me do it for everyone at the top of the stairs in front of chow hall one night, and at movie night as the warm-up before the feature presentation. My brother company even devised an official "Chubby salute" and a "Chubby dance." My new nickname didn't bother me like when my family used to call me "Chubs" growing up. I knew my fellow sailors were praising me.

When I wasn't telling jokes, I was studying the types of ships, putting out fires, and coughing in the gas chamber—we had to remove our masks, state our names out loud, and then run out of the room. Through it all, there was a shit ton of push-ups to do. I auditioned for the Bluejacket Choir (singing Mom's favorite, "Killing Me Softly"), and we had to get up at four o'clock every morning, an hour earlier than the others, to rehearse and march. If one person got out of step, we all had to drop and do 50 push-ups. I usually had 300 to 400 push-ups under my belt before eight.

I still wasn't used to the Florida heat, and during my entire time in boot camp, I'd be thoroughly sweaty by breakfast. (I'd always been tormented by sweat; simply walking from one end of the room to the other could leave me dripping, no matter how much antiperspirant I had slathered on.)

I progressed well in most areas, excelled in some, and messed up in a couple. When I was training to "stand watch" over the company and standing inside the barracks door, I was supposed to yell, "Intruder on deck!" if either Barlow or Mickler entered unannounced—which they did. I opened my mouth to yell but nothing came out. I froze. After Barlow walked past me, I started to yell "Intrud—"

"Too late, Lyzz-gaang!" he shouted. "Drop!" I assumed the push-up position where I was and waited to hear how many. Instead, he left me there and took the rest of the company through a bed-making drill.

Half an hour later, I was still in push-up position drenched in sweat. My hands were purple. "Request permission to recover, sir!"

No answer. I balanced on one hand and shook the other until the blood flowed, then switched. Another five to ten minutes went by. "Petty Officer Mickler, request to recover, ma'am!"

"Shut up, Lyzz-gaang!" Barlow yelled. "We heard you the first time!"

Fifteen minutes after that, he left the barracks and barked again. "Lyzz-gaang, get up!"

Chief Barlow looked at me with disappointment. He'd made an example of me in front of the company, and for good reason. Standing watch was one of the most important jobs in the Navy—one bad move could be your life and the lives of your shipmates, so paying attention to details was etched into our brains.

I felt so ashamed, as if I'd let my entire company die. We were supposed to have each other's backs and be able to fight together and trust each other with our lives. And we looked up to our commander like children do to their parents; I wanted Chief Barlow to be proud of me.

I earned his respect back the following week, when all the companies competed in an athletic weekend and Barlow bet the other commanders a case of beer each that we'd outdo them. I had stopped swimming for a year in high school after the Uncle Doug incident, but resumed it senior year and had been picked for the state champion-ship in freestyle. One of the swimming events during our boot-camp athletic weekend was the 25-yard sprint freestyle. *Piece of cake.* The other involved jumping into the pool holding our fire-retardant pants above our heads, inflating them with air, twisting them up into a flo-tation device, then holding them between our legs and backstroking the 25 yards. I won both races, making Barlow proud.

During a football game another day, he was the quarterback on the opposing team. During one play, he directed two girls to stop me, so they sat on my feet like little kids. I still pushed forward and reached him, dragging the women with my legs.

"Lyzz-gaang," he said, with awe, "what the hell is wrong with you? Are you a man?"

Yeah, yeah, like I hadn't heard that before. But I could tell he was impressed.

Boot camp was, like Dad said, a game—and if played correctly, it was easy to win. All you had to do was follow orders, not ask ques-tions, not talk back to those in higher rank, and do as you were told, whether you liked it or agreed with it or not. In the bigger picture, it was about putting yourself in the hands of your fellow comrades and trusting them with your life.

A few days before graduation, Dad and Debbie arrived for "lib-erty weekend" and came to the base for a meet and greet. I've only seen my father cry twice in my life: The first was when I was ten years old and he and Debbie briefly split up. The second was when he first saw me in my dress whites.

"I'm proud of you, Dana Leigh," he said, hugging me and patting me on the back.

Chief Barlow and Petty Officer Mickler spotted me and came over. Barlow introduced himself to my father and extended his hand. "Mr. Liesegang, I want to tell you that your daughter is the most famous recruit here at Orlando RTC. In fact, she's the most famous recruit I've ever seen go through Orlando RTC."

Dad and Debbie smiled, and so did I—Barlow had said my name correctly! He was surprised that they didn't know my Chubby bit and ordered me to perform it one last time, and we all had a laugh.

Before the evening was over, Barlow took me aside. I had worked hard during boot camp and was down to 150 pounds by graduation, a loss of 10 pounds. "Liesegang, I want to see you succeed," he said, "and I see that weight is a struggle for you, like it is for me. Keep up your running during apprenticeship training school, okay?"

I smiled. "Yes, sir!"

At graduation, I marched with the choir, and we sang "Anchors Aweigh." It was one of the best days of my life. I've never felt so proud of myself, my country, and my flag—ever.

IN AUGUST 1990, I STOOD ABOARD THE USS *McKee* stationed at Naval Base Point Loma in San Diego. I was 19 and an engineman in the Navy, and excited for my future to begin. As a kid I'd watched sailors tying ships to the docks when I went with Dad to the shipyards, thinking it looked adventurous and easy. Moored next to us was the USS *Ranger,* a huge, beautiful aircraft carrier that made our ship look puny. I helped pull the thick mooring lines of the *Ranger* out of the water and was shocked by how heavy they really were. Women weren't allowed on carriers yet, but I hoped that one day soon they would be.

As for the present, it took me a while to acquire my sea legs, you might say. My first day on the ship, I got lost. Weeks later, I had a run-in with one of the guys in my division, R-9. We started off as friends when he kindly loaned me money to buy clothes after I'd forgotten my civvies. A few days after that, though, he came up to me and for no reason at all, gave me Spock's Vulcan nerve pinch on my trapezius muscle. It really hurt, so I pushed his hand away from me and told him to knock it off.

He did it again, and I pushed his hand away again. This felt all too familiar. The third time he pinched me, I warned him, "If you don't stop, I'm going to punch you."

You can guess the rest. He pinched me again, and I swung around in my now-infamous 180-degree move and bloodied the guy's nose. (Men perplexed me. If a woman says to leave her alone three times, why don't they listen?) The guys aboard ship began making fun of me in the weight room, calling me names like "Lesbiangang" or "Pump-kinhead" after seeing me lift up to 155 pounds.

On ship the first two months, I didn't do any real duties of an engineman yet. My first month was spent studying to get my qualifications in order to do my engineman duties. After that, I was pulled to another division to learn computer skills . . . along with how to clean and remove "non-skid"—that gritty, rough flooring on a ship—from the vestibule steps. Then, I was pulled up to the main galley to do my time "mess cranking," which is essentially kitchen duty.

There was a bar on base called the Pump Room, which was a few minutes' walking distance from the ship. Beer was a dollar a pint, and the on-base legal drinking age was 18—how could I resist? We were a beer-loving family. (In fact, when I'd gone home on a two-week leave after graduation and apprenticeship training, Dad had picked me up at Portland International Airport with his black *Smokey and the Bandit*–style T-top Trans Am, and there was a six-pack of Miller Genuine Draft in the passenger seat as a "congratulations." He handed me a beer, and the car keys.) I was a typical 19-year-old sailor excited to be able to legally drink in a bar.

I slowly began making friends. Lena, a hull technician; Reynelle, an electrician; and Ron, a machinist's mate, were three buddies I'd go to the Pump Room and have a few too many cheap beers with, or we'd go to the movies off-base. Still, I felt a bit lonely and reckless those first weeks at Point Loma, maybe because things were so different from boot camp, where I'd been so popular.

In the back of my mind lurked a crazy wish, that maybe my male shipmates would be nice to me if I broke an arm or leg because who'd pick on a girl who was hurt? It was the fantasy of a child who felt powerless, I knew. I spent a lot of time humming the despairing "Killing Me Softly" to try to cheer myself up.

On Thursday, October 25, 1990—my brother Gary's birthday—I spent all day on mess-cranking duty, which included serving meals, throwing out trash, working the main galley, and any other job in and around the kitchen. Lena was on duty with me, and we finished mopping up around 7 P.M. She tried to convince me to go to the Pump Room with her, but I didn't feel like it. Reynelle wanted me to go with her to a birthday party off-base, but I didn't feel like that, either. I'd been up since 4 A.M. and was too tired to party.

I changed into a baggy sweatshirt, high-top sneakers, and stretch pants, and walked off-base about a mile to mail a birthday card. It was for my new long-distance boyfriend, Mark, whom I'd met at home while on leave a few months earlier.

It was a chilly evening, and I was shivering as I walked back to the base. A red pickup truck pulled up alongside me, and the driver asked, "Hey, do you wanna ride back?"

His name was Bruce, and he was a diver on the ship next to mine, the USS *Dixon*. I didn't know him, but I was tired and cold and he was a fellow military man. I thanked him and hopped in.

It was now about 8 P.M. as we drove back to base, and he pulled into the parking lot by the Pump Room. From the looks of the empty pint of Jack Daniel's on the floor of the truck, he'd already been drinking.

"Oh, yeah. I just drank that whole thing," he boasted. "Do you want to go in?" he motioned to the bar.

"Nah, I don't really feel like going to a bar."

"Well, do you wanna do somethin' else, then?"

Bruce was vaguely cute and 18, a year younger than I was. He was tall and skinny—his build reminded me of Davey, whom I used to fight at the dump in Three Lynx. In all my years slugging it out with boys and men bigger than me, Bruce was one of the least physically threatening males I'd ever met.

"Sure," I said. "I don't feel like going back to the ship, either."

Bruce decided to drive to nearby Mission Beach, stopping at a convenience store across the street from the beach's wooden roller coaster. He gave money to a homeless guy in the alley to go in and buy him another pint of Jack.

"Let's go someplace I can drink and not get caught. Someplace the cops won't find us."

"How about Sunset Cliffs?" I was so helpful.

I'd heard that Sunset Cliffs Natural Park—only a ten-minute drive away—had dramatic cliff formations and caves and beautiful ocean views along its bluffs. Of course it was already dark, so I don't know how much I thought I'd see. I just wanted to hang out and have a few laughs; I wasn't interested in anything else, and he didn't seem to be either.

On the drive, Bruce lit a cigarette and started telling me that he took drugs and dealt them, too.

"How do you deal drugs while you're in the Navy?"

"It's easy!" He laughed, a little too loudly.

I suddenly felt my stomach drop. *I shouldn't be in this truck. I should tell him to turn around and drive me back to base.* But I didn't want to seem scared, so I didn't say anything (I could hear Dad's voice in the back of my mind: "You're too macho for your own good!")

We parked by the cliffs and got out. Both of us had to pee, so I went one direction behind a little hill and he went another. A minute later, as I was crouched down, "copping a squat," I looked up to find Bruce staring down at me.

"Have you ever had anyone watch you pee before?"

Shit. Okay, now I'm in trouble. I stood up and walked past him, purposely bumping into him as I strode by to show I couldn't be bullied. Maybe not such a good idea.

We sat down and started chatting. I reached for his Jack Daniel's to try to look cool and tough. *We're two fellow military men, having a drink,* I told myself, and then he pulled the bottle away from me roughly.

"Let's go for a walk," I suggested, jumping up and heading down the trail. I wasn't sure what I was doing or where I was going; I just knew I had to get out of there. He followed me for a few seconds, and then lunged toward me from behind.

The rest is a violent, muffled blur of images and sounds: me swinging my fists wildly, trying to knee him in the balls . . . him pinning me down with his knees on my arms, punching my face as I tried to get him off me . . . his heavy breathing and the sound of clothes ripped from my body . . . *Don't! Don't! Don't!* screaming from deep in my gut . . . his fingers curling around my neck—squeezing, squeezing . . . and then blackness.

I was falling.

PART II

After the Fall

CHAPTER 7

Ears of Tears

When I opened my eyes, I couldn't move. I couldn't talk. I couldn't breathe on my own.

It was Friday, October 26, 1990—I'd been in a coma for 18 hours. I woke up in the intensive care unit at UCSD Medical Center in San Diego, flat on my back and in traction, hooked up to a respirator that did my breathing for me.

I stared at the cracked paint on the ceiling and thought, *How did I get here? What happened?*

I didn't remember a thing.

I didn't know that the night before, I'd been found at the bottom of the majestic Sunset Cliffs, naked and broken. I had no recollection of who'd found me or how, or that a Life Flight helicopter had raced me to the hospital as a Jane Doe—my clothes and dog tags were still at the top of the cliff where I'd struggled with Bruce—and I hadn't been expected to survive. Before sunrise, I'd been reported as AWOL (or UA, as the Navy calls it) to my commanding officer when I wasn't present and accounted for in the galley.

By then, police had found my clothing and military identification and dialed Navy officials, who called the emergency contacts on my file: Dad and Debbie. Within hours, while I was still in the coma, my family had flown or driven to the hospital—Mom, Dad and Debbie, Ken and Bonnie, Gary, Grandma Blanche, and even Chrissy from Hawaii.

I had plummeted 75 feet off the cliff to the sand and rocks below. When my parents first saw me in the hospital with tubes stuck all over my swollen body and oxygen being pumped into my throat and lungs, they didn't recognize me.

In those first 18 hours I had been heavily sedated, drugged and unconscious. But in my mind, I'd been lost in a fuzzy, limbo space between reality and imagination. I remember hearing nurses moving around the room, clattering objects and talking about me, saying things like, "Those are strangulation marks on her neck . . ."

At one point, Mom and Chrissy had sat at either side of my bed, talking to me and praying and singing, "Killing Me Softly." I heard them, but I also saw them gently put their hands on my damaged body as if to heal me. I could see them as if I were standing at the head of my bed watching them. I tried to talk to them and comfort them, attempting to say, "Mom, Chrissy . . . I'm fine!"

I had broken my neck and critically injured my spinal cord, had lacerations to my liver and spleen, and suffered severe traumatic brain injury. "She'll be lucky to live through the night," one specialist told my mother. "If she does survive, she'll most likely be paralyzed from the neck down and never breathe on her own and could possibly be brain damaged. She'll be a vegetable." (When there was talk at some point about taking me off life support, my father wouldn't hear of it.)

My mother gave the doctors her own prognosis—the correct one, according to her: "I was told by a higher source that she's going to be fine," she said. "I don't know what 'fine' means, but I know that's what she's going to be." *I* was that "higher source" she was talking about; Mom had heard me assure her as she and Chrissy put their hands on me.

"You don't know the spirit inside that little girl," Mom told the doctors. "I do. That girl can do the impossible."

It was a blessing that I had woken up with no memory of the night before, because I had more important things to think about— namely, how to stay alive. That is, when I could think clearly at all. The next several days and weeks overlapped and ran into each other like a never-ending nightmare. I was in and out of sleep and remained heavily medicated with no concept of days or nights or time, as I couldn't turn my head to look at a clock and the ICU had no window.

I knew one thing for sure without anyone telling me: I was para-lyzed. I heard the word *quadriplegic,* and I knew that I couldn't feel or move anything from my collarbone downward. In my daze, I could hear people come and go and do things to me, but I couldn't see or feel it; I could only look straight up at the ceiling or out of the corner of my eyes. I could see the worried expressions of my family when they stood over my face, looking down at me. But even that was confusing.

Those first days in the ICU, visitors could only come see me two at a time—and I don't know how else to say this, but my family was arriving in the "wrong" pairs. I had five out of my six parents show up, each of them announcing "I'm her mother" and "I'm her father" when they got there, confusing the hell out of the hospital staff . . . especially when each one confirmed the others were, indeed, also my mothers and fathers. Had I not been fighting for my life, I would have laughed my ass off.

At one point, Mom came in the room with Debbie, and another time with Bonnie—the women who had married two of her ex-husbands. That was strange. When Mom came in with Ken and both of them looked down at me with love, I looked up at them woozily with tears in my eyes, as the ten-year-old in me leapt for joy seeing them together after a decade.

"I know, baby, I know," Mom said, smiling.

It was weird seeing them all get along. Years later, I'd learn that they were putting on a strong front for my benefit and that outside the ICU door, Gary and Chrissy were busy dousing the tempers and defusing family arguments.

YOU DON'T FULLY APPRECIATE YOUR INDEPENDENCE UNTIL YOU LOSE IT.

I now had to depend on other people to take care of my most basic needs and bodily functions. Nurses, both male and female, inserted and removed tampons for me, fed me, scratched my nose, brushed my teeth and hair, shaved me, washed my bum and crotch. I couldn't even take a crap by myself like a baby in a diaper; I had to have someone manually stimulate me to have a bowel move-ment. The respirator—which felt like a baseball bat shoved down my throat—breathed for me, but because my lungs would fill with fluid, they had to be constantly suctioned, which was a necessary hell. The nurses stuck a vacuum tube down my throat to suck the fluid out.

As much as I hated it, I learned to ask for it so I wouldn't choke on my own mucus. How did I ask for it? "Sssssssssss," I'd say, when I could make any sound at all. *"Ssssss!"* And the nurses knew that meant I wanted the necessary hell.

Not being able to talk because of the respirator down my throat was a hell all its own. My family tried to use a blinking system so we could communicate—one blink for *yes* and two blinks for *no*—but we never could get it right and had to keep starting over.

"You know, Dane," Gary said, during one of his visits, "I think this is the first time since you learned how to talk that you've ever been speechless."

Not being able to talk to the doctors and nurses was even worse, because I couldn't tell them when something was wrong.

I was placed on a rotating bed that would eventually move me from side to side to prevent bedsores, but I wasn't allowed to rotate just yet—not until the doctors attached a "halo" to my head to keep my neck stable. One nurse came into my room in the first few days and didn't bother looking at my chart and flipped the rotation switch on.

No! I screamed in my mind to her. *Turn it off!*

The bed began to rotate to one side and my body shifted. The nurse looked alarmed, realizing her possibly fatal mistake, and quickly rushed to rotate the bed back to its original position in a panic, then tried shift my body back to where it was.

When the doctor arrived soon after, he looked perplexed as he examined me. "Did you rotate this patient's bed?" he asked the nurse.

"No, doctor," she replied.

Liar! I tried to choke out, through the respirator. I was pissed, and helpless.

The halo was a metal brace and vest that went around my head and chest to immobilize and support my neck while it healed, and getting it on was another necessary hell. To attach it to my head, the doctors had to put four screws into my skull—two in front and two in back.

Two doctors arrived on halo day with scissors to cut off my hair in the back. "We'll make sure we do this evenly so it'll look stylish," one of them said, trying to joke around.

Ha, you are so funny.

It wasn't so funny when they decided I didn't need any extra pain medication to numb my forehead before they screwed the pins into my skull.

I do need more! I do need more! I shouted to them in my mind. *Oh, God,* I braced myself.

They jammed the screws into my skull, and the pain was so unbearable—the sound of my skull bones cracking was horrifying, like bricks smacking against a stone tunnel wall—that I cried and shit myself all over the bed.

"Well," said the doctor with the sense of humor, "looks like we scared the shit outta you."

Go fuck yourself.

I actually cracked a smile, too—it was a pretty good one.

In my situation, I had a shockingly new perspective about people and their various levels of compassion and awareness. One day I opened my eyes to find five young male interns standing around my bed, staring at my naked body. A doctor had stripped the blanket off me and was talking to the students about my internal injuries as if I couldn't see, hear, or understand anything that was going on. As if I was a nothing, a lab monkey or zoo animal on display for them to look at whenever they wanted. When the doctor had finished with me, one of the interns tossed the blanket back onto the bed, and they walked out. They didn't even know my name.

Not only was I unable to breathe on my own or talk, but I couldn't drink and was continually parched with thirst. I was hooked up to an IV for water and the nurses used these awful lemon-glycerin swabs to dab the inside my mouth for moisture, but I was so thirsty that my family kept sneaking me ice chips even though I could have choked on them. I swore that if I ever got that damn tube out of my throat, I'd drink an entire lake.

Every day presented a new indignity, and I was in so much pain and misery that when my family wasn't around, I cried for hours. That caused an entirely new set of problems. When I was finally able to be rotated on that table—it moved in a semicircle from side to side—the tears that slid down the sides of my face and into my ears would slide in deeper, causing a massive earache in both ears. I was in agony and couldn't tell anybody. So I cried some more, making it worse.

I couldn't get that old Hank Williams tune "There's a Tear in My Beer" out of my head, except I sang it with my new lyrics: *There's a tear in my ear 'cause I'm cryin' for you, dear . . .*

Along with some people's insensitivities, I also experienced great compassion. After one especially difficult day, two nurses came in to give me a bath in bed. They gently washed my hair and sponged me clean under the halo vest with warm, soapy water. They talked to me softly and touched me tenderly, like I was a human being. I couldn't feel their touch, of course, but I could feel the kindness they were giving me and was grateful.

Yet despite the kindness of strangers and my mother's confidence about my fighting spirit, I decided somewhere in those first few days that I wanted to die. I didn't want to live the rest of my life with someone putting on rubber gloves and sticking their fingers up my anus to pull the poop out as I counted the dots on the ceiling. I didn't want to live the rest of my life not being able to even breathe on my own, as the smart doctors guessed would be my fate. So one night when I was alone in the dark after visiting hours, I bit down hard on the respirator tube to cut off the air being pumped into my lungs. Alarms on the machine went off, and a nurse came running in from their station.

"Stop biting the respirator!"

She wasn't surprised at all that I'd done it and was a bit annoyed. They'd seen all this before, I guess—many times. I tried to cut my air off again when a new nurse came on shift that same night. To avoid the alarms, I tried to spit the tube out. Instead, I managed to dislodge it upward just enough so that it hurt terribly, but kept working. *Fucking hell!*

I wasn't very good at killing myself.

IF I WAS GOING TO LIVE, it had to be on my terms. Like Mom, I refused to believe that I'd live the rest of my life like this. I'd never backed down from a fight in my life, so why should I start now? No matter what, I've learned that you take your core personality wherever you go, and I wasn't a quitter when things got tough. I wanted to get out of that bed and get my life back.

First, I had to learn how to do one of life's easiest, most basic functions: breathe. I had to get off that respirator, not just to breathe, but to talk. During week three in the ICU, we began weaning me off it—the hardest thing I've ever done in my life. I don't think the doctors and nurses thought that I could do it, but I fought and worked hard at it. A little bit at a time, a respiratory therapist would turn the air down so that my lungs would start working on their own. We started with five-minute increments . . . and then ten . . . fifteen . . . building up. One therapist would turn down my air while I was still sleeping, and I'd wake up abruptly laboring for air, feeling like I was choking to death—it was terrifying. I wanted to punch her in the face so bad (as I said, I was still *me* inside).

I learned to adopt a meditative mantra to calm myself down and train my lungs to work: *Nice and slow* [on the inhale], *that is the tempo* [on the exhale].

Finally, the day came when I'd worked up to four hours of breathing on my own, and it was time to take that respirator out. That same therapist who turned down my air as I slept was the one who pulled the tube out of my throat, then slapped a misting mask on my face.

"Cough!" she ordered, and then walked out of the room and shut the door before I could say or do anything. I had questions to ask and things to say after so much silence, and her abrupt departure pissed me off. My first attempted words after she left were brilliant, eloquent, and very Dana-esque.

"Bitch," I whispered raspily, "get . . . your . . . ass . . . back . . . here!"

Once the respirator tube was out, I could leave the ICU. Not only could I breathe and talk again, but I could drink! I guzzled water like someone who'd been lost in the desert for weeks and had found an oasis. I drank so much that they had to start limiting my intake because my bodily fluids got really diluted and my level of electrolytes got dangerously low. Whatever. I was so happy to breathe on my own and drink water and talk—things the doctors weren't sure I'd ever do again.

I started out speaking in a faint whisper, short words of one syllable at a time, with a big breath in between each word. I practiced my ABC's to exercise my lungs and voice, and at first could only reach C —by D no sound came out, but I kept going. I spoke as much as I could (again, I was still me), except with the doctor who came in to my room one day to give me a quickie test on how my brain function and memory were.

"Dana, can you name the last five presidents of the United States?"

Ha! Even if I hadn't been recovering from severe head trauma, there's no way I'd know those answers. Had I been able to speak better, I would have told him that.

Soon after I could breathe better on my own, Dad and Debbie helped get me ready for my first visit outside on the hospital grounds. Dad was gently combing my hair when he suddenly gasped and stopped. "Debbie, go get a nurse!"

"Dad . . . what's . . . wrong?" I whispered.

"Nothing's wrong," he said, with panic in his voice. It turns out that as he was combing, a chunk of hair and skin had fallen off my head and he'd stuck it back on with his hands while Debbie fetched the nurse. My father was horrified that he'd hurt me, but I'd developed a decubitus ulcer on my head—otherwise known as a bedsore.

Dad was in for another shock around that time.

That first month or so we'd all kept busy with the basics—that is, trying to keep me alive and keep me *wanting* to be alive. The next step was breathing on my own and talking, and then it would be eating. So we were all able to temporarily put aside the elephant in the hospital room: how I got there in the first place.

I didn't want to think about it. I later learned that not having a clear recollection of the events surrounding my injury—known as post-traumatic amnesia—was common with this type of severe head trauma. My memories had not been encoded properly in my brain.

I woke up not remembering, and now I didn't want to remember. I just wanted to get better and get the hell out of there. I wanted my life back.

I didn't want to deal with all of this, and I didn't know if my family could handle it. How would my father feel knowing that his "macho" daughter who had punched out men bigger than him had been beaten, raped, and tossed off some cliffs and left to die? The discovery of what happened that night, for both my family and myself, was inevitable. But it would take days, months, even years, for everyone to know everything . . . myself included.

My boyfriend, Mark, visited me around week four. After going to the San Diego police station to read their report on my case, he came to the hospital to tell me what it said.

"The report said you were making out with this Bruce kid," Mark began, "and he was on top of you and you slipped out from underneath him and fell off the cliff."

He took a breath and went on. "The police were doing a routine check in the area. They saw Bruce running away, carrying his shoes and shirt in his hands, and they stopped him. Your clothes were found later by the cops at the top of the cliff."

Dad and Debbie were in the room with me, and everyone was quiet. What I was thinking was: *Yeah, right. I fell off the cliff from underneath him. So why didn't both of us go down? You don't slip out from someone who is on top of you.*

What I whispered out loud, sort of, was: "That's . . . not . . . true."

I now remembered enough from that night to know that the report was incorrect and even a lie, but I didn't want to go into details about it. Not long after this, I had a visit in my hospital room from a female Navy advisor. Dad and Debbie were with me (they'd taken a leave of absence from work) because I'd given Dad my power of attorney.

The advisor got to the point right away. "We know it was foul play," she said. "Bruce told the police one story and he told the Navy six other, different stories. We know a crime was committed."

I couldn't see the expression on my father's face, but I could imagine it. I was picturing shock, then pain, then fury. Incidentally,

the Navy had already placed a restraining order on my family "to protect all involved." It was procedure, they said. Had they not, I knew, Bruce would not have survived to his next birthday, and my father and brother would have ended up in jail.

"If you take this to court," the advisor continued, "you will lose. You will get nothing. On the other hand, if you take your 'right to remain silent,' you will be 100 percent service-connected and be taken care of for the rest of your life by the Veterans Benefits Administration."

I was a 19-year-old woman with a halo screwed into my head, barely able to speak, paralyzed from the neck down. I could keep quiet and be taken care of for as long as I lived, or speak up and have the hope of justice and nothing else. The Navy advisor was making one thing very clear: it was my word against Bruce's.

I looked at my dad out of the corner of my eye, and he lifted his hand to his mouth and gave me the "zip it" sign. It seemed to be my best choice. I didn't want to talk to anyone about what had happened anyway. I didn't want to somehow get blamed for it. For once in my life, I *wanted* to be silent. If anyone asked, I could just tell them, "I fell off a cliff, and I don't know any more . . ."

Mom had it from a higher source that I was going to be fine, and the more I thought about it, the more I believed her. I knew that higher source was me. I wanted to walk and swim and climb and fly free on my bike again.

I will not spend the rest of my life in this prison.

The doctors didn't have faith in much recovery for me, and the Navy wanted to sweep my "accident" under the rug and pretend what really happened didn't. But as Mom had tried to tell everybody—myself included—they had no idea who they were dealing with.

CHAPTER 8

No Crying in Rehab

When I was a teenager, I plastered my bedroom walls with posters of Sylvester Stallone as Rocky Balboa. I first saw *Rocky* when I was ten years old, when Mom left Ken. I was a heartbroken kid, and watching Rocky bound up the 72 steps at the Philadelphia Museum of Art lifted my spirits. He was cool, and an underdog like me who could fight and didn't give up.

Two weeks before Bruce hurt me, I'd seen *Born on the Fourth of July* on the ship, the movie where Tom Cruise plays a paralyzed Vietnam veteran. There's a scene when Tom's character enters a VA (Veterans Affairs) hospital that looks like a slum, with rows of dirty, wounded military personnel, apathetic hospital workers smoking pot, and rats running across the floors. Later, as he is strapped into a bed and being refused access to a doctor, he freaks out and yells, "I want to be treated like a human being!"

I knew the feeling. When it was time for me to move from San Diego to the VA Puget Sound Medical Center in Seattle in December 1990, that horrific scene was stuck in my mind and *I* was freaking out. My fears disappeared, though, when I was wheeled into my lovely private room and met the two Filipina nurses who'd help lift me up—physically and spiritually—over the next ten months.

Merlita was a feisty, upbeat mom-type: "Time to get out of bed, baby!" she'd say in the mornings. "Mama's here to take care of you!" Lelani was sweet and gentle and assured me that I was safe in their hands: "You can trust us," she'd say. And she was right. When Merlita and Lelani moved me from the gurney to the bed in a "two-woman transfer" soon after I arrived—a move that had so hurt and traumatized me weeks earlier when two students attempted it that I'd thrown up —they performed it painlessly and with ease.

A few weeks later, 1990 ended with me in a new home, and the family visiting me for the holidays. Gary decorated my halo with tinsel to make me look like a Christmas tree.

Not so painless was the assembly line of x-rays and MRIs I endured that first month in Seattle. They'd put me in that freezing cold, claustrophobic tube with the jackhammering sound in my ears and say, "Don't move!" _Don't move? Um, okaaaay, I'll try not to move._

All of this agony ended up being well worth it, though. Often with injuries like mine you don't know fully what the damage is until the physical swelling goes down. When I met with Dr. Barry Goldstein, a specialist in spinal cord injuries, to view the results of my new tests, he had great news.

The doctors in San Diego knew that I'd broken my C1 to C5 vertebrae, which are the highest five bones (out of seven) on the neck, C1 being the highest. And they saw that I had a severe head injury, which is now commonly known as TBI (traumatic brain injury), but they were not certain what the extent of damage had been to my spinal cord. The higher the injury, the more parts of your body are affected. For example, if your spinal cord is injured at C1 and C2, that takes away your ability to breathe on your own, which is what happened to actor Christopher Reeve. A typical C5 injury has shoulder and biceps control and a little wrist function; a C6 injury usually has more wrist function; and a C7 injury generally has some triceps use, as well as partial hand and finger use.

Those doctors assumed I'd never even get as far as I already had—breathing and drinking liquids on my own. But UCSD was a training hospital and I don't think they had a spinal cord injury (SCI) unit; plus, while I was there my injury was still very recent. The fact that I'd been able to wean myself off the respirator while I was there was very telling.

Sitting in Dr. Goldstein's office now, he showed me the new pictures of my MRI scan on the screen. "You have an _incomplete_ injury at C4," he said, pointing to an image in front of us. "Now, look here in this area. I think you have an incomplete injury at C5, too, but we won't know for a while."

When I asked what all that meant for me, he replied, "It means that your spinal cord at C4 and C5 is bruised, not severed. The paralysis that you experienced from C1 down these first few months was due to swelling and shock."

I couldn't believe what I was hearing. This was why I'd been able to breathe on my own. This was why more was possible for me than what the staff in San Diego had suspected. Had I not fought hard to get off that respirator, I might still be on it since they thought my injury was worse than it was.

"Will I ever have bowel and bladder control?" I asked.

"With incomplete injuries, we just don't know . . . but anything's possible."

He was the first doctor to talk this way; most medical professionals would've only told me no.

I pushed further. "Will I ever walk again?"

"Again, we don't know. Anything's possible."

At that moment, I loved Dr. Goldstein more than anyone else in the world. The new information he'd given me meant that I could regain more motor function than anyone previously thought!

Hearing this was a *Rocky*-esque inspirational turning point. My spinal cord was only bruised. *Bruises can heal,* I told myself, *and that means I can heal.*

I PUSHED AHEAD; THERE WAS NO STOPPING ME NOW.

When I got off the respirator in San Diego, I'd only eaten Popsicles, watered-down Ensure, and once in a while soggy Froot Loops. When I first arrived in Seattle, however, Merlita and Lelani thought I was on a no-food diet because I refused everything. I lost my appetite, but I also tended to throw up anything solid that I attempted to get down.

Believe me, however uncomfortable vomiting is in general, it's ten times worse when you can't move and your diaphragm and stomach muscles are paralyzed. The irony didn't escape me one day, as I was barfing up beef Stroganoff while choking on it, that I'd spent the last three years making myself throw up food on purpose. Now I never, ever wanted to throw up again.

I'd been afraid to eat, but I wanted to build up my strength, too—so, ever so slowly, I started eating real food again. The cooks in the SCI unit spoiled me and made my favorite comfort foods, like plain noodles drenched in butter with Parmesan cheese, and crustless peanut-butter-and-honey sandwiches.

Another thing I did after arriving in Seattle was to brave the mirror once more. My family and friends had wisely kept them out of my room in San Diego so that I wouldn't see how horrible I looked. But once I was off the respirator and allowed outings, I took a look. Dad, Debbie, and Mark had taken me to a nearby Jack in the Box to coax me to eat, and on the way out we passed a mirror that was visible through the open bathroom door. I had been shocked to see myself—I had a round, pumpkin face, and both my face and body looked like a pasty, bloated blob. The halo around me made me look like an alien, or like Frankenstein with the bolts in my head.

Now a month later, I looked in the mirror and was relieved to see that the puffiness in my face had gone down, and my hair was growing back after they'd shaved it during the scaring-the-shit-out-of-me halo prep. Looking better made me feel better.

So did Dr. Goldstein's can-do, progressive attitude. He and another genius doctor, Dr. Little, were always trying new technologies to help people with spinal cord injuries, and I was their willing guinea pig. One day they came into my room and held a contraption over my head to try to measure what the nerves in my body were doing. (Years after I left, Dr. Goldstein conducted a study on the positive effects marijuana had on muscle spasms, after so many of his patients told him that smoking pot helped them.)

My physical therapist, Jennifer, was also just what I needed. She came into my room to introduce herself before we began our sessions. She was a petite blonde with clear blue eyes and a very athletic, fit physique. "What's your goal?" she asked me.

At that point—three months into my injury—all I could do physically was shrug my shoulders. Even though I had big plans for my recovery, the doctors had told me that there was no way to know what other muscle function I might regain. The goal of physical therapy was to teach me how to use the muscles I did have use of that were not affected by the paralysis. So far, that was my shoulders.

"I want to be totally independent," I replied. "That's my goal."

Jen gave me a surprised look, and then one of recognition—we were both no-bullshit, strong-willed types.

"Okay, then," she said briskly, "let's get you sitting up first. And don't even think about getting a powered wheelchair. Using a manual wheelchair will help you build up your existing muscles."

For the next ten months, rehab was the new boot camp. I had physical therapy (PT) twice a day with Jen, and our first goals were to teach me how to sit up in bed, how to go from a lying-down position to sitting up, how to roll from side to side—all using my shoulders. It's amazing what you can do with one muscle group used in different ways. I was taught how to push myself in my chair, slowly and one inch at a time, by using my shoulders to reach back and pull my chair. I learned how to lock my elbows and use my arm bones for support, as well as to lean on or push against.

Over the many months ahead, as the swelling around my spinal cord continued to go down, I was able to redevelop the muscles that were not truly paralyzed. As my biceps grew stronger and the nerve connectivity became more normal, my muscles were able to grow back some bulk and strength.

Meanwhile, over in occupational therapy, my therapist Susan taught me how to use my new "quad paws"—formerly known as functional hands. Using a technique called "tenodesis," which is a passive hand grasp-and-release technique that uses the wrist and other adaptive aids to help my hands "grip" things, I learned how to perform daily living skills like eating and brushing my hair and my teeth. We practiced using popcorn and Jelly Bellies as our equipment. (If you ever eat popcorn with me, you'll see that I only pick up one kernel at a time. But that means more popcorn for you!)

I was with three paraplegic veterans in the rehab unit—I was the only female and the only quadriplegic, meaning that all four of my limbs were affected by paralysis. The paraplegics, on the other hand, were only affected in two limbs—their legs—which gave them far more independence than a "quad" (we called each other "quads" and "paras" or, in general, "gimps"—a common slang term in the veteran SCI world). If you break your neck, you're considered a quad. If you break your back, you're a para.

The four of us were each at different levels of ability. Nevertheless, we took classes together that covered everything: skin care and pressure sores, bladder and bowel management, driver rehab, psychological adjustment, nutrition, exercise, and more. In wheelchair-skills class, we would learn how to get over curbs and up ramps and staircases, how to open a door with a key, how to take our chairs apart to stow in our cars, and how to teach others to take us up and down stairs and get us on and off curbs and escalators.

During my first few months in rehab, I had help with most of the wheelchair skills. Even so, we practiced our going-up-and-down-the-stairs skills with hilarious results. At the back of the hospital, we used a set of three steps to practice on that was next to a wheelchair ramp. Jennifer was pushing me in my chair and teaching the paras to do it on their own, and as we were slowly making our way up the stairs, at least a dozen people walked by and pointed out helpfully, "Oh, there's a ramp right there you can use!" *Duh.* We were paralyzed, not blind.

Several months later, when I was trying curbs on my own, I was ticked off to discover that this girl who'd ridden her bike with no hands and raced hundreds of miles to swim practice along bumpy highways had a "problem" with curbs. Every time I tried to go off one, I'd drop my front wheels too soon and go flying, with Jen diving to catch me. After too many close calls, I learned how to tackle them backward.

"Come on, quad, hurry up. You push like a girl!" the guys would tease me.

"I *am* a girl!"

At night, when I needed to, I cried alone in my room. I didn't want to do it in front of the guys, the staff, or my family. When we cried as kids, Dad used to say, "Crybaby, kick a rock." In other words, don't show weakness. But when I cried now, it wasn't for myself. It was because I felt I'd let my shipmates down. I got hurt and they were sent to the first Gulf War—Operation Desert Shield—without me.

They say crying makes you feel better, but it never did for me on those nights.

MY NEW COMRADES WERE THE STAFF AND PATIENTS in Seattle, and they were a colorful bunch. Like in boot camp, the camaraderie made our situation bearable and the hard work a bit easier.

Roger was a para in his 40s who'd been shot by his own sawed-off shotgun (by someone else) during a drug deal gone bad. He looked like Charles Manson, and I was his favorite; he couldn't resist my upbeat chattiness, and I couldn't resist his gruffness. Yes, I'd regained my infamous ability to chat up a storm, but I still took a lot of breaths and had to lean forward so people could hear me because my volume had remained low. I followed Roger around and he couldn't get rid of me, so he nicknamed me "the rodent." He was angry at the world, but I could get the old man to smile (over 40 was old as dirt to me).

Jen brought in other injured veterans over the months to show us how they managed the little and big things in their lives. For example, a fellow quad named Gary came in for an outpatient appointment and taught me how to pick up a penny from the ground or a table before I had any finger function or dexterity.

"You've got to lean over," he said, demonstrating, "and get the coin wedged against your thumb. Then you push it toward your other finger . . ."

One of my favorite cameo appearances on the unit was by a para named Ian, who came for his annual evaluation during my last few months in rehab. (I later referred to my own annual visits as my yearly "poke and prod, you're still a quad" sessions.) As soon as we met, Ian and I were like naughty schoolkids bound for trouble. He was 24 years old and cute, and he decided the staff was being way too easy on me. I fell in "tough love" with Ian.

"What? They're not making you make your own bed?" he scolded. "They're not making you open doors on your own? They're babying you way too much."

"Except Jen!"

"Whatever," he replied, rolling his eyes.

His visit lasted only a week, but we managed to get into trouble every day. One night, Ian got the brilliant idea that we should explore an old part of the hospital that was under construction. On one floor we looked at the old spinal cord unit. On another floor, it was the old gym and psych ward. We inched our way down empty corridors—me at my turtle's pace—and Ian made me press every elevator button and open every door we reached, both tasks a big struggle for me. But if you were a troublemaker as an able-body, you were a troublemaker in a wheelchair, too.

What I didn't realize while we were on our adventure was that I had to be in my room by 8 P.M. for the day-shift nurse to get me undressed, into pajamas, and in bed before the shift was over. The night-shift team insisted it be done before they arrived. Eight o'clock went by . . . and so did nine. At about 10 P.M., Ian and I were creeping around the psych ward when he eerily knocked on a closed door for fun.

Tap-tap-taptap-taaaaaap! it knocked back.

Ian and I looked at each other, scared to death. "Oh, my God! Let's get out of here fast!" we both said. Ian zoomed by me to the elevators to press the button (this was an emergency situation!), and I rushed at my turtle's pace.

When we returned to the unit, the nurses on the night shift were livid. "When you can change and get into bed by yourself, Dana, you can stay out as late as you want," they said. "But until then . . . !"

This led to one of Ian's other brilliant ideas the next afternoon. He was going to teach me how to undress and dress myself. I lay in my bed wearing a T-shirt and shorts as he instructed me from his chair at my bedside.

"Ya gotta put your leg up like this, Dana . . . try to get one leg crossed over the other like in a number four, see? And then you pull your pants on this one leg, and then you bring the other pant leg up around to your knee . . . and then you kinda gather it up around your leg like this, see . . . and then you *flop* right down here, and then pick up the other leg over here and shove it into that pant leg. You got it?"

Huh? It used to be so automatic. This looked like a game of bed *Twister.*

I was in the middle of trying to roll on to my side and get my hand in my pants to pull them, while Ian was trying to give my pants a yank, when in walked Nurse La. She was a tall, broad-shouldered Samoan and, next to Roger, the grumpiest, sternest person on the unit. Every day she was on duty, I tried to make her smile. She took one look at me without my pants and at Ian yanking at them, spun on her heel, and left the room—slamming the door so hard the clock fell off the wall. Ian and I laughed our heads off, and the incident sparked quite the rumor, even though there was no hanky-panky going on.

I was beginning to wonder about that, however. During one of Gary's visits, he'd picked up an object he'd seen on my bedside table—a plastic ring with a metal circle and a protruding "finger" in the middle. I knew what he was thinking; it looked like a sex toy.

"What's this?"

"Umm, you don't want to know."

"C'mon, what is it?"

"We call it the 'fickle finger of fate'—we stick it in my bum and then manually pull out the poop."

"Ohh, grooossss!" he groaned, dropping it. "But too bad you can't have sex anymore."

"Why not? They didn't sew me up down there, you know. Of course I can have sex." Pause. "I just can't *feel* it."

"Ah," he said, adding his signature crassness without missing a beat, "and *that* would make you the perfect girlfriend. Four feet tall and a place to set your beer down."

"You are sick!" We laughed.

But seriously, I wasn't sure who to ask about all of this. Although I'd been raped, I had pushed that memory so far down that it didn't get in the way of me wanting to be a normal, healthy young woman, with a normal, healthy sex life and drive.

We had sex-ed class in rehab, but it was mostly for the guys' benefit. Jen talked about papaverine—the "erection injection"—a medication they could inject into the shaft of their penis to get an erection. All I learned for myself was that I could still get pregnant, and that an orgasm could cause autonomic dysreflexia in quads like me; that is, blood pressure so high, it could be life-threatening. Great, thanks. Maybe sex *was* over for me. It was a sobering thought for a 19-year-old.

I'd broken up with Mark after I got to Seattle so that I could concentrate on my rehabilitation, which meant I didn't have a boyfriend I could try things with. I needed to ask a woman who'd been in a chair for a while and had, er, hands-on-experience.

When Danette—a pretty, slender, brunette former Marine with a vivacious personality—rolled into the VA hospital for surgery on her hand, I pounced. Danette was a para in her early 20s who'd gotten hurt a few years before me. In the coming years, she'd teach me more about being a female in a chair than any doctor and all the classes combined ever could. While at the hospital that week, she shared my room, and I started the girl-talk immediately.

"Hey, Danette. Can we still have sex?"

She cracked up. "Yes, absolutely," she said.

"But . . . what does it feel like? *Can* we feel it?" I had a million questions.

"It works differently for everybody. The first thing to do is to concentrate on the areas of the body that do have sensation. Start from there."

I started off by doing some sassy flirting. During an outing with a very cute recreational therapist from our unit, I followed Danette's lead and made use of my new tenodesis skills by pinching his butt as he walked by. Even with limited mobility, this award-winning flirt hadn't lost it.

Danette was one of a handful of female role models who helped me enormously during that time. Laurie, a C5 quad like me, but a "complete" injury, was another. She taught me a small but very useful skill—how to open a carton of milk using thumbs and teeth. And she showed me something much, much bigger and more valuable.

I went to Laurie's home one afternoon and watched every detail of how she lived: I saw her lowered countertops, her bathroom setup, her wheelchair ramps, and how she moved around in her world. She had an attendant come in to help for bowel care and other daily activities, but she lived alone and accomplished almost every other task by herself that an able-bodied person could.

I returned to the hospital that evening with stronger resolve than ever before. Even with Laurie's "complete" injury diagnosis, she was living on her own. My "incomplete" injury meant that I would eventually be even stronger and have more ability than she had, which meant I wouldn't need attendants at all.

To me, Laurie was living proof in front of my own eyes that not only was my goal of total independence a possible dream to reach—it was my inevitable reality.

CHAPTER 9

We Are Family

My family and friends kept my spirits up and my body well fed during my stint in rehab.

Mom lived five hours away in Friday Harbor, and Dad was four hours away in Hillsboro; they both took shifts so that one of them was usually with me.

Mom made arrangements with her boss at the restaurant she'd been working at to take Monday through Thursday off each week, and we'd wander around the hospital together or watch comedies on TV like *The Simpsons* or *Cheers,* keeping our conversations light and upbeat. If there was something my mother knew how to do, it was the positive pep talk. Now that I was eating, she'd also bring me her healthy foods like pita bread and hummus, but that didn't cut it. She soon broke down and started arriving with my favorites, like takeout Mexican, hamburgers and fries, or pizza. One of my fellow patients would bring me contraband beer poured into a water container, hidden in his power chair—because you can't have pizza without beer.

Even on cold winter nights during those first few months, Mom would sleep under a canopy on the back of her blue Toyota pickup truck in the hospital parking lot. It wasn't allowed, but the VA police officer patrolling the area was cool about it and kept an eye on her to make sure she was safe.

Dad and Debbie would arrive on Fridays to take the weekend shift. He'd leave right after work from the shipyard, pick up Debbie at their home with bags packed, then drive the 180 miles to meet me, through rush-hour traffic and rainstorms.

The first time they brought their orange Pomeranian, Bobo, to see me, I was in for a sad shock, though. Bobo and I had been great buddies. Before I joined the service, I'd come home for lunch from Scottie's Auto Body and hop up on the kitchen countertop, and Bobo would follow me, springing into my lap to share whatever I was eating. I hadn't seen her since my two-week trip home after boot camp and was so looking forward to seeing a dog that loved me.

Dad set her on the floor next to my wheelchair, and instead of springing into my lap, which is what I expected, she barked like I was a stranger.

"It's me, Bobo!" I said.

She didn't recognize my voice, my scent, or how I looked in the halo—she was afraid of me and wouldn't come near me. It broke my heart.

Gary told me years later that the change in my voice was one of the hardest things for him to get used to after I was hurt. Apparently my voice was much lower before—so low that the high school choir teacher made me second alto and almost had me be a bass. "Oh my God, how low can you go?" she had asked. My brother also said that I had talked slower. "Now you talk like you can't get the words out fast enough," he told me recently, "as if someone is going to take away your ability to talk." That's what a few weeks on a respirator not being able to swear out loud at people will do to a girl, I guess.

I was rarely lonely, between Mom and Dad and other relatives and friends who made the trip: Uncle Kent and Aunt Jeanne with their kids, Kyle and Connor; Uncle Butch and Aunt Betsy; Ken and Bonnie; my dear friend Amy; my cousin Patrick and other cousins, too. (My cousin Little Jim was in the Army, so I didn't get to see him, and Chrissy couldn't come much because she was still living in Hawaii.) Everyone arrived bearing my favorite order of the day: McDonald's Quarter Pounders, hold the onions.

One day, in walked Gene, full of new jokes to make me laugh. When I was home on leave after boot camp, I'd told him what a hit his jokes had been and how they'd made me famous. When he finished this visit, though, it was on a note of tenderness. He knew I loved to dance, so on the way out the door, he said, "Hey, dumbshit, don't forget. You still owe me a dance."

Susanne visited me during her spring break from school, and it was difficult for her to see me as I was. I'd always been the physically stronger one, and now I was over the moon that I could use my arms to pick up my right leg and cross it over my left—a move that had taken me 15 minutes during her visit. But we laughed and talked like we used to.

She had sent me a package right after I got hurt that contained two precious items: a letter-on-tape that she had recorded for me, and a 4" x 4" piece of cloth. It was Bankie! She had cut out and sent me a little square of her baby blanket that she had loved as a child! Susanne knew my Banana Blanket had mysteriously gone missing while I was in boot camp, so she'd sent me a bit of her own security blanket. Mom had held it up to me as I lay in bed in the ICU, unable to move, and I cried.

"I hope this makes you feel safe," she said on the tape. "I love you."

Our relationship had been rocky since high school, when I began hanging out with the stoners and she was with the cheerleaders. And then when Mom left Ed, both our hearts had broken. Yet when I listened to Susanne's tape, I realized that our love as sisters ran deep, no matter what.

"You are strong, and I wish I had your courage," she said on the tape. "During our years growing up, you were always there for me—cheering me on from the stands." Then she sang that Bette Midler song "Wind Beneath My Wings" to me.

I never knew she felt that way about me. It was such a gift.

BY SPRINGTIME, I WAS ALLOWED weekend visits home. On my first one at Dad's place, I was celebrating a milestone: the doctors had taken the halo off my head. After wearing a hard collar and then a soft collar around my neck, I no longer needed those, either—my neck was stable. It was a little miracle of sorts, because x-rays a week before the halo came off had shown that my neck was not healing well enough, and I'd need surgery to fuse the bones and stabilize it.

After they told me the procedure was set for a few days later, I went to my room and closed the door, then blocked it with my chair so no one could get in. I needed a moment, by myself, to hide and cry. The idea of doctors opening up my neck scared me. *What if something goes wrong? What if I come out worse than I am now? What if the doctors mess up my "incompleteness"?*

Dad and Debbie were due to arrive any minute, and I couldn't let my father see me like this. Not because of his old "Crybaby, kick a rock" taunting from childhood, but because I didn't want to worry him. I always tried to be so strong and positive—whenever I did cry, my family knew it was something very, very serious. I didn't want to upset Dad, so I allowed myself five minutes of tears behind my door. Then I dried my eyes, sucked it up, and put on a smile. No one knew how desperately I did not want this surgery. Or so I thought.

The day after those x-ray results had come in, I was sitting outside in front of the SCI unit doors, upset, when a man I didn't know walked up to me. "I am an angel from God," he said, holding his hands above my head and halo, "and I am going to pray on you and heal you."

A few minutes later, a nurse rushed over and gently pulled the patient away. "I'm so sorry," she told me. "I've got to take him back up to the seventh floor."

Ah. The psych ward.

"I am an angel from God!" he repeated, as he backed away with a smile. "And you are now healed!"

I laughed it off, and never saw him again. But I thought about him a few days later when I went in for a round of presurgery x-rays. The doctors were shocked by what they saw—my neck had healed.

"We must have read the other x-rays wrong," they mumbled to each other. But I knew better. The angel from the seventh floor had healed me.

Dad picked me up the following Friday in his black '88 T-top Trans Am. My physical therapist, Jen, had trained him how to transfer me in and out of the car—he'd also installed a ramp at the front of the house and widened the bathroom door so that my chair would fit through.

Debbie spoiled me with feasts of pork chops, mac and cheese, and pizza. She also bravely took on nurse duty for the weekend by bathing me, dressing me, and doing my "bowel care." Thank God, she had a good sense of "toilet humor." She'd stick her rubber-gloved index finger up my rectum and swirl it around. "Heeeeere, poopy-poopy," she's say, in a little song, as she waited for the poop to come down the chute. I should have joined her in a reprise of "Mellow Yellow" as the encore. "Come out, poopy-poopy, wherever you are!"

Debbie was a real, dare I say it—*pooper trooper.* Her sense of fun made it less humiliating for me. Mom, Bonnie, and even Ken were also pooper troopers that first year. Dad did the handiwork in other ways, building things around the house and carrying me. He fixed all sorts of things, but he couldn't fix me and that devastated him.

The family decided that we'd all meet at Christie's restaurant for breakfast one Sunday morning, before Dad had to take me back to the hospital. A bunch of aunts and uncles on my father's side got a table ahead of time by the front window as he and I drove over in his Firebird. We parked across the street and Dad transferred me into my chair, like a pro. All we had to do now was cross the street and get to the restaurant. Everyone was waving from the window, watching us.

As we approached the crosswalk, Dad sped up. If there was one thing the Liesegangs liked, it was speed—fast cars, fast bikes, so why not fast wheelchairs? I'll tell you why. Because the people who build sidewalks and curbs don't realize that if they leave a lip that makes the transition from road to curb uneven, it's hazardous for those of us in chairs.

Dad slammed into the one-inch lip on the curb cut—the ramp at the corners of sidewalks—and my chair flew forward. He immediately grabbed my chair to pull me back toward him so I wouldn't fall, but my Velcro seat belt had already split apart and I went flying out of the chair like a projectile rocket.

"Oh, shit! Goddamn it!" he yelled.

And onto the ground I went with a thud, face-first.

"Are you okay? I'm so sorry!" Dad was horrified. He gathered up all 160-plus pounds of me and wrestled me back into the chair. I was like a limp, wet noodle.

"Dad, I'm okay, I'm okay," I kept repeating, as he kept apologizing. Thankfully, I'd only scraped my knees and elbows. But by the look on my father's face, you'd have thought that I'd been thrown to the middle of the street and hit by a car. He fastened my crappy Velcro seat belt, and we stood by the curb for a moment as cars sped by us.

That look on Dad's face was one I'd see many times in the future— it was the look of a father whose child was hurt and he couldn't fix it. My father reminded me of a country song I'd heard a few years before called "Daddy's Hands." It was about a woman remembering how much her father's hands did, and that they were "hard as steel" when she'd done wrong, but "soft and kind" when she was crying. When my father was in soft-and-kind mode and got that look, it was sometimes followed by a tortured declaration.

"Dana," he'd say, shaking his head and looking at the ground. "I never should've let you join the Navy."

"What? Dad!"

"I never should've let you go."

"Oh, c'mon. It wasn't your decision."

"I should've stopped you."

"Dad, do you really think you could have stopped me? Besides, I kept it a secret until I was sworn in. It was too late for you to do anything. Hence you calling me a dumbshit."

That usually lightened the moment, and we'd laugh. But I knew that deep down inside, he felt it was his fault I was in a wheelchair.

It was something I never talked about with anyone—whose fault it was that I was in that chair. Not with my father or my mother or my friends—who never asked anyway—and not with the doctors, who did ask.

Soon after I got settled in at Seattle, I began getting visits from social workers and psychologists. My social worker, Marge, was a big, strong woman with a booming voice and one of the few people in this world who could intimidate me.

She was busy trying to get all the important information from me and from the Navy to ensure that I would be 100 percent service-connected through the Veterans Administration, meaning that all of my medical bills and needs for the rest of my life would be paid for by the VA—including a monthly paycheck more than sufficient to cover my cost of living. I had assumed that when I'd taken my right to remain silent, the service-connection was a done deal. But that's not how it works.

At the moment, the Navy was covering all of my medical expenses (including paying for an attendant when I needed one) and giving me 75 percent of my base pay until I was discharged from rehab and the military. After that, I'd be left with only social security disability benefits unless I got service-connected. Marge was working hard on that, but she was having a difficult time getting records from the Navy, interestingly enough.

I had already told any official who'd asked the details of what happened on the night of October 25, 1990, that I'd fallen off a cliff . . . somehow. I wasn't sure how.

Marge wasn't buying it. "So what happened, Dana?"

I was sitting across from her desk at her office in the hospital. "I don't know."

"How did you fall?"

"I don't know."

"Do you remember anything?" she pressed.

I shook my head. She looked at me silently for a minute.

"Try to think. Tell me what you remember."

"I fell off a cliff."

"Is that all?"

"Yup. I don't remember anything else."

My weekly sessions with the hospital shrink yielded even less information, if that was possible. He was an older man and he wanted to talk about my feelings. Well, I didn't want to talk about my feelings. And if I did, I wouldn't be discussing them with him. I wasn't feeling so trusting of men I didn't know these days.

"So, Dana. How do you feel today?" he'd ask.

"Fine."

"How would you describe your spirits?"

"Good."

"Nothing is upsetting you?"

"No."

"Nothing at all?"

"Well," I'd say. I knew I had to give him something or else I'd never get out of there. "I don't like being in a wheelchair."

"Is that all?"

"I don't like being a quad."

"How does that make you feel? Are you . . . angry?"

"Yeah, yeah. It makes me angry. Can I go now?"

I was like a hostile witness on the stand at my own trial. I'd just shut down and tell him what he wanted to hear in order to make the sessions end as quickly as possible.

WHATEVER PROGRESS I WAS LACKING ON THE EMOTIONAL FRONT, I was making up for on the physical front. By early February 1991, soon after I had arrived in rehab, I got full function of my biceps back, but they were very weak and atrophied. By April—around the time I started going home for my visits—I was able to feed myself and was beginning to push my chair farther as my biceps slowly built back up. By early May, I could get up the curb cuts.

By late May, I learned to stop whining.

Jen had been taking me in my wheelchair up little inclines on the hospital grounds, where I'd *slowly* make my way up what seemed like an enormous hill (but was really an anthill to anyone else). To push myself, I'd press my wrists against the push-rim of the chair because I didn't have finger function to grip them. Technically, I was pulling instead of pushing. Jen would walk behind me to make sure I didn't go backward and give me little assists if I needed them.

One morning, Jen and I went outside so she could teach me how to transfer in and out of a car in preparation for when I left rehab a few months later. It was a difficult maneuver, and until that day, I'd always used a transfer board for support and leverage. Jen thought I could do it without the board. Normally, I'd be as bold and gung ho as she was and push myself out of my comfort zone. But I was having an off day—it was one of those days where everything felt impossible, and I was moaning about it.

If Gary were there, he would have called me a brat. He never could stand it if I copped an attitude while I was growing up, and damned if he was going to stand it now. During one of my visits to Dad's, I'd been complaining about something throughout the weekend until he finally took me aside.

"Bitch!"

"What?"

"You heard me. Knock it off, Dana! You are not the only one going through this, you know. We *all* are."

I had my days where I got moody and frustrated. As I worked with Jen, it was clear that this was one of those days.

We began the transfer, and I managed to get from my chair into the car on my own, which was good. But once in the car, I started whining and bitching about the getting-out part. I'd been whining and bitching all day, in fact. "How am I supposed to do this? My arms are too short. I don't have any triceps. This is stupid."

Jen had been diligently coaching me from the side of the car, and now she'd enough.

"Fine," she said, straightening up. "I'm out of here. You can figure out how to get out of the car yourself. And after you do, don't bother coming to see me for your appointment this afternoon." She turned around and walked back into the hospital, leaving me sitting in the front seat of the car with my chair parked next to it.

I was pissed. *I cannot believe she fucking left me here.* And for about half an hour, I stewed in my grumpy, angry mood until I thought, *Oh, shit . . . maybe she really isn't coming back! Ah, hell. Maybe she's right . . . yeah, okay, maybe I'm a jerk. But is she really gonna just leave me here? Won't someone come out and get me? Looks like I'm stuck out here. . . .*

I wasn't about to ask passersby for help—hell, no. I had too much pride. After an hour passed and I'd gotten good and humbled, Jen did come back and help me into my chair. I was so happy to see her and very, *very* apologetic, but she was still playing the hard-ass.

"Whatever," she said, pointing to the hill right next to us. "Go push yourself up the hill. I don't want to see you this afternoon." Then she left. Again.

I was devastated. I looked at the hill—it was about 30 yards of slight incline, but it looked like Mt. Everest. I'd never done a hill like that alone before. Today, apparently, was the day to try. It took me a good 30 minutes to push up the hill by myself.

Inch by inch by inch by inch . . .

People walking in and out of the parking lot asked if I needed help.

"Nope, no, I got it," I panted. I wanted to be able to tell Jen that I'd gotten to the top without help. When I finally got there, I smiled—proud of myself. Then, inch by inch by inch, I pulled myself to Jen's office to let her know I'd done it. I also begged her to take me for my afternoon session, promising there would be no attitude.

"I'll be good, I promise! I won't be a whining brat!"

She took me back, of course. The people who loved me loved me tender, pushed me when I needed it, called me out on my crap, and forgave me my trespasses. Because that's what friends and family who give each other tough love do.

CHAPTER 10

Curbs and Wheelies

Jen often told me about the National Veterans Wheelchair Games, a yearly summer sports event put on by the U.S. Department of Veterans Affairs and the Paralyzed Veterans of America (PVA). It gathered together hundreds of veterans from all over the country and was the largest wheelchair sporting event in the world at that time.

Even though I had a month more to go in rehab, I was discharged for one week and on a plane to Miami for my first Games in June 1991. Jen and one of my nurses, Deb, were the coaches taking the Northwest team, which included about 15 other people in chairs . . . all men. We also had a third nurse as part of the entourage to help take care of the guys who were still learning their ADL's (activities of daily living), as well as Deb's 14-year-old daughter, Mary.

I packed colorful shorts, shirts, and shoes—it was time to put my "moon boots" and the drab sweats I'd been wearing every day for the last several months to rest—and embarked on my first plane ride since getting hurt. I wore what's known as an "indwelling" catheter and leg bag so we didn't have to worry about getting me in and out of that tiny airplane bathroom to pee—thank goodness for that. When the plane landed, Deb held on to me so I wouldn't fall forward, as I wasn't strong enough to stay in an upright, seated position.

I was nervous. More specifically, I was scared to death. Here I was, this little 19-year-old, roly-poly kid, who wasn't even old enough to have a beer with the others who'd be there. It would be my first time being around such a large number of people since getting hurt, but it would also be my first time being around so many people—hundreds and hundreds—in wheelchairs.

When we went to register for the Games, I stuck close to Jen and Deb. I looked around and saw that I was definitely the youngest veteran there (and would be for years to come).

Registration was in a large exhibition hall close to our hotel, where all the competing athletes got muscle-tested, classified, and put into groups according to injury and level of function, to make sure everyone was on a level playing field. They had three general levels in the manual-chair divisions for quads—1A, 1B, and 1C—with 1A being the least amount of function and strength.

At that point, I had use of my biceps, which were getting a bit stronger. After six months of rehab, my left hand was showing more mobility than the right; in fact, from that point on, I'd relearn everything I used to do as a right-handed person with my left hand, becoming a lefty.

Despite this progress, I didn't have use of my triceps or trunk at all, or any finger function yet—I had nothing there. I was definitely in the A category, which was standard for a C5 quad like me. (However, during the Games, I'd happily discover that I had use of some back extensors, so I was able to develop what little I had from then on playing rugby.)

We approached one of the classifiers, who was a friend of Jen's. Jen was highly respected and trusted by everyone there, as she'd been going to the Games for years.

"So, let's see," the classifier began, "Dana—"

"Dana's a 1B," Jen broke in, unquestionably. "You don't have to muscle-test her. She's a 1B," she repeated, knowing full well that I should be in the 1A division.

"Oh, okay."

Being with Jen was like hanging around a female Gary—she was always bumping me up beyond my level, certain I'd rise to the occasion. Now she was throwing me into the event to sink or swim.

They filled out the necessary paperwork. It turns out that I was the only female in that division that year (and, again, would be for many years to come) in the sports that I picked, no surprise. We picked out swimming, slalom course, and quad rugby for me; they also had events like basketball, softball, and track and field. I was perplexed by how I was going to do any of it.

The next day at opening ceremonies, the teams from each VA in every state lined up in a procession. I walked with my Seattle team, the Northwest PVA. Jen pushed my chair so I wouldn't get tired out, but she let go when the cameras were on our team so that I could look and feel more independent.

Any fear I had upon arriving was washed away by the exciting sea of energy, momentum, and camaraderie I experienced those first few hours, and would continue to feel for the duration of the Games. Almost 500 veterans at various levels of injury in wheelchairs surrounded me—some new like me, some 30 years post-injury—cheering each other on and welcoming me into the fold. It was like a family reunion.

The next feeling to overwhelm me was something I didn't expect. The able-bodied people walking around who weren't missing a limb or didn't have a chair or weren't maimed in some way—well, that week, they were the odd ones out. With hundreds of people roaming about in chairs, the able-bodies were the abnormal ones. It was an odd feeling, and one I couldn't place at first. Then I realized what the feeling was, and I was so grateful that I nearly wept. I'd been sequestered in hospitals for eight months after having my life ripped away from me in minutes and had felt like a freak. But now, surrounded by multitudes of people who were just like me, for the first time in eight months I felt . . . *normal.*

THE NEXT DAY, I WENT FROM LEARNING HOW to sit up in my chair and not fall out of it to using my chair to slam and crash into people.

Quad rugby is like demolition-derby soccer on a basketball court, but using a volleyball. You have four players per team, and the goal is to get any two wheels of your chair across the opposing team's "back line" in their key. Each team had players within a wide range of ability; some were even Paralympic athletes.

When on defense I was given the position of "rover" because I had the least amount of function, not because I was the newest or worst player (which I was). As the team's rover, I had to move back and forth, side to side, and try to block the opposing team. Everybody was crashing and slamming into each other—it was great! I totally sucked at it, but I loved it.

Players would rush from one end of the court to the other—at my snail's pace, I'd get to half-court, and they'd already be turned back again and passing me by. In my non-haste, I clipped another player by accident and was sent to the penalty box. Ha! I took it as a compliment, since that's always where the cool kids ended up.

Jen had been taking me into the pool at the VA hospital, and now I was in a swimming event at the Games. Both Jen and Deb had to hold me up by the arms before the starting gun went off because I wasn't strong enough to hang on to the edge of the pool myself. It was hard to imagine that one year earlier I'd cleaned up in the 25-yard swim event at boot camp and had been picked for state championship a year before that. Yet this event was almost like going home again—25 yards across a pool doing the backstroke. The way I did it now, though, I looked like I was flailing about and drowning. I never liked the backstroke, even as an able-body, but it felt great to be moving across the water again.

It took me a ridiculously long time to swim those 25 yards, and I was the last person to finish, but when I did, the crowd cheered as if I'd won. To me, finishing was winning at that point in my life.

Next came the slalom course, which was really an obstacle course. It was set up inside to simulate outside challenges like wheeling over rough terrain, trying to open doors while in a chair and on an incline, or hitting the uneven curb cuts that demand a good wheelie to get up and over them—real-life situations that someone in a chair faces many times a day.

The organizers set up four-inch curbs, thick mats to simulate grass and plush carpet, and sheets of plywood with blocks, ropes, and pieces of garden hoses nailed to the wood—all of which we had to navigate over, going both forward and backward. In one section, they'd put door frames with cones on top, and you had to open the door (a feat in itself), go through it, and close it without knocking the cones off.

I was doing fairly well, until I reached a wooden ramp that was a bit steeper and longer than a curb cut. Damn the curb cuts! I tried to get up and over it in a forward motion, like everyone else did . . . up, up, up . . . then back down. Again . . . up, up, up . . . and down. This went on for a while, because I could not get up that sucker.

"One more time! One more time! One more time!" I kept telling the spotters. I didn't want their help; I wanted to do it myself. But after five times, the official and spotter, Frisco, gave me a little nudge over the ramp to keep the event moving.

"Good try. Way to hustle," he said with a smile.

The most difficult part of the slalom course was getting over the wooden ladder on the floor, rung by rung. It was worse than curbs! I had to stay in a wheelie to get over each rung. My lack of triceps made this event kick my butt, as did my minuscule hand function. Yet I didn't care how long it was going to take me or how hard it was, I wasn't giving up. It was Jen's hill all over again.

The average time for the obstacle course that year was three minutes, and the fastest time was two minutes. It took me 22 minutes to do it, and when I finished my wrists were bloodied because I'd worn the skin off. The crowd watching on the sidelines was screaming and applauding my efforts once again.

The Games, I soon learned, were also a big social scene for everyone to meet and flirt and drink and dance all night (yes, people can dance in their chairs), but I was too young and too newly injured to venture out. I didn't feel ready to jump into those social waters yet, so I mainly hung with Jen, Deb, and Mary. I was more focused on observing and learning from the others in wheelchairs. These people were all role models for me—they showed me what was possible in the near and far future for myself. When I saw an athlete do something particularly amazing, like the way the quad rugby players zipped across the court so fast, I thought, *If I work hard, I can do that, too!*

The Games were a place and a state of mind where all things were possible, where everyone helped and cheered each other on to reach new goals. For me, it was perhaps the most important week I had post-injury. It was a place where my life began again.

At the closing-night ceremonies, we watched a video of highlights taken from the week. And there I was, brow furrowed and determined, wrists raw and bleeding, as I pushed myself up the ramp with that Tom Petty and the Heartbreakers tune in the background, "I Won't Back Down."

An appropriate theme song, I thought.

BACK IN SEATTLE, I FINISHED MY LAST MONTH IN REHAB with a flourish. After weeks of intense concentration and determination, I mastered the all-important wheelie. This skill would be needed to get over life's curbs, big and small, in the outside world.

In the PT room and out in the hallway, I performed a static wheelie, where I sat still and popped the wheelie; and a dynamic wheelie, where I moved while staying in the wheelie. Those two moves earned me a reward: Jen removed the "anti-tip" bars, which were like training wheels in the veteran-gimp world, from my wheelchair so that I could be one of the cool kids. That was momentous.

And so was what happened next.

Most medical staff told me that even as an incomplete C5 injury, I wouldn't regain any use of my hands or my legs. But they'd told me a lot of things along the way that ended up not being true. They said I wouldn't breathe on my own, but I did. They said I'd never be able to feed myself, and within four months, I could.

"You guys keep saying I'll never do things, and then you're wrong," I said to one doctor, who was telling me yet another thing on the list of what I would never be able to do. Like my usual stubborn self, I didn't listen from the beginning, and I'm sure that's a big reason why I kept improving. Had I believed it was impossible to make progress, I might not have tried.

I remember one doctor telling me that I could continue to see recovery for two years and then, whatever function I had at the two-year mark would be what I'd have for the rest of my life. By why put a limit on a person? (Doctors have since upped the "limit" they tell patients from two years to five after seeing many patients progress beyond that.) I knew I was going to do what I wanted to do, and no one else was going to dictate *my* life.

I'd reached a lot of milestones while in rehab. Sitting up without passing out was a milestone. Pushing my chair five feet by myself and feeding myself without wearing the food were milestones. Getting the halo off, brushing my own teeth, pushing the elevator door button, and pushing up curb cuts were momentous. Opening my own doors and dressing myself—the second-hardest thing to learn after teaching myself to breathe again—were major accomplishments I was closing in on.

I was aware of other small moments, too. At one point, I thought I could wiggle my left big toe a little. Then I thought I noticed a flicker in my left index finger. But I didn't say anything to anyone about it because in an SCI rehab center, their job was to teach us how to be as independent as we could be in our wheelchairs, with the muscle function we had. They had it set in their minds what we could do, so that's what they taught us. They didn't want to hear if we were planning to walk one day.

At the end of rehab, at ten months post-injury, I was functioning as a typical C5 quad and had use of my biceps, deltoids, and trapezius muscles, as well as some forearm use for tenodesis. I was having leg spasms, which are normal for people who have spinal cord injuries, so doctors put me on a drug called baclofen to stop them. Even though these movements were involuntary, to me it meant that currents or nerve messages were getting through. And something else was happening: Before I left rehab, I could feel pressure on my left leg when someone pressed hard on my thigh, and I was hypersensitive to touch in my right leg.

During one of my last PT sessions with Jen, I showed her something I was excited about.

I moved my leg into a twitch. It wasn't an involuntary spasm; it was *voluntary*, something I was doing myself. We watched together as my leg, which had been still for nearly a year, moved. I was ecstatic, but Jen was cautious.

"Dana, try not to let the other patients see this, okay? So they won't feel bad that it's not happening for them, too."

I went to sleep that night wishing I could yell it out loud: "My body is healing itself!"

CHAPTER 11

Out in the World, Shit Happens

My first solo bus ride after getting sprung from rehab was a comedy of errors.

I was living in an apartment in West Seattle with my mom—she was to be my official "attendant" for a year, paid for by the Navy—but for the first six months I was out of the hospital, I still had to go back and forth to the VA hospital for outpatient rehab. I'd been home for only a few weeks when I attempted to take the bus by myself to go visit my old pal Roger in the SCI unit. At the most, it was a 15-minute trip.

My misadventure began before I even left home. The spring-loaded door slammed into my chair before I cleared the doorway, wedging my front wheels outside the door and my back wheels inside. It took half an hour for me to get unstuck and on my way. Then as I made my way on the sidewalk toward the bus stop, I came to a parked truck blocking the curb cut, with barely enough space for me to squeeze by. That's when he decided to back up, right into me. He didn't hear me screaming as he pushed my chair and me into the busy street and sped off, with me flailing my arms and yelling quadriplegic-like—which means that no one could hear what the heck I was saying or see what I was doing.

Thankfully, I wasn't hurt. I finally got to the stop and boarded the city bus, telling the driver where I wanted to go as she strapped my chair down, and away we went! Phew!

All was calm until a young woman boarded the bus, took one look at me, paled, and collapsed on the seat next to me. "You look like my girlfriend who just died!" she cried. What followed was a teary monologue about the woman's lost love, until she got off the bus about ten stops later.

I checked with the bus driver to see if we were nearing my stop yet, as I had to get on a second bus from there.

"Oh, honey, I'm sorry! I forgot all about you. We missed your stop. You'll have to ride the entire route again with me."

Two hours later, Driver #1 dropped me off at my stop, and I made my way to the next one a block away. On the way, I accidentally ran over a hot-dog bun and it stuck to my tires and got them all gummy. I had to wiggle my chair around and around in circles, like a doggy chasing his tail, to get it off.

I reached the stop just as the bus arrived, but I couldn't board it because the lift wasn't working. The driver struggled with it as the passengers grew impatient, shooting me looks. Luckily, some random dude walked by, gave it a yank, and got it going. *Yes!* I was on my way again . . . until a bus in front of us broke down, and we couldn't get around it.

"Everybody off!" yelled out Driver #2. "We have another bus coming to pick you up across the street!"

As an aside, this is the problem when you're 20 years old but look 12: people think you're a kid. And you're in a wheelchair, which makes it worse. Not only do you look like a child, but a helpless one to boot.

For example, when I was in rehab, Roger and I were scheduled to go on an outing to a dance studio nearby. The instructor was a para, and she was teaching a class in wheelchair dancing! I was so excited, and I dragged Roger with me. Actually, my dear and gruff friend usually insisted on coming with me on my outings because he'd worry about me if I went alone.

He wasn't the only one. The new resident physician, who'd only been there a week, refused to sign off for me to go to the dance studio. "You have to call your parents to get permission."

"What? Why?"

"You just have to. I'm the doctor, and it's my call."

"But I'm not a kid. I'm 19 years old and I'm a veteran—*hellooooo!*"

"I don't care. Call your parents, and if they say it's okay, I'll let you go."

I grumbled and called Dad, who laughed and had a few colorful expletives about the clueless resident, and got the permission. It was the last time I had that problem in rehab, but my baby face caused mayhem quite a few times once I was out in the world.

"I can't let you off here alone, young lady," the bus driver told me now. "You shouldn't be wheeling around by yourself."

Out the window, I could see the relief bus coming. *"Lady, let me off this damn bus!"* I yelled.

"No, no. You need to wait."

I finally convinced her to let me out and raced across the street, nearly getting hit by a truck whizzing by.

"Whoa there!" A cop who was directing traffic ran over, helped me cross the street and board the bus, and told the driver what my stop was. *Just a few more minutes and I'll be at the VA hospital,* I told myself. But *noooooo.* Within those few minutes, the bus stopped and a new driver boarded, relieving the first one. But Driver #3 didn't tell Driver #4 what my stop was, and as we approached it, he showed no signs of slowing down.

I yelled out, and luckily he heard me (then again, I was the only person on the bus at this point). Even though he'd passed the official bus stop, he was able to let me off right in front of the SCI unit doors. My 15-minute trip had taken a total of five hours.

Mom was so relieved to hear from me when I called her from the nurses' station that she rushed over with a big plate of nachos with jalapeños from 7-Eleven—my favorite junk food at that time— to make me feel better. *And* I got my period during all that, by the way, so those nachos were right on the money.

That, ladies and gentleman, was a typical day in the life. Out in the world, I learned, shit happens—especially as a young female quad who's navigating a whole new world from her wheelchair.

And not only did I have to adjust to being out in the world again, but so did my parents. For example, all I wanted to eat was cereal and nachos—I'd been spoiled by the nurses and all my visitors bearing Burgerville cheeseburgers at the hospital. Yet Mom was determined to heal me with her organic foods like dandelion salads, vegetable soups, and hummus (the emergency, post-bus nachos were a rarity). She also gave me a good dose of tough love when I needed it. One day when I was trying to put my pants on, I got so frustrated and pissed off, I screamed and cried.

"Dana Leigh! Do you want your independence or not?"

"Yeah."

"Well, no amount of crying and screaming is going to get those pants on!" she said, then turned around and walked out of the apartment.

Mom was always good at kicking my ass in the rare moments I ever felt pity for myself. Dad, on the other hand, couldn't stand to see me struggle for a second and was constantly trying to do everything for me.

"Dad," I'd remind him, "don't open my door! Don't push me! I have to learn to do it myself!"

"*Goddddammmn it,* Dana Leigh!" was typically his response.

IT WAS ODD TIMING FOR ME TO BE RELEASED from the protective, isolated environment of the hospital walls in August 1991. Just a month later, the "Tailhook scandal" was all over the news. At the Las Vegas Hilton early that month, more than 100 U.S. Navy and Marine Corps officers were alleged to have sexually assaulted or engaged in "improper or indecent" conduct with at least 83 women and 7 men at an annual aviators symposium. Critics accused the U.S. military culture of having a "hostile attitude" toward women.

Some of the details splashed on the news included this tidbit: The centerpiece of a hospitality suite at the symposium was a drink-dispensing dildo affixed to a mural of a rhinoceros, and women were prodded or even forced to drink the "Rhino spunk." If that wasn't "hostile" enough, one of the lieutenants supposedly involved in the sordid mess was reported to have told the media, "Everyone needs to seriously lighten up. What do they expect? This is Vegas, baby! They call this symposium 'Tail' hook for a reason!" At that, the TV news showed images of outraged protests and demonstrations by the gates of military bases across the country.

I tried to ignore all of this. I was busy focusing on surviving my own life, and had the details of what was going on registered in my mind, they would have consumed me. I was trying to stuff my own trauma down, trying to be quiet.

Meanwhile, if Marge was having trouble finding records for me before, it got much more difficult after the Tailhook scandal exploded. The Navy wouldn't have wanted any of my records coming out now, for sure. I imagine they were busy hiding and perhaps destroying all sorts of records in those months. My own case was still under investigation; ironically, had I taken my case to court, I would have had Tailhook on my side now. The truth was, I was still having trouble getting service-connected because the Navy was trying to find ways to make Bruce raping and almost killing me my fault.

Let me repeat that: *my fault.*

Marge worked hard as my advocate, and for a moment there we worried I was doomed when the Navy claimed I got hurt due to "willful neglect" on my part because a sign somewhere in the area had said something to the effect of, DANGER: CLIFFS. Right. I ended up 75 feet below on the beach because I hadn't paid diligent attention in the dark to that sign while a man was beating, choking, and raping me.

Thankfully, by early '92 I got a "medical honorable" discharge from the Navy, and all my paperwork was in order for what I needed. I was 100 percent service-connected, which meant that I would get a good salary (better than had I still been employed there) and wouldn't have to worry about medical or dental bills for the rest of my life—I would be covered. Now I could focus only on healing and getting better. Not many in my situation had that blessing.

AROUND THE SAME TIME AS my discharge and service-connection, I made another move that changed my life in my quest for independence. I could dress myself, eat, transfer myself in and out of bed and the shower, and brush my hair and teeth. The only issue in the way of my becoming fully independent and not needing an attendant was my bladder situation.

As soon as I started drinking lake-sized vats of water after getting off the respirator in San Diego, the nurses were emptying my bladder every half hour. They decided to put an indwelling catheter in me, which stayed in my bladder all the time and the urine drained directly into the leg bag. It made it easier on them but was a pain when I had to do it all myself. I hated the leg bag—it took a lot of work to go to bed at night and change from a day bag to a night bag. Then I had to soak the day bag in bleach and rinse it in Scope to keep it from stinking. I also had to go to the hospital and have it changed every few months. Plus, having the catheter stuck in my urethra day and night could lead to a lot of infections.

Ideally, I'd want to learn how to do "intermittent" cathing myself, and I certainly tried. I spent a month in "advanced rehab" to learn how to cath myself. We used every little gadget and trick: I had this strange-looking device that had a mirror on it so that I could see my crotch, and it would spread my legs to get them open enough. Then, I needed a flashlight for the detail work. I'd use a bendable hair clip to try to hold the catheter as I attempted to insert it and . . . well, it was ridiculous. And every time I tried to do it, I would take so long that it was too late and I'd piss myself. I was supposed to do this every time I needed to pee?

"How is this going to be functional in the real world?" I asked the nurse helping me. "This is not going to work!"

"Well, there is one other way," she said. She told me about a surgery I could have that would reroute my bladder to a spot next to my belly button, making it way easier to stick a cath tube in, in order to reach my bladder and empty it.

"What the hell are we waiting for?" I asked. "Let's do that!"

The surgery was scheduled a few months later, and when it was done, my world freed up to another level. I would get a new sign that my bladder was full—not the pressure others get, but a tingly sensation in my head and an urge to yawn, strangely enough—and I could get to a bathroom in time to quickly take care of business all on my own, with no struggle. I didn't even need to drop my drawers to do it.

"Number two" was a whole other ball game. I could transfer onto a raised toilet seat (I packed one in my suitcase when I traveled— a shower bench, too) and was pretty good at using my "fickle finger of fate." But after my bladder surgery, my digestive tract was pissed off that it had been jostled in there. For two months, I had bowel accident after bowel accident because everything I ate went right through me. I was scared to leave the house!

Mom had moved out after my surgery, and my cousin Sally (who's Little Jim's sister) moved in; in exchange for rent, she was to be my new helper.

One night when she was out of the house, I had one of my now-infamous bowel accidents—I shit the bed, to be blunt—and needed help cleaning up, so I called Debbie. When she got there and I went to answer the door, poop was dropping out of the back of my chair like a trail. Debbie counted 29 little piles of poop, like deer droppings—"Dana droppings" would be more apt. Debbie was great about cleaning it, and me, up.

I must say that most of my family and friends those first few years rose to the occasion and emptied pee bottles or cleaned up nightmare bowel accidents. It could happen anywhere, I'd learn over the years: on a plane, on a train, in a bus, in a car, during sex . . . I was like the *Green Eggs and Ham* of bowel accidents.

Chrissy and I may not have always seen eye to eye—we've had fights with fists and words—but we have a loyal sisterly bond that nothing and no one can break. And that kind of bond comes in handy when you've just had an accident all over Dad's Trans Am. Actually it was *my* Trans Am, which I'd bought from him.

I had set my sights on driving—I'd learned how in rehab and was certain I'd be able to do it. I knew that being able to get around on my own would give me a whole new degree of freedom, but I was in denial about what kind of vehicle I'd realistically be able to drive at first. Oh, the stigma of driving a van! The common belief is that a quad uses a power chair and can only drive a van, if at all. But vans are not cool to someone in her early 20s, so I got Dad's Trans Am and intended on adapting it with hand controls.

Chrissy and I wanted to take it for a spin, but right away it was obvious that the car was too low for me to get in and out of. Even so, she drove and we went for a bite to eat. Just as we pulled back up to my place, I pooped my pants. I was mortified.

My sister, however, didn't skip a beat. She started singing the diarrhea song from when we were kids:

When you're driving in your car,
And your house is just too far,
Diarrhea, diarrhea.

When you're sliding into home,
And your pants are full of foam,
Diarrhea, diarrhea.

She kept going and going—how many verses did this song have, anyway? We laughed all night long. In the moments when I felt most humiliated, my friends and family could always make me laugh.

IN THE WINTER OF '91, I STARTED WORKING OUT at a gym and hired a trainer to help me build upper-body strength. Once the weather got nice, I'd go outside and push myself in my chair for a mile at a time, until I'd worked up to two to four miles a day, which took two to four hours. One unexpected bonus that came with my surgery and bowel mishaps was that, combined with all the exercise I was getting, I lost tons of weight. I pooped myself skinny!

By the time I went to my second National Veterans Wheelchair Games in Dayton, Ohio, in the summer of '92, I was looking good. I weighed 115 pounds, which was the slimmest I'd ever been as an adult. And I was feeling like myself again—ready to get out and talk to people, not shy like the year before. Deb's daughter, Mary, who was now 15, came with us again, and she and I snuck into bars and convinced the bartenders to give us beers. Even after all the beer drinking I'd done in my day, I was still under the drinking age—my 21st birthday was weeks away.

At the Games, I also hung out with pretty Danette, the vet who'd answered my sex questions in rehab. Little did I know that she was the "popular girl" at the Games, which meant that soon I became popular, too. It rained the entire week, and we hung out in the local bars and went to events and flirted with guys. Since the accident, my flirty mode was pretty much on "pause" but Danette was a great at it, and I watched and learned.

At one event we were watching, she called over a tall, handsome guy—Frisco, the man who'd be instrumental in my coming-of-age in this brave new world. I recognized him immediately as the official who'd given me a nudge during the slalom course the year before.

Frisco was a quad rugby referee at the USQRA (the United States Quad Rugby Association) and at the Games, where he was pretty much considered the coolest guy on campus. He was also a ski instructor at the National Disabled Veterans Winter Sports Clinic every March. When Danette introduced us, she asked Frisco what type of ski I should try.

He gave me the once-over—in a professional sense—and said, "I can see you on a bi-ski, and we can duct-tape your hands. Maybe we'll use fixed outriggers, maybe not . . ."

I could feel the flirt pause button disengaging. Later that night, in the hotel bar, Frisco saw me from across the room and yelled out with a smile, "Hey, are you even old enough to be in here?"

I was smitten with this Frisco. So when I discovered that he was to be my ski instructor at the Winter Sports Clinic the following March, I was off-the-hook excited.

The National Disabled Veterans Winter Sports Clinic is a five-day event where military veterans develop winter-sports skills and take part in workshops to help with their rehabilitation and reentry into the community. It's not competitive, like the Veterans Games. It's more of a "ski, play, drink, and have a good time" thing. It's also not only for those in wheelchairs. The WSC is for everyone—visually impaired, amputees, people who have had polio, veterans with head traumas or injuries of all different types. And like the Games, it's another place where people like us feel "normal."

Like the Veterans Games, the Winter Sports Clinic was a revelation to me. From the moment I arrived, and for the next two decades until this day, the Clinic became my inspiration to work hard all year so I could gauge my progress in strength, skill, and function every March.

I arrived for my first Clinic in Crested Butte, Colorado, in March 1993. And there was Frisco in fluorescent-pink ski pants, standing tall on the slopes next to a bunch of skiing contraptions I'd never seen before. He had a mountain-man bi-ski ready to put me in, and he told me about the other types of equipment and ways for people with disabilities to ski: monoskis, three-tracking, and four-tracking, for example.

True to his first assessment, he determined that the bi-ski would fit my injuries and function level at the time. On a bi-ski, you sit with your legs extended out in front of you on a seat that has two skis affixed to the bottom. You hold on to two short poles with cuffs that wrap around your forearms and ski-tips on the bottom ("outriggers").

Frisco duct-taped my hands and arms from the handgrip up to the cuff. Then as I sat in the chair, he strapped my legs and chest in. I grew up skiing in the Pacific Northwest and always loved racing down the sides of mountains and flying through the air coming off a jump. This time, Frisco was to ski behind me, but we would be tethered together. He'd control my speed and turns until I learned how to do it myself using the outriggers.

At the top of the ski run called "Painter Boy," Frisco gave my bi-ski a little push and sent me sailing down the hill through the crisp air. I felt like I was flying: *Woooooo-hooooooooooooooooo!*

I broke out into a Carole King song, changing the words a little: "I feel the snow . . . move . . . under my skis!" I'm sure the day I woke up in that hospital room in San Diego and couldn't breathe on my own, no one thought I'd ever ski again. And here I was, zooming down the mountain faster than I'd moved in almost three years. I couldn't stop smiling!

The next day, I tried scuba diving for the first time in my life. Hardly anyone was in the pool, and it was a beauty—a steaming, outdoor oasis on the side of the mountain. The instructors lowered me into the warm water with air tanks, and I sat at the bottom of the pool for a while, looking up at the sky in the silence. In the water, I always felt free and like I was *me* again. From the time I swam across the Clackamas River to meet Gary on the other side to the time I sliced through the water for the swim team as a teenager to the time

I made Chief Barlow proud during boot camp, those moments were pure me. When it was time to come up from the bottom of the pool, I surfaced to cold snowflakes on my nose and the majestic awesomeness of Mt. Crested Butte in front of me.

Back on the mountain each day, I couldn't help but flirt with Frisco as he zipped and taped me up and strapped me down. The night before our last day—"Race Day" is what we call it—after a drink and a dance at the bar, we went back to his room and shared a first kiss, and more. I was happy to discover that Gary's worry that I'd never have sex again was nothing to worry about at all.

The next day Frisco and I went up the mountain by snowmobile and once we got to the top of the slope, we found ourselves in the middle of a whiteout and couldn't go down. We couldn't even see a foot in front of us. As the snow piled up on my legs and skis, Frisco opened his coat and wrapped it and himself around me to shield me and keep me warm.

CHAPTER 12

Dance with Me

What happens on the mountain stays on the mountain; that's what I learned after my wonderful evening with Frisco. And for those who are curious, as Gary and I were, it turns out that sex as a quad isn't all that different than it was before. I may not have sensation in some areas, but the sensation is crazy heightened where I do have it. Everything from my sternum—the C4 and C5 area—upward is hyper-sensitive to touch. So kiss my face and neck, and I go berserk. I had my neck kissed for hours by the hottest guy on the mountain, and it was the best night of my gimp life so far.

Since I was a 21-year-old female, of course I romantically imagined Frisco and me skiing off into the sunset together, happily ever after. It was not to be, because that's not how it worked on the mountain. After that night, Frisco would remain my instructor and dear friend for the next 20 years, and I hope for the rest of my life. And even if our romance could not continue, I will forever be grateful for what he gave me that night: the gift of confidence about my sexuality and attractiveness. I wasn't so sure about those things *before* I got hurt, never mind after. One night of TLC from Frisco gave me the courage to go forth and date.

Three months later, in the summer of '93, I met the man I'd marry.

Sally and I were now living in an apartment in Hillsboro, near Dad, and I'd been going to school part-time at Portland Community College. I took remedial math, reading, and English, retraining my mind from the brain injury (to this day, I still forget to punctuate my sentences). I surprised myself by doing very well: I had a 3.8 GPA, and for a girl who did okay in high school and didn't feel smart enough for college, I was proud of myself. Now that I didn't have to worry about getting a job, I wanted to spend my time not just healing but also learning. I wanted to better myself and create my future using my mind. So much of my life had been about how strong I was physically; maybe the universe was telling me it was time to focus on my brainpower.

No one around me seemed to care too much that I was getting good grades, though. They figured I was taken care of for the rest of my life, so why bother? My father in particular was worried that I was isolating myself and not having any fun.

"You're living your life through your books!" he'd say. "You're too goddamn young to stay inside all the time and study. You need to get out and live!"

I took his advice and starting hanging out with Gary and his friends more, going out to pubs. One night I felt bold enough to go to a local country-music honky-tonk bar all by myself. It was a first for me, something I never would've been brave enough to do before my life-affirming night with Frisco.

After my Trans Am fiasco, I got myself a Ford Econoline van, which was exactly what I needed at the time. I had it adapted with a lift on the passenger side for my chair, and I could transfer into the six-way power driver's seat directly from my chair. I used hand controls that looked like a bike grip—they had a metal rod attached to the gas pedal and another rod branching out from that one to the brake. I pushed forward to brake or down to accelerate.

I got myself a table by the dance floor. The DJ put on the Judds' "Girls Night Out" when a handsome, swarthy-complexioned gentleman approached. He reminded me of Chief Petty Officer Barlow.

"Would you like to dance?"

"Sure!"

His name was Rick, and out on the dance floor, he began spinning me around in my chair. He held my wrists snugly and pushed and pulled me around like a shopping cart—twisting my chair side to side and using his foot to give it a little kick. At one point, he let go of one arm to spin me in a circle and then caught my arm as I spun back around. If my buddy Gene could see me now! This guy didn't care one bit that I was in a chair.

When we sat down, Rick told me all about himself. He was 39 and had joined the Army in the early '70s and been stationed on Okinawa in Japan. More recently he'd worked in a casino on a cruise ship and traveled a lot; he'd also been married and had a son. His current job was as a security officer for the Portland Metro City Building.

At the end of the evening, he wrote down his phone number and gave it to me. "Honey, you're as cute as they come," he said with a smile.

Interestingly enough, one thing I'd discovered my first few years out in the world after rehab is that being cute, outgoing, in a wheelchair, and in a bar intrigues a lot of men and piques their curiosity. It surprised me to realize that there are so many guys out there who will try to hook up with someone like me because they wonder what it's like to have sex with someone in a wheelchair.

The next weekend, Rick and I met back at that same honky-tonk. We'd just started dancing when the owner of the bar came over to us and looked at me.

"I'm sorry, but you can't dance here. You're taking up too much space on the dance floor."

We were shocked, but Rick said, "She's not taking up any more space than anyone else. And we're having a good time, so we're going to keep on dancing!"

We had a great night, and the bar owner didn't approach us again. But the next day I was so pissed off that I went back to the bar to have a talk with her. When I pulled into the parking lot, I noticed a pink Mustang parked in the handicapped zone. It was hers.

Once inside, I laid into her for asking me to leave the dance floor and for parking in the handicapped spot. "Are you familiar with the Americans with Disabilities Act?" I asked.

This is a civil rights law that had been enacted three years earlier in 1990, just in time for me to learn about it from the Paralyzed Veterans of America. The ADA prohibits discrimination against people with disabilities in all public areas, as well as in private ones that are open to the general public.

"You would come under Title III," I told this woman, "and what you did last night is discrimination on the basis of disability by a public accommodation and commercial facility. Which means," I took a breath, "that I have the same right to dance on your dance floor as anybody else."

That honky-tonk bar owner certainly didn't see it or me coming. She apologized, and I continued to dance at her club many times after that.

A FEW WEEKS AFTER I MET RICK, Gary and I embarked on a two-week trip to Sweden and Norway, my first-ever trip outside of North America. We went with a group called "Wilderness Inquiry," an adventure-travel organization that specialized in active sports and "access, inclusion, and opportunity." Danette had talked me into going with her but had to cancel at the last minute, so my brother stepped in.

He had no idea how much he was going to have to help me in the pooping and bodily function department, but I knew. He got a hint on our flight to Stockholm: It was my first overseas plane ride, and I had to pee in the worst way but couldn't get to the bathroom. My chair had been gate-checked and stowed in the belly of the plane—even if I'd had it near me, though, it wouldn't have fit down the narrow width of an airplane aisle or in those tiny bathrooms.

I was stuck, and I had to empty my bladder into something, anything. "Gary, I've got to cath and I don't know what to do."

"Well, I'm not touchin' it," he said. "Gross!"

I waited until he fell asleep and grabbed the barf bag in front of me, stuck one end of the plastic tube in my belly button and the other into the bag and emptied the urine from my bladder into it, figuring it had to be waterproof if it held vomit, right?

Gary woke up just as I was apologizing to a very gracious flight attendant while handing her the near-bursting bag. "Ewww!" he groaned.

At least it was just pee. After a mishap I had years later when eating a poppy-seed muffin on my way to the Games in Puerto Rico, I learned never to eat solid food during a flight or there could be trouble. Fortunately, the bowel accident happened as the plane was landing. After everyone got off, I was able to use an "aisle chair"— a chair specifically made to fit along the narrow aisles of an airplane— to get to the bathroom and clean myself up. Ever since then, I'm sure to pack my carry-on bag with an extra pair of pants and shirt, a pile of baby wipes, extra catheters, and a high-caloric snack like a candy bar that will sustain me but not go through me.

During our European sojourn, Gary and I rode in planes, trains, cars, canoes, and rafts. He carried me and pushed me and pulled me; he lifted my chair, with me in it, over fallen trees and across mud and up flights of stairs and over streams like a superhero. During one part of the trip, we rode through Class IV rapids and the boat ride was so rocky that I was about to fall out, when Gary dove from one side of the raft to the other in a split second and grabbed me.

We were also troublemakers during our canoe trip. Gary did everything possible to piss off our guide—standing up in the boat, rocking it back and forth—to make his little sister laugh.

"Sit down!" the guide yelled. "You can't stand up in a canoe!"

I paddled a canoe for the first time since my injury on that trip. The able-bodied people carried the canoes and pushed me when needed, but for the most part I pushed myself. Gary kept a close eye on me and helped when I needed it, kept me safe, and would have carried me the entire time if he could.

"If I could put you in my back pocket," he said, "I'd keep you there."

My brother is strong as shit, but when it came time to help me in the actual shit department, we really separated the men from the boys. At one point we were in a tiny bathroom in our host's house in Sweden and the toilet was so awkward and I was in such pain that Gary had to hold me up and spread my legs apart while I "had a dig" with my fickle finger of fate, and I was crying and he was crying because I was crying. What an ordeal. My brother was a total rock star, and halfway through the trip he'd become a pro.

"Here, Dane, pee into this," he'd say, handing me a water bottle with a smirk. "And you better not be a bitch to me or I won't spread your butt cheeks for you."

He always made me laugh. Near the end of our camping trip in Norway, the mosquitoes were so bad that my hands had blown up like little balloons. Gary was pissed off because the guide—the same one who told him to sit down in the canoe—wasn't doing anything about it and dismissed Gary's concerns.

"Listen, you can fuck right off. Do you see my sister's hands?"

"Why don't you be more like your sister, huh? She doesn't complain. She deals with it."

Uh-oh, I thought.

"Fuck you, we're outta here," said Gary. He packed up our stuff and grabbed hold of my chair and walked off, taking me with him. We were supposed to stay that night in a teepee or tent, but we were tired of being cold and bitten. Plus, it was my 22nd birthday, and Gary wanted to take me into Oslo so we could tie one on.

It was one of those days in the season when the sun doesn't seem to fully set and it stays dusk all night. We got into the city, got a hotel room, and went straight to the local pub. The entrance was at the top of a huge flight of stairs and the two bouncers at the door carried me up.

Inside, the band was playing American pop tunes, and everyone was singing along to Elvis and John Denver. By the night's end, the mild-mannered Norwegians were dancing on tables and I joined them on the floor, a cute boy gave me a birthday kiss, and Gary passed out at the table. When we finally got back to our hotel, it was still golden outside. We slept a bit then hopped in a cab to get back to our rafting group. The guide was livid, but we didn't care. Our trip was epic.

I CONTINUED DANCING AND HAVING FUN at the Veterans Games that August in San Antonio, and earned my new nickname: "Problem Child."

When I returned, Rick met me at the airport with roses; he had big plans for us. He wanted us to go boating together, sure it was going to be the greatest thing in the world. We went out on his motorboat on the Willamette River by Portland's waterfront. All was going fine until we went flying over the wake of someone else's boat and I fell out of my seat and onto the floor, getting my leg stuck underneath the seat in front of me.

In a panic, Rick quickly yanked me up from the floor and I could hear the *crrrraaaaaack*. At the hospital, doctors told me I'd broken my leg above my ankle and put me in a cast for three months. I was crushed. The addition of a bulky, heavy cast plus the loss of being able to put even the slightest amount of weight on that foot for balance would make transferring impossible for me—which meant I couldn't get on a toilet or in the shower or in and out of bed by myself. I would need help with everything.

All the freedom I'd worked so hard to get, bit by bit, over the last three years was temporarily gone. The broken leg took me out of the independent-living game. I was going to need a lot of help, a lot more than what my cousin Sally could give me on her own.

"Why don't you move in with me?" Rick suggested.

That's how it came to be that only three months after we'd started dating, I moved in with him. He took great care of me and helped me with everything I needed. He was also in love with me; he'd said so from the get-go. *Maybe I could love him*, I thought. *We've had a lot of fun together and he's a great cook and so nurturing.* But I told him one thing from the get-go, too, and it was that I never wanted to get married. After watching my mother marry and divorce so many times, I couldn't believe in it anymore, and I never wanted to put kids through what I'd gone through.

So when he said he wanted to buy me a ring for a Christmas present and took me to a jewelry store to pick one out, I made sure again he was clear on my position.

"It's not an engagement ring," he assured me. "It's a promise ring."

"Okay, but I'm not marrying you," I reminded him, as I put on the ring to see if it fit. We spent Christmas with his family at his brother's house in Santa Maria, California, and they were wonderful people who loved him very much. When we got home, I went into the kitchen to think good and hard about the situation while he was in the living room packing up the holiday decorations.

Rick was a good man. He'd gone out of his way to help me over the previous three months in which I'd been completely dependent on him. Losing my independence really threw me for a loop—it was hard to go back to square one and not be able to do anything by myself, and scary to think it could happen again. I thought about Frisco, whom I was still crazy about, but he didn't want to be with me.

Fuck. I'm 22 years old, and I'm a quadriplegic. Who else is going to want me?

I went out to the living room, where Rick was taking down the tinsel from the tree, and shocked us both.

"Okay," I told him. "I'll marry you."

CHAPTER 13

Nightmares and Dreams

Not long after Rick and I got engaged, the nightmares began.

Each time was a variation of the same scene: Bruce's face loomed above me as he forced my legs apart and choked me. I kicked and punched and tried to scream. I couldn't see his eyes. It was too dark, or he wasn't looking at me—one of those, I'm not sure which.

He looked right through me, as if I wasn't there . . .

After the first nightmare, I woke up next to Rick, sobbing. I could feel the imprint of Bruce's fingers wrapped around my neck.

"Dana, what's the matter?"

It was time to tell him about that night on the cliff. If I was going to marry him, he had to know what happened to me. I didn't give details, just the basics: "That boy. He raped me and threw me off the cliff."

Rick was shocked. He could see I needed to say something about it but didn't want to say any more than I had, so he just wrapped his arms around me until I felt safe enough to fall asleep again.

So far, Amy had been the only person I'd told. The day had come when I needed to tell someone, and I didn't want to keep it from my dearest friend anymore. After I told her, we cried together, and she assured me that it wasn't my fault and that she loved me.

She asked me if the man been caught. "No," I said. "Nothing happened to him. Nothing at all."

After the nightmares began, it got more difficult for me to contain the memory inside myself. Slowly, one by one, I began telling those closest to me.

"I want to kill him!" Chrissy said, shaking her head in tears.

And then she told me that she had also been sexually abused—twice. "First time it was by a friend of Mom's when I was nine," she said. "I told you about it at the time, but you didn't believe me. You were only seven."

The second time it happened to her was when I was in rehab. She was 22 and had too much to drink at a party she'd thrown at her own home. She passed out, and woke up to one of the guests raping her. When it was over, he told her not to bother telling anyone because no one would believe her.

"*Did* you tell anyone?" I asked.

Chrissy shook her head. "Not for a long time. No one believed me when I was nine, so why would they believe me as an adult?"

Just as Rick was shocked to hear about me, I was shocked to hear about Chrissy. And to have it happen to you as a child! It explained something about my sister that I couldn't have understood before, how she was as a child and as a teen—as if there was an invisible wall of pain around her that kept the two of us from fully connecting. I was sick, thinking about all those times she just wanted to fit in and play with Gary and me, and we made fun of her and excluded her. Now my sister and I were heartbroken for each other, and we cried and hugged, knowing that we were forever bonded as members of a club that we both wished we didn't belong to.

After Chrissy, I told my mother.

"Sweet Pea, I know," she said softly. "When I got to the hospital that day and the police told us that another serviceman was involved, I knew."

Dad and Debbie, of course, had known since that day in the hospital when the advisor had urged me to take my right to remain silent in order to get my service-connection. The advisor didn't spell it out, but they could read between the lines when she said, "We know it's foul play" and that a "crime" had been committed. Like the others, my father and stepmother followed my lead on not talking about it.

So now, six people close to me knew the truth, and the telling had given me some relief. I had been afraid to say anything to anyone for fear of being blamed, but thankfully that didn't happen. I was also afraid to say anything because I still wanted to hide from the truth myself. It had now been three and a half years since that night on the cliff, and I didn't want to go back there ever again.

Perhaps that's why the nightmares had begun—the memory was bubbling to the surface like hot lava that eventually had to erupt.

BY EARLY 1994, RICK AND I HAD MOVED to Cove, Oregon. Rick's mom had been diagnosed with brain cancer soon after we got engaged, so I quit school and we packed up our stuff. We moved into his parents' barn—"the tack room," as they called it—which was really a very nice apartment, and helped take care of her.

I loved Rick's parents, Bob and Laura, right away. Laura was an amazingly strong and elegant woman, and a lot of fun. She used to love visiting Rick when he worked casinos in Vegas and on cruise ships; now, as her health deteriorated, it was her last wish to go gambling in Winnemucca, Nevada, which was about six hours away.

All four of us piled into my van soon after we got there, and road-tripped to this tiny town that Johnny Cash sings about in his version of the country song "I've Been Everywhere." I lay down on the backseat that became a bed and chatted up a storm with Rick's mom.

When we got to the casino and cased out the slot machines, Rick's dad, whom I called "Pop," handed me a plastic tray that held 100 one-dollar coins. "Go have fun!" he said.

Not only was his family wonderful, but Rick was a very good influence on me in the beginning, too. He was into health, so after we started dating we began drinking green juices together and he urged me to get off that muscle-relaxant drug I was still taking. The purpose of baclofen was to stop involuntary muscle spasms, and it's commonly prescribed to patients with multiple sclerosis or Parkinson's disease. Yet when Rick researched it, he discovered that the side effects were poisonous for the nervous system and insisted that we wean me off it.

It was a good instinct, as I felt better right away. I had more physical mobility and was able to use my muscle tone and spasticity to work *for* me instead of against me. For example, by locking my left knee when my muscle contracted during a spasm, I could stand on it! Once I saw that was possible, I began training myself to make the same contractions/spasms voluntarily. Each new movement I could make was progress toward my ultimate goal: to walk again.

Rick was uniquely and strangely in tune with me whenever I was in trouble. I started riding a handcycle that spring, and a few months later had worked up to riding 12 miles and two hours at a time. However, on at least five different instances when I was riding, I ran out of food and water and started to fade, and I thought, *Rick, please come and get me! I need you!* A minute later, he was driving up next to me.

"I heard you," he said.

But with his nurturing side also came his jealousy, temper, and drinking.

That March, I took Rick with me to my second Winter Sports Clinic. Jen was my ski instructor this time, and speeding downhill was as exhilarating as the first time . . . even though I didn't have Frisco keeping me warm, which was just as well. Rick had no idea any dalliance had ever occurred between Frisco and me, but it *was* obvious that I had a crush on the guy.

Rick did a few runs with me, but for the most part, he went skiing on his own. At the end of one day on the slopes, we met the gang at a bar and I was chatting with Frisco, when someone tried to get past in the crowded, narrow aisle behind me. I scooted forward a bit toward Frisco, who was standing up and leaning against our table, then scooted back. From across the table, a drunken Rick seethed. He had the crazy notion that I'd put my head onto Frisco's lap, became angry, and left. When I got back to our room, he did plenty of yelling.

A day or two later I was getting dressed to go skiing just as he returned from a few hours on the slopes.

"Dude," I said, "you've got your ski pants on backward and your zipper is undone."

He looked surprised, but didn't say anything.

"How do you put your pants on backward?" I asked.

"I don't know."

We went home from the Clinic that year without further mention of it. But I was beginning to wonder if I could wiggle my way out of the engagement. Rick wasn't a bad guy, but I could see that we weren't the best match. He could be kind and gentle, except when he was drinking—and then he was not. The dueling extremes sounded very much like my father, I guess. I wasn't a piece of cake to live with either, I'm sure. I wanted my independence so bad and was such a wild child that the more loving he tried to be, the more smothered I felt and the more I pushed him away.

Before I had a chance to think on my dilemma some more, Rick's mother passed away—she died in Rick's arms the day after I arrived at the Veterans Games in Kansas that July. In our last conversation before I left, Laura asked me to make her a promise: "Please, take care of Rick."

When I got home from the Games, Pop put her diamond-and-emerald wedding ring in the palm of my hand. "She wanted you to have it," he said through his tears.

The irony was that here I was, a quad, and Laura clearly saw my relationship with her son as me taking care of him instead of the other way around, which is how *he* saw it. It was in fact a complicated combination of both, I think. I further suspected that Rick's need to take care of me and my need for independence and increased mobility were doomed to clash.

By that summer, I had reached an athletic overdrive. At the Kansas Games my rugby team played so great, we won a medal for third place. While there, I told a friend, Hayes, all the sports I was up to: my hours of handcycling per day, wheelchair racing, skiing, and playing quad rugby.

A fellow quad, Hayes designed the slalom course and was an official at the Games. "Dana, let me give you one word of advice," he said. "Don't try to do it all. Your shoulders have to last you the rest of your life."'

Slow down? No way. I wanted to do more; I needed to keep moving. There are 10,000 things you can do in the world, I discovered, and when you're in a chair you can still do 9,000 of them.

If you have the will, you can figure out an adaptive way to do almost anything. Paralympian Mark Wellman was the first para to climb the arduous granite faces of El Capitan (in 1989) and Half Dome (in 1991) in Yosemite National Park, for instance, and wrote about it all in his memoir, *Climbing Back.* I looked around at people like Mark and Hayes, and countless other inspiring examples, and truly understood that there were no limits. No dream was too big or impossible.

Every day, I'd drive out to the middle of nowhere (which is redundant, since Cove *is* in the middle of nowhere) and park on a deserted road to do laps in my wheelchair for hours, back and forth. The people in the area got used to seeing me, and they'd drive by and wave. Once in a while, my training would alarm a passerby, such as when this one guy stopped and got out of his car to make sure I was okay. I assured him I was.

"Say, how'd you get that disabled veteran license plate on your van?" he asked.

"I *am* a disabled veteran."

"No, you're not. You're too young—and you're a girl."

"If you can join the military at 18, you can be a veteran at 18," I told him, as I got into my van and started my engine. "And women serve their country, too, you know."

I drove away and left him standing there, speechless.

AFTER RICK'S MOTHER DIED, HE QUIT HIS JOB and told anyone who asked that he was my attendant. We had enough money coming in with my benefits that he didn't need to work, and this way he could spend more time "taking care of" me. He also took over my bank account—reminding me that my math was shit and I couldn't balance a checkbook, which was true.

For a one-income household, we sure bought a lot of expensive toys that fall, including a FL70 business-class Freightliner truck, a Champion race-car trailer, and a Waverunner. Rick sold his house and, combined with my savings, his plan was to build the trailer into a wheelchair-accessible fifth-wheel RV to be pulled by the Freightliner. The trailer was an empty shell when we bought it, and he did all the work himself: he insulated it; cut out windows, built stairs, and extended the floor; installed a roll-in shower, full kitchen, and washer and dryer; and added wheelchair lifts and automatic doors. He basically turned it into an apartment, with a garage, on wheels (today people would call it a "toy hauler").

The truck already came with an Allison push-button automatic transmission, and Care Medical Equipment in Portland installed hand controls and the lift on the truck—so I was good to go. The deal from the start with the 18-wheeler was that if I was going to pay for it, I damn well was going to drive it! Ever since I was a kid in Three Lynx, driving a truck had been my childhood dream ("I'm a trucker!" I would tell my mom, after my cookie rounds). I thought that dream had been lost to me, and now here it was, parked in front of my face.

First was the matter of a license to drive that apartment-on-wheels, though. I already had my regular driver's license—I had retaken the test when I got my hand-controlled van and passed with flying colors. Now I needed a Commercial Driver License and had to take a whole new test, both written and driving. I went to the DMV in nearby La Grande and did everything I was supposed to—inspected the truck and trailer before driving, drove around town and on the freeway, backed up around a 90-degree corner, hooked up my trailer, and more. The examiner gave me a score of 94.

But that wasn't enough for the Oregon Department of Transportation. They told me I wouldn't be driving my rig until I sent them a medical waiver and they had seen me drive with their own eyes. They couldn't wrap their heads around the idea of a quad driving a big rig; apparently, it just wasn't done. So they were sending one of their own people to come and test me again. I got Dr. Little, one of the genius doctors from the VA hospital in Seattle, to sign my waiver, and I prepped for my next test. Not only were they going to make me redo what I had already done, they informed me, but they were going to make me take a special "endurance" exam as well.

The very serious-looking examiner arrived from ODOT and took me on the narrowest and windiest roads he could find, and I didn't let my trailer cross any of the white lines on the road, even as I turned tight corners. This testing guy couldn't believe he was seeing a quad—and a female quad who looked 12 years old at that—drive a rig.

"We'll put up some cones now," he said, "to simulate you backing up to the dock."

"Well, why don't I just back up to a real dock?" I asked. I drove around to the local Walmart and backed up to their loading dock with only one pull-up and reset, and I did it perfectly. I was poetry in motion.

"Young lady," said the test guy, closing up his notebook when we were done, "you drive better than most truckers I've ever tested. And I was trying to make you fail!"

In 1995, I became the first quadriplegic to obtain a Class A Commercial Driver License in the United States, and maybe in the entire world. The proud staff at the VA hospital pinned a local newspaper article about me on the bulletin board of the SCI unit's physical therapy room.

AROUND THE SAME TIME THAT I REALIZED MY DREAM of being a trucker, another dream from childhood materialized in front of me. When I was newly out of rehab, my buddy Gene had gone up to my special place in Three Lynx—the waterfall that Gary and I used to hike to as kids—and taken a photo for me. I put that photo up on my wall at home and would gaze it, daydreaming that I'd climb back up to the falls one day.

It was Mom's idea that while a bunch of us were at Grandma's in Estacada having a little family reunion, we should drive to Three Lynx and take a walk down memory lane, and then hike up to the falls. One of my aunts and a few cousins (including Sally and her younger brother, Christopher), piled into cars with Mom, Gary, and me; once we got there, Mom led the way on our hike.

We took my chair as far as we could on an old back road, for about a mile. Then once we got to the dam, Gary attached a sleeping bag to a backpack frame so that he could haul me up on his back and my butt and legs would be supported. Kind of like what he said to me in Sweden—he wanted to put me in his back pocket to keep me safe.

He strapped me in and up we went, knowing the way like a map forever etched in our hearts. Gary climbed the ladder up to the dam, crossed over on the boards, hopped over onto some rocks, and then stepped on the deer trail that led up to the falls. Once we got close, he climbed over fallen trees, then up another hill.

My brother wasn't taking me close enough to simply *see* our waterfall; he was taking me close enough so that I could hear it, smell it, and touch it.

Everyone was behind us as Gary carefully walked along the slippery, mossy ground until we were both directly behind the thundering waterfall, like we used to do as kids. It was our magical place. We stood there together in silence, me hugging his back, as droplets of water splashed onto our faces and mixed with teardrops.

As always, we didn't need any words.

CHAPTER 14

Snow Angels

Rick and I got married on April 22, 1995. He was excited, and tried to make everything nice for me. He built little side guards out of PVC pipe that went over the wheels and cushions of my chair so that my dress wouldn't get caught as I pushed myself down the aisle. He'd also picked out a poufy Cinderella-type dress for me to wear, and I felt like an idiot.

"Oh, you're so beautiful!" Mom and Debbie said, like mothers are supposed to, as they did my makeup and sprayed goop on my hair. Thank goodness, though, that I'd picked my own rebellious footwear to go under the traditional gown—a pair of white, lacy Keds.

My nurse Merlita, from the VA hospital in Seattle, came to the wedding, as did Deb's daughter, Mary. Amy made the very long drive from Arizona State University to be there for the ceremony and do a few dances at the reception, then had to turn around and drive back for her classes the following Monday.

Before I took the plunge, another friend pulled me aside. "You can still back out of this wedding," she whispered. "Everyone will understand." Some of my friends and family members didn't like Rick so much—they were afraid that he was with me for my money, and they knew I didn't really want to marry him deep in my heart. But I had made my decision, and I was going to stick with it.

Soon after we got hitched, Rick and I took our newly built rig out on the open road and blared Steppenwolf's "Born to Be Wild" as we went off to look for adventure. We went all over the place—Vegas for a few months, Arizona to visit Amy, a two-month stop in Texas to work on the trailer and visit other friends and relatives. During a stop on Padre Island we met up with Grandma Blanche's sister and brother-in-law, who asked us to go in on some property with them in a town one hour north from there.

By early December, Rick and I had parked our rig in the flatlands of no-fucking-where in Odem, Texas, population about 2,000. It was a dusty, isolated spot, but we started out in good spirits.

We had been exploring all sorts of holistic therapies and remedies as we drove through the Lone Star State: We went on a 14-day liquid cleanse, drinking only a tea of boiled flaxseeds (it had the consistency of slime), unsweetened cherry juice, and bouillon broth—chased down with psyllium husks and loads of vitamins. We did a one-day liver cleanse, drinking only a small bottle of olive oil mixed with pineapple juice, and buckets of water. And to expunge all those pesky toxins from our systems, we gave ourselves high colonics and coffee enemas three times a day, using a bucket and a colema board.

Poor Rick. One day we were in the shower, and I unceremoniously pooped on his foot. Talk about cleansing. "A family that poops together, stays together," he said with a smile. "Now that you shit on my foot, we're sure to stay together, right?"

I tried something called Electro-Acuscope/Myopulse Therapy, in which a practitioner delivers microcurrents of electrical charge into the cells to help the body heal its nerve and brain tissue. Then I did a series of light, color, and tone therapies. I went to a chiropractor who tried to adjust my coccyx, but ended up breaking my tailbone while performing an "internal alignment" by sticking her finger up my rectum. Personally, I don't recommend getting your coccyx straightened from the inside. What she did hurt so bad that I shit myself right on her table. Well, she asked for it.

Of everything I tried, the only combination that had any effect on my body's function and sensation was a mix of juicing, vitamins, minerals, healthy food, Reiki, and "One Brain Method" kinesiology, which is a blend of psychology, meditation, and exercise.

At one point, I was on the floor of the trailer learning to crawl. Rick held me up in the middle of my tummy to keep me from falling on the floor and Mom, who was visiting, moved my arms, while two homeopathic practitioners moved my legs. I concentrated on keeping my head up and arms locked enough so I wouldn't fall as they supported and moved my body.

Did I actually crawl? My body *thinks* I did. From what I'd learned so far about the mind-body connection from all the holistic practitioners I'd met, my body didn't know that I wasn't doing it all myself. And thinking I could do and was doing it was the first step to actually doing it.

ONCE WE WERE SETTLED IN ODEM, I began to feel trapped and isolated. Rick had convinced me to leave my van in storage back in Las Vegas (and yet we hauled the Waverunner and his truck with us inside the back 28 feet of our trailer), so I had to depend on him to go everywhere. Not only could I not drive his truck because it wasn't adapted, but I couldn't even get into it on my own—he had to lift me up and carry me in. I could drive the big rig, of course. But anytime I suggested he unhook it from the trailer so that I could drive it around, he got all pissy.

It was bad enough that I couldn't drive anywhere myself; worse was the fact that I couldn't even get out to use my wheelchair to get around! Our trailer sat on a concrete pad set back from the road, and between the trailer and road was an uneven patch of 50 feet of grass and spiky goathead stickers that I couldn't get through with my chair. I felt like a caged animal unable to leave the dimensions of that trailer and concrete pad.

Day after day, I felt more helpless and depressed. It was that same sinking feeling I'd had when I broke my leg with Rick and couldn't do anything on my own—as if all the hard work I'd done to find every inch of independence possible was being sucked down the drain.

Once in a while, Rick and I toured the area. I also bought one of those blow-up kiddie swimming pools to play in. And I played dress-up with clothes and makeup (which I didn't even do as a kid!). I knew I was really, really desperate when I called in to a radio station and clucked like a chicken to try to win tickets for a concert. I mowed the lawn with one of those riding lawn mowers a few times, and that was fun. But mostly I sat in the trailer, looking out the window, bored to death.

I reminded myself of that nursery rhyme:

Peter, Peter pumpkin eater,
Had a wife but couldn't keep her;
He put her in a pumpkin shell
Away from her family, and there he kept her in hell . . .

Okay, I changed the last line a bit. But by February 1996, I did feel like I was in hell. I remember thinking, *Is this how things are going to be forever?* Then, after ten months of begging to get my van, Rick took it out of storage. And I knew exactly where I wanted to go first —and last—with it.

One sunny afternoon, I drove to a stop sign on the two-lane road where the train tracks crossed. Then I parked in the middle of the tracks and sat there, waiting for the train to come and hit me. As I waited, I thought about my grumpy old pal from rehab, Roger. He'd gotten out of the hospital a few months after I had, and even briefly lived with Mom and me in our apartment in West Seattle. He was in terrible pain all the time—gunshot wounds tend to have more neurogenic pain than other spinal cord injuries. Some days, it was more than he could take.

"If this pain doesn't get better in one year," he confided to me then, "I'm going to kill myself."

He knew exactly how he was going to do it, too—with an overdose of drugs. "It's better for the people who find you," he insisted. "It's the least messy and least traumatizing. Shooting yourself is not a nice way for people to find you."

Other people might have said, "No, Roger, don't talk that way!" but not me. I respected his decision. I remembered the moment I'd tried to bite down on my air tube in the hospital those first few weeks in San Diego. I feel we all have a built-in survival mechanism and sometimes we reach a point where we are just done. Who am I to judge someone else's exit from the world? If it's their time to go, it's their time. If they want to go, it's their choice.

I had only one request for him: "Roger, if you're going to do it, will you please say good-bye to me first?"

He promised.

Apparently, he did try to reach me before he killed himself a year or two later by OD'ing, but didn't find me. I got a phone call afterward from a mutual friend with the news of his death, telling me that Roger had left a note with specific instructions to call to say good-bye to me from him.

Now as I sat on the train tracks, I watched a train speed toward me. I thought of my family and how they would hurt. I thought about the train engineer blowing his horn at me, and how unfair this would be to him and his own family. I decided it wasn't my time yet, and I drove away.

A FEW WEEKS LATER, I WAS ON A PLANE TO CRESTED BUTTE. I'd spent the last three months feeling trapped, and I needed more than ever to speed down a mountain. I'd missed the Winter Sports Clinic the year before because it was so close to my wedding date and Rick didn't want me to go. Honestly, I think he was jealous of the close friendships I was forming there and feared he'd lose me if I went. This year, there was no talking me out of it.

When I tell people that the Veterans Games and the WSC saved my life, I mean it on so many levels and in countless instances. The people involved, and the life-affirming beauty of the sports, have helped me mentally, physically, and emotionally over the many years; I owe my life to them.

In the spring of '96, the Clinic helped to pull me out of isolation, and to feel alive and hopeful again. After my experience on the train tracks, it put me back on the *right* track. When I arrived, I sat on a back deck of the hotel to have a beer and take in the beautiful surroundings. Gazing at the top of a snowcapped mountain on a beautiful spring day with a beer in hand does a lot to immediately put a girl in a good frame of mind.

One of the cross-country ski instructors, Anita, came over to chat and convince me to give cross-country sit-skiing a try that year. I didn't like cross-country skiing as an able-bodied teen and had no intention of liking it now, but she said, "It's good to try something new, Dana. What have you got to lose? And besides, we have really cute instructors."

One of the life-affirming qualities of the Clinic was that everyone always encouraged you to try new things to see what you were capable of—often, you'd be so surprised by what you could do. The gang here was especially geared toward independence; if you let an able-bodied person push you up a hill and someone saw it, you'd get so much crap from other people in chairs that you'd never hear the end of it. Like, "Oh, really? Poor thing! You need help?" Trying something new and finding that you're able to do it was crucial to one's sanity after you've been thrown into a situation where suddenly everyone tells you that you can't do anything. As for cute instructors . . . well, that was a bonus.

The next day, I was on the other side of the mountain to meet my new cross-country ski instructor, Jim. He had blue eyes and a sweet smile, and he wore tight ski pants—he was hot as hell. I sat in a sit-ski, which looked like the frame of a wheelchair but attached to skis, and my feet were stretched out in front of me. Jim taped my hands to the poles and strapped my feet together and to the footrest. Then he leaned over me to strap my torso to the seat because I still didn't have enough core strength to sit up on my own. He looked at me and gave me a big smile.

Crap, I'm married!

That didn't stop me from flirting up a storm, nor did it stop him from flirting right back. And I don't know if Jim's cuteness factored into it, but I was surprised that I liked cross-country skiing right away— I felt like I had more control and independence than with downhill. Even though Jim and two other cross-country instructors, Cliff and Phil, were doing all the work, they let me think that I was doing a lot of it. I also loved how much fun this Nordic (cross-country) gang was, way on the other side of the mountain from the Alpine (downhill) skiers. They were totally up for my giddy, childlike personality.

"Hey, can you put me in the snow? I want to make a snow angel!" This was something you definitely couldn't do on the downhill slopes. Once I was on my back, Jim moved my legs and I moved my arms.

We laughed as he piled snow on top of me, and I kept waving my arms and he kept moving my legs.

"*You're* the snow angel," he told me, and that became my nickname for years after that day. But the truth was, he was my angel that year. The sense of accomplishment I had trying a new sport and succeeding, coupled with Jim's flirty attention, gave me new inspiration. When I left the WSC that week, I was invigorated with a brand-new goal for myself for the following year when I returned: I was going to stand up and cross-country ski.

"I know I can do it!" I told a bunch of instructors. Standing-up downhill skiing didn't seem doable yet to me, but cross-country—yes! I could feel the real, kick-ass Dana back again.

"Okaaaay," they all told me, with encouraging smiles, but I could see that they weren't so sure about this. Their mouths may have smiled, but their eyes said, *I don't think so. You know you're a quad, right?*

My eyes answered back, *And your point is?*

Back in Odem, I told Rick that it was time to get out of that trailer and out of that town. He didn't want to go back to Oregon, telling me, "Your family has too much influence on you." So we set our sights on the big city of San Antonio, two hours to the north.

By August we were living in our own new house, which Rick had helped to build and adapt for me. True to my word, I worked on ideas that would enable me to stand up and cross-country ski the following March. I was going to focus on this type of skiing for now because I felt there was more I could do with it at that time (and it didn't hurt that hot-as-hell Jim was a Nordic instructor).

I was inspired by the mechanical "standing frame" that the VA had bought for me and I used every day at home. On the frame, I'd transfer to a padded seat and put a seat belt on, then hand-crank myself to a standing position. It had a padded knee holder to lock my knees in position and make me stand up straight with some weight on my legs and feet, and it had little wheels on the bottom. I would actually move about the house in an upright position, using a steering-wheel device that I manually pushed. It was kind of like a stand-up wheelchair.

My legs didn't move like I was walking, but I was standing up as I moved on the wheels. It was like "practicing" standing up, and it helped me build muscle memory.

I'd also had a good look at "ski legs"—adaptive equipment in which the tips of downhill skis attached to a bar in front, like a heavy-duty walker—at the Clinic. *It looked like a walker with downhill skis under them,* I thought. *Why can't something like this be used for Nordic?*

I got to work in our living room in San Antonio, building my contraption. I bought a pair of skis, and got Rick to mount a walker to them using fabricated metal brackets. Then I put tinfoil on the bottom of my socks so that my feet would slide across the living-room carpet, as if I was wearing skis myself and there was snow underneath. I used the walker to stand up, and with my elbows locked out, I held myself up using strength from my shoulders. I shifted my right hip to get my right leg forward, then I shifted my left hip to get my left leg forward, leaning on the walker to help me get the alternating-leg function going. Soon enough, I was shuffling across the living-room floor on my tinfoil skis . . . it worked!

"Hey, Rick! Look at this!"

He came in and watched me shuffle in my walker-skis with foil on my feet. "That's never going to work," he said, shaking his head, and left the room.

The difference between Rick's defeatist attitude and the positive encouragement I found with the instructors at the Games and at the WSC was beginning to gnaw at me. I didn't understand it, until one night when he said something that connected the dots.

He'd had a few glasses of wine at dinner and was a bit tipsy, and I'd had an exhausting day with my various exercises and therapies. We were both in bed, minutes away from passing out, when I heard him softly say, "Dana, I don't want you to walk. If you walk, you'll leave me."

He whispered it under his breath as if I wasn't meant to hear it, but I did. A few minutes later he was asleep, and I drifted off with his words in my head. Rick needed me to be dependent on him; he needed me to stay in that chair. I'd realize years later, after several failed romances, that my wheelchair attracted a type of insecure man who wanted a needy woman to make him feel strong: *If you're in a wheelchair, you'll always need me and never leave, right?*

Rick needed me to stay in that chair, and the thing I wanted most in the world was to stand up from it. This was going to be a problem.

WHEN I SHOWED MY CONTRAPTION TO THE INSTRUCTORS at the next WSC in March 1997, the word *never* didn't cross their minds. They were excited, and we got to work brainstorming and building. One instructor donated a pair of Nordic skis; another screwed them to the walker. Then we took a piece of plastic sled we found at a local shop and sewed a pad and fabric onto that to make a seat for me to sit down on or lean against when needed.

Early one bright morning, we took the walker configuration out on the trails, with me— the original inventor—as its first guinea pig. We got duct tape in all sorts of funky colors, and the instructors wrapped my knees with Ace bandages to help lock them out and taped my boots for extra support and stability. And off I went, moving my hips from side to side, and shuffling myself across the snow.

I could see the look of total surprise on the faces of Jim, Cliff, and Phil. Apparently, no one from my level and severity of injury as a quad had ever done this before. Even a few of the downhill instructors came over from their side of the mountain to see if it was going to work. I was slow as a slug in sand that first time and only went about 50 yards, *but I was skiing standing up!*

At the closing ceremonies that year, Jim and I got to the auditorium late. We slipped in a door at the back right as the Winter Sports Clinic's founder and director, Sandy Trombetta, was talking about the winner of the Linnie Howard Spirit Award. This was a great honor given out every year to the person who most captures the spirit of the WSC and serves as a role model for both veterans and staff, who anonymously nominate and vote on the winner. The room was jam-packed with at least 300 people, so it took Jim and me a few minutes to realize that Sandy was talking about me! He announced my name as the award winner and everyone looked around for me. We were in shock!

One of the PT's from Seattle, who'd come that year instead of Jen, spotted me at the back. "There she is!"

I was supposed to go to the front of the room, but the aisles were blocked with people and chairs. The PT got up and weaved her way over to me, scooped me up from my chair, and carried me through the thick crowd to the front. She plopped me on a chair onstage next to Sandy, to the applause of everyone in the room.

"Wow," he said with a laugh, "that was the best transfer I have ever seen."

The audience roared. Sandy handed me the Spirit Award, which was a big eagle so heavy I could barely lift it with both hands. It was engraved with these words: IF YOU DON'T LEAVE A LITTLE BLOOD ON THE MOUNTAIN, YOU HAVEN'T BEEN THERE.

After the ceremony, Jim came back to my room with me, and we talked—and then our flirtation crossed over into cuddling and kissing. Even though I was still married, our connection was so strong that it was overwhelming, and I couldn't deny it.

As the sun rose, Jim took a small paper bag out of his jeans pocket and handed it to me. He knew how much I loved the water, so he'd given me a beautiful silver necklace with a little dolphin on the chain. The dolphin's spirit, I knew, was a symbol of protection and resurrection. And its playful nature was a reminder to approach life with humor and joy.

Back home in San Antonio, I arrived floating on air with my Spirit Award in tow and Jim in my heart. When I told Rick about my award, he was anything but congratulatory: "What did you have to do to get *that?*" He made a vulgar gesture. He'd been drinking.

"I won this award because I actually have this much spirit in me."

It was getting bad between us . . . and it was about to get a lot worse.

One afternoon, in the middle of an argument, he walked over to me and—in a very calm, controlled fashion—tipped my wheelchair over backward, causing me to fall out. He left the room with me sprawled on the floor.

"Rick! Come back here! *Come back here right now and pick me up off this floor!*"

"No. I'll come get you when I'm good and ready," he said from the other room.

I lay there for 15 minutes before he was "good and ready" to come back and pick me up. I felt incredibly helpless and vulnerable—and pissed off. I couldn't continue with this abuse. Something had to change.

Snuggling with
Dad #2, Ken,
at age 2.

An early '70s hippie family.
From left to right: Chrissy,
Gary, Ken, me, and Mom.

Singing
"Mellow Yellow"
on the toilet
at age 3.

At age 7 with my "snot cast" . . . and a beer, to ease the pain.

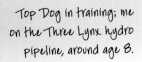

Top Dog in training; me on the Three Lynx hydro pipeline, around age 8.

Clowning around with my new
sis, Susanne. We're both 13 and
on summer vacation by the lake.

Pretty in pink; at my eighth-grade
graduation with Ken and Mom #3, Bonnie.

Curled hair and
makeup with
Dad #3, Ed.

At age 16, in Dad's
kitchen with Gary
and Chrissy.

My official Navy portrait taken during boot camp, when I was 18.

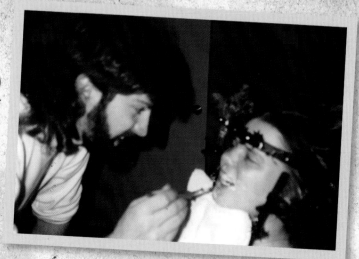

Christmas 1990; Gary decorated my halo with tinsel and brushed my teeth for me.

Gary piggybacking me up to "our" waterfall in Three Lynx.

Mom readying a reluctant bride in 1995.

I realized my dream of being a trucker in 1995.

With cousin Jim, circa '96—finally cowboys!

At the Winter Sports Clinic in 1997, I captured
the Spirit Award, while Jim won my heart.

Partying as Baby Spice for Halloween with best buddies
Sean (left) and Mary (right).

Tethered and ready to speed downhill on a bi-ski, age 25.

At age 27, conquering the slalom course at the Veterans Games in Puerto Rico.

Tipper Gore treated me as a dear friend at the
2000 Democratic National Convention.

With three of the Ponderosa Boys in 2000.
From left to right: Wes, Cliff, me, and Phil.

Scuba diving with my BFF Amy in Australia in 2002 . . . shit happens.

Braving and surviving the Grand Canyon in 2002.

Dancing in the street in Beijing after receiving stem-cell treatment in 2004.

On a cruise with my beautiful sister, Chrissy, in 2004.

At Burning Man in 2007, where the men thanked me "for being a woman"!

Riding a camel in Africa circa 2010—it's harder than it looks.

My awesome aunt Jeanne always helps keep me grounded.

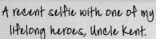

A recent selfie with one of my lifelong heroes, Uncle Kent.

With the best little grandma, Grandma Blanche.

Jack and me with neighbors Bob and Carolyn—my little, loving Grand Junction family.

Independence!
Standing up while
Nordic skiing in
2014, with the
genius Bobby Palm.

With Wayne Dyer—and "our"
purple hat—telling my story in
front of an audience.

May 2015, getting ready to soar like a bird in the ultralight.

At Crater Lake with Jack, the love of my life!

PART III

Falling Up

It's amazing what we can do when we put our minds to it. Most people don't know how powerful their thoughts are; I certainly didn't. Sure, I'd always had determination and found that thinking positive got me results. But I had no idea that the mind worked on making our thoughts happen even when we weren't aware of it.

That spring of 1997, after Rick left me on the floor, I attended a health expo and heard people talking about a motivational speaker named Wayne Dyer. He'd apparently given a life-changing lecture that was all the buzz, but I'd missed it because I was too busy having a consultation about my disintegrating marriage with one of the many psychics who'd set up shop at the expo.

"So, will my marriage last?" I asked, as the woman laid down her tarot cards. I knew psychics rarely answered questions like that with certainty—how could they? What if they were wrong? And they usually pumped you with positive stuff so you'd come back for more.

"Not a chance," she said, shaking her head. "Your marriage is over, over, over."

I guess it was obvious even to a $10 fortune-teller.

They say that when the student is ready, the teacher appears. A few weeks after the expo, I was hiding out in a bookstore before closing time—I'd been keeping myself out of the house most days until Rick went to sleep at 10 P.M. to avoid him. I was pushing my chair down one of the aisles when a book fell off the shelf, narrowly missing me, and landed at my feet.

I picked it up and saw that it was called *Manifest Your Destiny,* by Dr. Wayne Dyer. I recognized the name as that guy everyone had been talking about at the expo, so I flipped through a few pages. *Hmm . . . interesting.* I decided to buy the audio version, and slipped the cassette into the tape player in my van as I drove home.

Talk about a bolt of lightning. Dr. Dyer's words about changing your life and visualizing the future you want were so strong and true to me that by the time I got home half an hour later, I was exploding with energy. That was it; I was done. I wanted to change *everything.* I wanted to get rid of all that was draining my life, and direct my energy to focus on what I wanted as if I already had it. And just as important, I realized with a shock, was the way in which I visualized my future.

As I listened to Dr. Dyer's book, I realized that I had been manifesting all along and had created my present, which had taken shape from my own thoughts and desires. For instance, in the few months before I got hurt, I had three wishes I thought about over and over:

1. To be skinny and petite like other girls

2. To be popular

3. To stop sweating

I was astonished to realize that within a few years of crystalizing those wishes in my mind, they had all come true. I had lost at least 70 pounds and now, in my chair, was four feet in height—and many of the bulky muscles I had worked so hard to build in the weight room had atrophied to nothing. I was popular—I'd just won an award voted on by all my peers and instructors and had been with the cutest and most popular guy on the mountain. And since my accident, my broken neck had affected my ability to sweat.

We create our world, for good or bad, it dawned on me. *Had I manifested myself getting hurt?*

Now that I knew just how powerful visualization and thoughts were—and how good I evidently was at making them a reality—I was pumped. I said the following words out loud as I drove home that night from the bookstore and repeated them in my mind as I fell asleep. It was my mantra; it was my prayer; it was my future, and I knew it:

I am walking. I am walking. I am walking.

Whatever I'd been doing healthwise that had led to even small progress, I began again and cranked into overdrive. I juiced, I upped my colonics, I worked out more and harder and longer. I injected myself in the legs with vitamins B_6 and B_{12} every other day—I'd pick a spot that I couldn't feel, close my eyes, and stab the needle into each thigh. It gave me a buzz and filled me with energy.

I also listened to Wayne's soothing but directive voice whenever I could throughout the day, especially when I was on my way to the San Antonio VA hospital to work out. That's when I did the "aah" meditation he talked about, which was filled with a lot of affirmations, such as: *My past is nothing more than the trail that I have left behind. What drives my life today is the energy that I generate in each of my present moments . . . I know that my highest self is always ready to lift me up beyond the world I experience with my senses . . .*

At home, I piped Enya's greatest-hits album, *Paint the Sky with Stars,* into my headphones while pumping the arm ergometer (a stationary tabletop handcycle) at full throttle for an hour or two. And with every exercise that I did, I affirmed: *I am walking. I am walking. I am walking.*

I took charge of practical matters—selling the truck, the trailer, the Waverunner, and getting back control of my bank account. And then I finally got back control of my personal life as well.

THE NIGHT BEFORE I LEFT FOR THE WINTER SPORTS CLINIC in March 1998, Rick and I had another argument while he was drunk, and he did it again. I was talking with him and one of his friends when Rick got angry about something—I don't even remember what it was—and he turned to me, tipped me over backward in my chair, and walked away. That kind of blow was worse than a punch to me. His friend called him an asshole, and lifted my chair and me upright.

I wanted to think that this sort of abusive act wasn't normally in Rick's nature—that it came from insecurities made worse from drinking. That maybe if he had a job he wouldn't have gotten lost, as he seemed to be. He wasn't the Rick I knew, who only a few years earlier would intuitively know when I needed help and never hurt me. It now seemed that the more independent I got, the angrier he got.

When we went to bed that night, I tried to talk to him about it. I said that we needed to make a compromise or our marriage wasn't going to work.

Rick turned to me, and in a cool and measured voice, replied, "Didn't I already compromise by being with someone in a wheel-chair?"

His words were a stab in the heart and a twisting of the knife. I'd never been so hurt in all my life . . . and that's saying a lot, all things considered. I'd finally had enough, and there was no going back from that one. I had already left enough blood on the mountain.

"This marriage," I told him, "is over right now."

Rick tried to apologize the next day as he drove me to the airport, but I didn't want to talk to him; my decision about us had been made. And I was too busy manifesting something else fantastic in my mind before I even got on the plane: This year, not only was I going to stand up and cross-country ski, as I had done the year before, but I was also determined to stand up and ski going down the mountain, too.

Once at the Clinic, I got on the Nordic trails and in my walker configuration. Everyone could see my improvement in just one year. I was standing taller and stronger after all my working out (as tall as you can be at 5'3"). I was still shuffling my legs, but I was moving them faster. Now more than ever, the cross-country skiing gave me the sense of being able-bodied and free as I glided through the snow with the cold air on my face.

Jim, Cliff, and Phil were part of the able-bodied Nordic ski instructor team at the WSC known as "the Ponderosa Boys." They were a funny, good-natured, bighearted lot who got their name because for the duration of the Clinic, they all roomed together in a condo complex by the slopes that was called the Ponderosa. Of course that was the name of the fictitious ranch on the TV show *Bonanza,* home of the Cartwrights. Each of the guys had a character name: Jim was "Little Joe" (who, coincidentally, was the one I had a crush on as a kid). Cliff was "Pa" because he was the eldest and most serious of the bunch. Phil was "Hop Sing" because he'd cook up big dinners for the gang. Dr. Bob was "Adam" and, like the character, would make cameo appearances at dinner. And Wes was "Hoss," which I could never figure out because he was tall and skinny.

I had a lot of fun with the Ponderosa Boys and flirted my ass off with them in a friendly way—I couldn't help it. They became much more than instructors to me over the years. These guys were my mentors, friends, colleagues, brothers, and biggest supporters. None of them ever said "No" or "Don't try that." They may have been hesitant a few times, not wanting me to get hurt, but they always let me try.

So when I broached the subject that year of skiing downhill while standing up, they were all for it. After seeing me stand up and ski cross-country, they didn't doubt me when I said I was going to do something.

Molly, the downhill ski instructor at the Clinic who'd invented ski legs, and I got ready at the top of the hill for the big event. And it *was* a big event, because no one usually progressed in this way. Usually if you're sit-skiing when you arrive for your first time at the Clinic, you're still sit-skiing ten years later. They don't expect you to go from sit-skiing to standing, never mind both cross-country and downhill. This was huge, as no one had done it as a quad, at least that I know of. I was about to change the norm yet again.

Before we went down, Molly stuck a wad of toilet paper onto my butt as if I were a snow bunny. I had two other instructors with me in addition to her—one on each side to help me turn and one behind me, tethering, to control my speed. My job was to lock my knees and stay standing. As we skied down the mountainside together, we sang out loud at the top of our lungs that Chumbawamba song "Tubthumping," with its message of "I get knocked down, but I get up again!"

I was elated. I loved downhill skiing as an able-body, and to stand up and do it again, to feel that power of being upright and looking down a mountainside as I glided down, was a dream come true; a wish manifested. I was a little over seven years post-injury, and I'd gone from not being able to breathe to standing on my own two feet and skiing down a mountain.

When I got to the bottom of the hill, all the team leaders were excited, and several instructors on the lifts cheered. Later on, Frisco gave me a big hug and a special smile. "Only you could do something like that," he said. "Way to go."

The support and joy my dear friends at the Clinic offered that spring lifted my spirits after I'd decided to leave Rick, and helped me continue to believe in myself and manifest a happier future. One new friend in particular made an impact on me that would change my life.

I'd seen Lucy at a few Clinics and Veterans Games, but we hadn't really talked much until this year. She was a very beautiful, auburn-haired girly girl from Arkansas a few years older than me. She loved offering me advice on hair, makeup, and clothes—advice I desperately needed, it seems. I'd always been happy wearing shorts and waffle-stompers, whereas she was ultrafeminine with every hair in place.

"Oh, honey pie," she'd say to me. "Don't you know how to look like a girl?"

"I'm wearing lip gloss. Doesn't that count?"

"Well, bless your heart."

In front of the mirror, she'd style my hair with the curling iron and do my makeup. I appreciated her help, and we bonded as new friends. But what truly drew me to her was something I couldn't immediately put my finger on—yet it was something I recognized and felt a kinship with.

One night when we were having drinks, I watched her behavior and subtle body language as the men swarming around us flirted, and I knew. The next day we were both at a meeting with some instructors and other participants when this guy made a sexist remark that everyone laughed at. I turned to look at Lucy and saw that she was halfway out the door. I followed and caught up with her at the elevator.

"Hey," I said.

"Hey!" She smiled brightly.

"So . . . when did it happen?"

Lucy's smile froze. "What are you talking about?"

I just looked at her, and her face crumbled. We got into the elevator fast and went up to her room, where both of us cried like a dam busting. Lucy told me her horrific story of rape, which had happened a few years earlier when she was in the Army, and about the resulting cover-up among her superiors.

"You're the first person I've told," she said through her tears. "I thought I was the only one. I've felt so alone."

She wasn't alone, of course. I'd met a handful of women at that point who'd been sexually assaulted but had spoken about it in hushed tones, feeling embarrassed or as if it were their fault. I found them the same way I found Lucy—we recognized something in each other, and then someone was brave enough to ask. So many of the stories were the same, and we all shared a common reminder of our assaults: We felt a sense of shame, we felt no one would believe us, and we felt we'd be blamed. And worst of all, the guys had been good enough to let us into their previously male-only club and now we were going to complain? To tell on them and be tattletales?

I had a momentary childhood flashback of my brother reminding me that I was in the club, but I had to remember to keep my mouth shut when I got hurt. It was pretty clear that in a man's world, if a woman got hurt and talked about it, she would be banished from "the club."

By the time I got hurt, I was already very good at not telling.

SEVERAL WEEKS AFTER THE CLINIC, I DROVE TO JIM'S PLACE in Ashland, Oregon, to spend a few romantic days with him. We'd shared more kisses and late-night cuddles at the Clinic, and now that I was ending things with Rick it was time to consummate our passion.

Jim unplugged the phone, and for three days we had the most energetic heart-body connection I'd ever felt. In the mornings, he'd run out for lemon–poppy seed muffins and make tea and bring them back to bed. In the afternoons we went to the nearby forest and

strolled the bike path. It was a precious moment in time because Jim wasn't up for a relationship with me, even though he would profess his undying love . . . for the next decade.

I didn't mourn the romance with Jim for too long. By the end of the summer I'd moved to Eugene, Oregon (Rick stayed on in our house in Texas), and met my handsome and very able-bodied neighbor, Matt. He was in his 40s and I was 27, and while he insisted I was too young for him, this Class Flirt couldn't help herself. We became platonic running partners until he kissed me one day while helping me out of my race chair.

That sweet kiss began the most romantic year of my dating life *ever*. It included love notes written in letter-shaped cookies on his coffee table, chocolate truffles with love notes in my fridge, long bicycle rides, home-cooked dinners (by him), and on and on. I spent so much time at Matt's that he built a ramp and deck onto his house and ultimately asked me to move in with him, so I did. Soon after that, I went deeper into my quest for healing.

Matt and I had flown to Vegas for Christmas, and I'd sat next to a doctor of internal medicine on the plane who told me about this "renegade" he knew who was doing "experimental and interesting" things that were getting good results with cancer patients. Apparently, he was this brilliant, hippie doctor who worked in Mexico and used an alternative treatment called "Enderlein remedies." I booked a trip to go see him in July.

In the meantime, I was getting ready to see a doctor in Seattle who did a technique called NeuroCranial Restructuring, which involved putting balloons up the nose to expand the skull and connective tissue around the brain and spinal cord. That expansion was meant to release tension caused by trauma, allowing the body to unlock, shift, and return to its "original design."

Both treatments were a far cry from my enemas or vitamin B shots of the past, and I didn't know any quads who'd tried anything experimental or radical like this. But since I was currently manifesting my destiny at warp speed, I took a leap of faith and brought it to the next level.

In February 1999, I sat in the doctor's office in Seattle as he stuck balloons up my nose. It burned like hell and felt like someone had punched me in the nose. After he got the balloons up there and expanded, I heard a loud *pop!*—the bones in my head were cracking, as if a chiropractor were adjusting my skull bones. I had the treatments three days in a row, and I saw results immediately. When I went to the VA for my annual evaluation the day after my treatments, I stood at the parallel bars with leg braces on and saw a marked improvement in my balance.

The improvement continued at the WSC the following month. My balance and endurance were even better when I skied, and we didn't have to lock out my knees using Ace bandages for support as we usually did. Every little improvement was a giant step.

I wore my new favorite T-shirt all week at the Clinic, which said: I CAN TALK THE TALK BECAUSE I WALK THE WALK. That week, I also got to ski with a celebrity.

Tipper Gore, the wife of Vice President Al Gore, was scheduled to join the veterans for a ski at the end of the week, present medals, and give a speech at the closing-night ceremony. Six veterans were invited to have lunch with her after the ski run, and because I was improving so well and one of the few female veterans there, I'd be one of them.

I was also chosen to show Tipper some of my skiing. It was tradition to dress crazy on our last day, so I wore the silliest outfit you could imagine: hot-pink pants that I'd won at a singing contest the night before, a neon-yellow-and-pink fleece sweatshirt that I'd stolen from Rick, and a pair of kooky kid's sunglasses with multiple lenses that flipped to the side.

I skied halfway down the run with Molly and waited to meet Tipper there. It was a beautiful sunny day, and as soon as she arrived from the top of the mountain on her skis, I pulled a total Forrest Gump. I had to pee so bad that my instructors had to make a human wall around me while I did my business into a water bottle, with Tipper waiting a few feet away.

After I was done, the wall opened and Sandy Trombetta and Tipper's Secret Service guys brought her over. Molly explained

about the ski legs she'd invented, and the tremendous progress I'd made since my first Clinic six years earlier.

When Tipper knelt down to talk to me, I asked, "Can I call you 'Tipper'?" My fellow veterans had dared me to call her that, while the Ponderosa Boys told me that I should not, under any circumstances, call her "Tipper" to her face.

"Yes, of course you can!" she said, sweetly.

We chatted a bit and then I showed her how I skied down the rest of the hill.

Even though they'd dared me to do it, my co-veterans gave me hell later for being so informal with the vice president's wife—but it made sense considering what happened next. We had lunch out-side on the hotel deck, sitting slope side, and I was seated next to Tipper. Under the magnificent view of the 12,162-foot-high Mt. Crested Butte, she asked all of us how we got hurt and listened intently as one by one, we went around the table.

When it was my turn, she was scooping chicken and potato salad onto my plate.

"Dana, how did you get hurt?" she asked.

It was a question I had answered the same way for more than eight years, and I had my routine answer to shut people up: "I fell off a cliff. I don't remember anything else. Let's change the subject."

Yet ever since my illuminating conversation with Lucy and a hand-ful of others, and the relief we all felt sharing our story with another woman, something had been stirring inside me. It was that feeling of not wanting to be quiet anymore. Perhaps a part of me thought Tipper could help. I could see that she was a genuine, loving human being whose only agenda was to help others, and I made an instinc-tive decision to be totally honest with her.

Very quietly, so no one else could hear, I told her. "I was raped by another sailor," I whispered, "and thrown off a 75-foot cliff."

"Oh my God," she whispered back to me, her eyes tearing up. "I am so sorry."

No one else at the table knew how I got hurt, and they couldn't hear this exchange. But they were all looking up from their plates, wondering what was going on. Tipper and I pulled our attention back to the table and she put another scoop of potato salad onto my plate, her eyes still filled with tears.

We had shared an unforgettable moment between two women, as Lucy and I had. When a woman is sexually assaulted, it's a pain we all share together, and Tipper clearly understood that. On the mountain she had said something I'll never forget: "Dana, you are such an inspiration to me."

That night at the post-closing-ceremony party, we had a fantastic band playing some great tunes, and everyone was dancing. When Tipper arrived and spotted me, she came over and gave me a big hug as the band struck up that classic Tokens song, "The Lion Sleeps Tonight." Most people don't know that it was inspired by an old warrior chant about a hero lion that may be sleeping now, but will one day awaken to fulfill her destiny and lead her oppressed fellow lions to freedom.

It was the perfect song for two warrior Leos like Tipper and me, and we began to sing together. When a conga line formed on the dance floor, we looked at each other and nodded. The Secret Service guys hovered and looked nervous, but she didn't pay attention. Together, Tipper and I made our way to the line and *wimoweh, wimoweh, wimoweh-ed* the night away.

CHAPTER 16

Mad Mexican Scientists

On my 28th birthday in July 1999, I boarded a flight to Tijuana to meet the renegade doctor for a two-week stay in his clinic. Only Matt knew where I was going; I didn't tell friends and family. I didn't want anyone to worry, and I didn't want any negative input. Other times when I'd mentioned trying experimental treatments or wanting to progress beyond my level of injury, I usually got one of three reactions from my fellow gimps:

"You're chasing a pipe dream!"

"You're wasting your time and money!"

"Just be in a chair, like us. Play wheelchair sports and accept that you're a quad. *You are a quad!*"

I wasn't going to accept it. I was manifesting a different future for myself.

I am walking. I am walking. I am walking.

I had no idea what to expect when I got to Mexico. I didn't know anything about the experimental or newfangled stuff they were doing down there. It turned out that the clinic itself was a white stucco house—formerly the home of a drug dealer—surrounded by a high, concrete wall. My quarters were very nice—a master bedroom with my own bathroom, and a small living room.

On the first day I arrived, I got blood tests, x-rays, and an MRI; then I had a meeting with the man himself. Dr. B had long silver hair and a handlebar mustache, and wore a soft paisley vest—he was a flower-child version of Albert Einstein. He looked at my blood and showed it to me through a dark-field microscope, and then showed me my MRI pictures. His protocol was to show patients what their blood reveals to be wrong with them and then tell them how he was going to treat it. But as I sat in his office, he was flummoxed.

"I don't know what I can do for you, if anything," he said. "I'm going to hand you over to my colleague, Dr. Mondo. Let's see what he can do."

Along with Dr. B, Mondo was doing innovative, mysterious work with "cytokines"—the proteins in our body involved with cell signaling and behavior. Or something. He wasn't actually a medical doctor, he admitted to me at one point; he was a scientist. I didn't care what he was if his treatments worked.

Mondo said that he was going to look at my blood every day to determine what combination of remedies to give me that day and where. He showed me my blood through the microscope. "See, your blood looks tired and the cells are clumping together and moving very slowly," he explained. "And the outer membranes are wavy instead of nicely rounded, which is what we want."

The next day, I lay down on my back on a hospital-style table in his office, and he injected me with "Enderlein remedies"—named after the German scientist who'd invented them, Günther Enderlein, Ph.D. Yet it wasn't just one shot, in my arm; Mondo injected needles up and down my body. In my mouth, in my throat, on my head and neck, in my scars . . . every crazy-ass place he could find, he stuck a needle. There were maybe 30 shots in all, and they hurt like hell.

Mondo was so polite and compassionate, he apologized each time he stuck the needle into me. Yeah, there was no way this guy was a medical doctor.

"I'm sorry!" he'd say, in his thick Mexican accent, after each stabbing.

"No pain," I'd squeak, "no gain!"

Mondo nicknamed me his "Little German" because I was so blonde and tough and had a German last name. And since he didn't know or understand all the best English cuss words, I taught him a choice few and explained in detail what they meant.

"Little German," he'd say, when we were done with the shots for the day, "you have a sweet face, but your mouth doesn't match it."

After that first session, I began using a Hindu mantra I'd learned from a healer I met back at that health expo two years earlier: *Om Namah Shivaya.* I was told that it was associated with the qualities of divine love, grace, and blissfulness, and it did calm me down and help ease the stabbing pain. So bring it on, Dr. Frankenstein.

Sometimes the mantra didn't help, though. One day something went horribly wrong after my injections. My head began to pound after I got back to my room. I went into the bathroom thinking if I emptied my bladder and bowels, I would feel better. But as I sat on the toilet, my head felt like it was going to explode, and I started sobbing. Another patient heard me and alerted Mondo, who came rushing to my rescue and flung open the bathroom door with a giant needle in his hand. As I sat on the toilet with my pants around my ankles, wailing, he jabbed it into my head, and moments later the pain subsided.

Another day, Mondo had instructed the nurses to give me an injection intramuscularly, but by accident they gave it to me *intravenously* and then desperately tried to flush it out of my system right away. They searched in vain to find a vein to get IV fluids into me but couldn't find one. I started having a very bad reaction, and Mondo made a move to stab me in the jugular, but found a regular vein just in time.

After everyone left the room, I lay on the table and hurled everywhere, puking all over myself. *Oh my God,* I thought, *I'm dying. No potential gain is worth this agony. And there may be no gain at all! What if there isn't?*

I soon got my answer. A few days later, about two weeks into my stay, I was in the shower and had turned off the water when I felt ants crawling down my back.

Wait a minute. I don't feel it when ants crawl on my back. I don't feel anything on my back! I don't have sensation there!

I turned the water on and off again and felt that same feeling again. *It's the water trickling down my back!*

I could feel sensation where I hadn't felt any for nine years! What-ever they were injecting in me was working! I was so euphoric, I was crying and laughing at the same time. I spent the next several min-utes in the shower, turning the water on and off, simply to feel the sensation. Then I dried off and got dressed as quickly as I could, and rushed over to the doctors' offices to tell them what had happened. I found them huddled over a microscope looking at a drop of my blood on a slide.

"I have great news!" I yelled, bursting into the room.

What I didn't know was that Mondo had been watching that drop of blood for a few days. Right at the same time that I was feeling the trickling in the shower, they were all simultaneously watching "den-drites" growing in my blood, and were already off-the-wall excited before I stormed in. I peered through the microscope myself, and what I saw looked like the pictures of nerves from my school biology textbooks. When we looked at the same drop of blood the next day, the dendrites had grown even more.

I intended to stay only two weeks, but I was so excited about my new sensation that I couldn't leave and wanted more treatments. After this exciting development, I hadn't made any new progress for a while, but that didn't worry Dr. B. He was concerned about some-thing else.

I'd recently told him and Mondo about what had happened to me on the cliff, figuring that the information might factor into what treatments they used. And it did, unfortunately. With that informa-tion and their analysis of my blood every day, Dr. B had a lightbulb of an idea, which he shared with me around week six.

"You're too happy," he informed me.

"What?"

"You're too happy!" he repeated. "You're way too happy all the time—happy, happy, happy. For the trauma you've been through, you should not be this happy. You're not letting go of something, which is essential for this treatment to work to its full capacity. Your body wants to deal with it, but you're not letting it."

To remedy my "happiness problem," the doctors decided to give me their Enderlein injections at specific acupuncture points on my body to help release whatever embedded thoughts or deep emotions I was holding back. Only they didn't warn me ahead of time that they were doing this.

Mondo gave me what I thought were the usual injections that day, and I went to bed. I woke up at midnight distraught—I was unhappy, unhappy, unhappy. I cried my eyes out and felt a whole range of negative emotions: despair, confusion, pity, and *anger.*

Anger? But why? Who was I angry at? I had a long list, but the top three were:

God. The military. And Bruce.

I wanted to kill the motherfucker. No, I didn't want to kill him— that would be letting him off too easy. I wanted him to go through what he'd put me through. I wanted to make him suffer. I wanted to make him a quad.

I sobbed as I figured it all out in my mind. I could hire people to find him and break his neck. First, though, they'd beat the shit out of him. Then they'd rape him. And only then would they break his neck and leave him on the ground the same way I'd been left on the beach, unable to move. Maybe I would put the phone on his chest and dial 911 for him—I'm not a monster, after all. Not like him, who'd left me no chance at all. If he couldn't reach the phone, that would be too bad for him. He'd have a good, long time to think about what he'd done to me before he died. If someone found him in time, well, his fate would be to spend the rest of his life as a vegetable. My goons would have made sure that when they broke his neck, it was a clean and complete break at the C5 level.

I was shocked by how angry I was. And then, I was in tears again. At 2 a.m., I telephoned my father. I had gone AWOL on the family, and no one had heard from me in over a month, which was very unusual for me.

Dad answered the phone with a worried tone, surely expecting bad news. "Hello?"

"Dad, why me?"

"Dana!"

"Dad," I said, bawling into the phone, "Why did this happen to me? *Why?* I was nice. I never hurt anyone."

"Dana, where are you?!"

I explained where I was and what was happening—of course he was happy to hear from me, but not happy to know where I was and what I was doing.

Dad and Debbie went on to spend the next hour on the phone calming me down. If the injections I'd received were acting like a truth serum, then I guess the truth was that I was holding a lot of anger inside. But it was too much for me to deal with at that point in time; I wasn't ready. The only thing I wanted and needed in that moment was to be loved; that would help me. Half-asleep, my father and stepmother delivered.

"I love you, Dana Leigh," Dad said, from a thousand miles away. "I always have and I always will. Know that."

The next morning, Mondo came into my room with a present: a furry little teddy bear for me to hug and hold on to. "This is for you, Little German," he said, handing me the bear and giving me a hug and a kiss on the cheek. He then explained what he and Dr. B had done and told me that's why I'd felt so bad throughout the night.

"I'm so sorry, but we needed to do it. Just stay in your room today, and it will pass," he said. Mondo checked on me periodically throughout the day and brought me food as I continued to cry and rage. By the next day, I was back to my happy, happy, happy self—which I'm sure they were all grateful for. Dr. B never complained about my peppy outlook again.

AFTER TWO MONTHS AT THE CLINIC, my time as an inpatient was over, but I continued injections three times a week as an outpatient. In October '99 I rented a house in San Diego so that I could be a mere 30-minute drive from the clinic. Throughout the next nine months I didn't see any more improvement like the water-trickling moment, but Mondo told me it would take time to see additional progress and it would come gradually. In the meantime, I kept myself busy with Matt, who'd moved to San Diego to be with me, and I hobnobbed with celebrities.

After Tipper Gore and I had bonded at the WSC in March, she'd taken my contact information. I was pleasantly surprised to receive an invitation for Al Gore's presidential nomination–kickoff event in

Seattle a couple of months later, with hotel expenses taken care of. I took my mother, and we had a blast. Tipper introduced us to Al, who hugged me so hard, I felt like I was getting hugged in half. He was funny and awesome, not stiff like everyone thinks (when I asked him, "Can I call you 'Al'?" he responded, "Of course you can!"). And I met a hero of mine, Bill Nye, the Science Guy.

At the WSC the following March, I chatted with the beautiful Bo Derek. She posed in photos and gave out participation medals, and we talked about the horses she has on her ranch. (A few years later, she would bring her boyfriend, *Sex and the City*'s John Corbett, with her. Lucy and I went gaga, getting all dolled up and asking him to pose in a photo with us. He happily obliged and sprawled across our laps.)

And then, in the summer of 2000, I was ecstatic to receive yet another invite from Tipper, this time to the Democratic National Convention in Los Angeles as her guest! Debbie went shopping with me for new "business attire" clothes so that I wouldn't show up in my usual jeans and T-shirt looking like a redneck from Oregon. During the four-day convention that August, the Secret Service guys (who all knew my name by now) ushered me behind velvet ropes and into VIP sections all over the Staples Center in Los Angeles. It was like being a celebrity myself!

At one party, Tipper's daughter Karenna introduced me to actor Sean Penn: "This is Dana, my mom's friend!" It was one of those rare moments where a chatterbox like me was speechless. The Oscar-winning actor attempted to have a conversation, but all I could eke out was a one-syllable squeak—"Hi"—and a lot of blushing.

For the big finale, a nomination-celebration concert with headliner Barbra Streisand, my name was on the guest list for a seat in the handicapped box section at the Shrine Auditorium. Even more thrilling, though, was whom I spotted in the audience—Christopher Reeve. The actor had been injured five years after me in a riding accident and was a C1-C2 injury, the most severe level. He was doing a lot to promote stem-cell research in the United States; and that year, after many experimental treatments he'd undergone elsewhere, he announced that he could move his index finger and that other sensations were returning.

There wasn't much security around him, so it was easy to approach him and his wife (who was also named Dana), and introduce myself. I excitedly told him a bit about what I was doing in Mexico with Mondo's injections and about my improvement, then got back to my seat as Streisand appeared onstage.

A few weeks after the convention, it was time to say good-bye to the mad Mexican scientists.

"Okay, my Little German," said Mondo, giving me a kiss on the cheek, "I've done everything I can do. Now you must go out on your own and work on your muscles!"

I DID AS I WAS TOLD AND BEGAN WORKING OUT intensely at the gym at the SCI unit in the VA hospital in San Diego, patiently waiting to see more results.

During my visits to the gym, I noticed a fellow veteran quad. Although he was a new injury of about a year, he had been improving his walking ability every week, and I asked him about it. He told me about a trainer he'd been working with, Ned, who had been trained by "anatomical physiologist" Pete Egoscue, a chronic pain and sports specialist who'd written several books about pain and body motion.

I immediately began training with Ned three times a week, starting with one-hour sessions and increasing to three-hour sessions. Ned's a genius when it comes to knowing the body. He has an innate sense of it, and combined with his study of the Egoscue techniques, we were getting results. I shared with Ned all I knew about spinal cord injuries, teaching him about the levels of injuries, complete versus incomplete, how baclofen affects the body, bowel and bladder issues—everything I had experienced and learned.

I worked so relentlessly during my three-hour workouts that Ned nicknamed me "the Cockroach." As he said, "You see that brick wall over there? If that was the only thing standing in the way of something you wanted, you would get through it. If there was no way out of this building except brick walls, you would find your way out."

I took it as a compliment. By the spring of 2001 I was making great progress, and Ned wanted to videotape me taking steps while holding on to his hand. In a moment of confusion, he got on the wrong side of me—the weaker side, my right—and my legs gave way. I fell straight down on my foot, and heard the same terrible sound I'd heard in Rick's boat years earlier.

Ned took me to the VA hospital. You'd think that of all places they'd be the most helpful to a quad with a broken leg. But the doctor we saw in the SCI unit just shook his head when I explained how I broke it.

"What? You were trying to walk? Why are you trying to *walk?*" he asked, almost angry.

"Uh . . . because I can?"

"I'm sorry," the doctor said, "we don't do anything here with spinal cord injuries that break their leg."

"Why not?" I asked.

"We just don't."

It made no sense. I got on the phone and called my doctor buddy in Seattle, Barry Goldstein, and explained the situation. Thirty minutes later, that VA hospital in San Diego was giving me x-rays and putting me in a cast.

I didn't let the cast cramp my workout style, though. Cockroach, remember? I duct-taped my cast to the pedal of the stationary bike and kept going. My doctors were amazed by how fast I healed.

I DIDN'T LET MY BROKEN LEG SLOW ME DOWN at the gym, and I didn't let it stop Amy and me from taking a trip to Ireland. And as I would find out, a cast on my leg could have unforeseen benefits I never imagined.

To celebrate our 30th birthdays that year, Amy and I had found a spring special for one week in Ireland, which included our flight, car rental, six nights at quaint bed-and-breakfasts, and one night in a castle. We fell in love with the country as soon as we landed, and they gave us big mugs of boozed-up Irish coffee at the hotel. Yeah, we could get used to this.

We didn't get used to the cold, though. Our first night, we were freezing so much that no amount of whiskey could thaw us. We kept cranking up the heat and giving the radiator a kick, and finally rang the front desk in the middle of the night.

"Hey, can we have some heat on in our room?" Amy demanded.

"It's on."

"Oh, Jesus."

Amy was coming from Arizona, and I was coming from San Diego—to us, April in Ireland was like winter in Alaska. We survived that first night by steaming up our room with the little teapots we found and making it into a sauna.

Other than being perpetually cold, we had a great time living on chocolate and boozy coffees, and driving around County Galway and County Cork and seeing Blarney Castle. We took a boat tour around the Aran Islands, where we'd heard the Black Irish like Amy's mom came from. I was terrified to get on the boat because the gangway wasn't wide enough for my chair, so two guys on the dock had to hand me over the gap to two other guys on the boat.

"Trust us, trust us," they kept saying, but the gap was wide enough for me to drop into the black Galway Bay and never be heard from again, so I was freaking out. The four strapping youths had no idea I was a quad as I weeble-wobbled in my chair (even though my legs were starting to work, I didn't have a lot of core strength still). In fact, for one glorious week, I cruised around Ireland in a wheelchair and no one had any idea I was a quad—they assumed I was in the chair because of my broken leg!

Once I realized what the people I met were thinking, I didn't bother correcting them. The "normal" feeling I got twice a year at the Veterans Games and the WSC was now happening outside in the real world, and it was precious. I'd forgotten what it was like to be treated and talked to and looked at like a "regular" person by the able-bodied masses. It was like a little gift.

All was going great on this trip to the Emerald Isle, until we got to the Cliffs of Moher.

We drove to the end of a parking lot to get as close to the water's edge as we could and parked to take in the view. The cliffs ranged from 400 to 700 feet high and a few feet next to us, the ocean was crashing and frothing against the rocks like a water symphony.

To Amy, it was heavenly; to me, it was my worst fucking nightmare. My chest began to constrict and I couldn't breathe. I had a vision of the waves and white frothy water in front of us rising above our heads like Poseidon leaping out of the water to attack us.

"Amy, we've got to get out of here," I gasped for air.

"What's wrong?"

"I can't be here! I can't! I don't know why, but I have to go!"

I was terrified and in the middle of a full-fledged panic attack. As soon as we drove away, I was fine. I honestly didn't know what had happened at the time. But looking back, it's so obvious—it was post-traumatic stress disorder (PTSD). Being so close to the Cliffs of Moher, with the waves crashing against the rocks, had unearthed a snippet of memory from my subconscious, a scene I'd buried but had now risen to the surface: Me, ten years earlier, lying at the bottom of Sunset Cliffs naked, the sound of waves crashing against the rock forever embedding into my sense memory as I waited for help, or waited to die.

My memories had been slipping to the surface in my nightmares, and now they were coming to me when I was awake. As the mad Mexican doctors had said, there was something I had to let go of, or I wasn't going to heal as fully as I might. I knew what it was, but I still wasn't ready for that.

I SPENT MY ACTUAL 30TH BIRTHDAY IN JULY with my father, and had an enlightening experience that day. Even though Dad had broken three of his ribs weeks earlier when he and Gary had wrestled drunk, and even though his entire chest was in pain and he could barely breathe, he and Debbie still showed up on my birthday to take me to Six Flags Magic Mountain, north of L.A., with my friends Mary and Sean (a para and Marine veteran).

Dad held on to me as we rode the roller coasters all day long and didn't complain about his own pain—he just wanted to keep me safe. He tried his best, but Sean and I both passed out because the g-forces wreaked havoc with our blood pressure.

My relationship with my father had been as up-and-down as the roller coasters we rode that day. Sometimes we didn't like each other, didn't understand each other, disagreed with each other, hurt each other's feelings, and clashed monumentally. Other times we were exactly alike. Sometimes we hugged; other times we slugged each other. But through it all, we loved each other. I had broken my father's

heart as much as he'd broken mine when I'd insisted that Ken was my "real" dad. Yet now my father was the one holding on to me and keeping me safe, while the other men I'd called "Dad" had gone AWOL.

Ever since my injury, Ed hadn't been proactive in getting in touch with me. And because of a misunderstanding between Bonnie and me, she'd kicked me out of Ken's life a year earlier, when I was 29. I was devastated—especially because Ken didn't do anything to stop it. I lost Ken, I lost Mom #3 whom I'd loved for so many years, and I lost two stepsiblings. By my 30th birthday, I thought, *Fuck it, I'm not going to chase these fathers anymore. If they don't want me in their lives, then so be it.*

Meanwhile, my father, flaws and all, was loyal like a German shepherd.

Then, three months later, on the anniversary of my getting hurt and on Gary's birthday, my brother came to visit me in San Diego. I'd broken up with Matt a month or so before, so Gary had come to console me and help me do some work on the house.

Ever since I got hurt, my brother had hated his birthday. This year, though, I had a special present for him. I was going to turn October 25 into a happy day again, a day to celebrate.

After he arrived, I took him to Ned's gym to show him where I'd been working out. Then I slid a walker toward me. "Hey, Gare," I said. "I want to show you something."

Using my shoulders and legs, I stood up and leaned on the walker with the palms of my hands. I took one step toward him . . . then I took a second step . . . and then a third.

I was walking, with no braces on my legs.

I kept going until I passed him and walked the length of the gym. When I turned around to face him and walk back again, my brother was crying.

CHAPTER 17

Great Walls

In 2002 I went rafting with a group that takes people with disabilities on trips to do rugged outdoor activities. We were on the Colorado River, rafting through the Grand Canyon, for 14 days and 226 river miles, on the water by 8 A.M. and rafting all day until dinner-time. The Grand Canyon was absolutely breathtaking. Miles of winding, red-streaked sandstone, shale, and limestone towered beside us— I felt minuscule next to the awesome power of nature.

One morning I was in a two-person inflatable kayak (or "ducky") with an able-bodied woman behind me who did the steering. Bobby Palm, one of the downhill ski instructors at the WSC whom I had befriended, was in the ducky in front of us with another quad. We'd duct-taped my right hand to the paddle because of my lack of "grip ability," and because I insisted on doing some paddling anyway.

We bobbed up and down the frothy waters of the President Hard-ing Rapid until we approached a rolling wave that seemed bigger than our boat. As I dug my paddle into the water, it rushed over my hand and dragged the paddle and my arm backward, pulling me with it and popping me out of the boat like a champagne cork.

I plunged into the water and then rose to the surface, thanks to my life vest. But with very little leg and stomach muscle, I couldn't keep my face above the surface. My rubber-soled shoes kept floating my feet upward and throwing my head back underwater.

Inches below the surface, I looked up at the brilliant sun and sky through the water. An eddy pulled me under farther, and I thought, *Oh. I guess this is how I'm going to die.*

I wasn't panicked. I felt peaceful and warm, like people always say dying is.

The next thing I knew, I was on my back in the boat with everyone's worried faces hovering over me.

"Oh my God, Dana! Are you okay?"

"Well, I'm alive," I answered nonchalantly. I was either in shock or still in my near-death euphoria. "So I guess that's good, right?"

I was now a dozen years post-injury, and I was putting my new abilities to great tests and attempting death-defying feats. Often, I was successful; sometimes, I got dumped overboard. For example, Amy and I went scuba diving that spring, and when I got to the bottom of the ocean, the pressure was too much on my organs and large intestine and, well . . . shit happens. My instructor pulled me to the surface so fast, my body couldn't adjust, and I blacked out.

But I didn't let any of these little inconveniences stop me from trying anything. I was a fearless athlete while growing up, and I was still that way—not holding back, always pushing my physical limits. Like my skiing at the WSC, rafting would become a way for me to gauge my abilities and progress over the years. When I first started, I'd take my chair with me, and someone would push me over the sand when we were on land. After a few trips, I was able to take my walker and walk a bit more each time—until finally, I was able to leave my chair behind altogether and only use my walker on a three-day rafting trip.

It was a thrill to see my progress, however long it took. That summer it was even more of a thrill to teach someone else how to progress. I had certainly learned a lot by the time I met an 18-year-old kid named Joey.

Joey was a six-foot-eight-inch surfer who had become injured two years earlier in junior-lifeguard school. He was an incomplete C5 quad like me and worked out with Ned. But while he was doing well with his gym sessions, he wasn't doing so hot at home.

"What's your problem?" I asked when I visited him at his home one day. "Why are you letting other people push you? Push your own damn chair through the house! Take your own dishes to the sink! Brush your own teeth! Your family is being too soft on you!" (I could hear Ian's voice in my head, scolding me back at rehab: "What? You're not making your own bed?!")

Joey's father didn't take it easy on him, but his mother and sister definitely did—they were doing way too much for him. A little tough love, that's what this kid needed. His family made me an offer I couldn't refuse: stay the summer and teach Joey some independent-living skills, and in exchange, they'd teach me how to surf.

Deal!

For the three months I stayed with Joey and his family in Redondo Beach, California, my main goal was to teach him to get his upper body from lying on his lap to a sitting-up position, and then show him how to transfer in and out of my car using a sliding board that bridges the gap between car and chair.

My instruction began with the little things, though. One day as we pushed around the block, Joey was thirsty, so I handed him a Gatorade. He asked me for help, but I said, "No, I'm not helping you open *or* drink it. Nor will I let you go any farther until you do this on your own. I have faith in you. You can do this . . . use your teeth."

I knew his mother would kill me if she found out I was telling him to use his teeth, but teeth are a quad's third hand.

"Balance with one arm around the back of your chair so you don't fall over," I continued. "And use the other to open the bottle and take a drink."

"You're a bitch! I hate you!"

"My job isn't for you to like me. My job is to teach you. You will learn, and you will respect me in the end."

He did it, and this was the beginning of a feeling of accomplishment for him. That kid might have been stubborn as a mule, but like most people, he didn't know who he was dealing with.

When it came time to learn how to transfer, I pushed him to the point of tears. He had to get himself upright in his chair before we attempted the car. As he was sitting there, I pushed him forward until his face was in his lap. All he had to do was reach his arm behind and pull himself up.

169

"Dude!" Joey yelled, his voice muffled in his blue jeans. "Dude! I'm falling out of my chair!"

"Dude," I replied. "You are not falling out of the chair. Put your arms up there, sit up, and start wiggling your butt forward!"

He cried, but he got himself up. By the end of the summer, he'd done the transfer by himself, and I'd gone out in the ocean to surf with his family. I lay down on my belly as his uncle held on to my board, and I sailed through the water. It was such a great feeling.

Yet of all the progress I had made for myself—including learning to surf—I'd never done anything more satisfying in my life than to help Joey make progress, too.

I MET MY NEXT BOYFRIEND, DAVE, on a kayaking trip that fall on Lake Powell, a reservoir on the Colorado River. We'd all set up our tents the first day and I was exiting mine when Dave walked by shirtless in little running shorts, six-pack abs on display. That night as we sat around the campfire, he poured Kahlúa on everyone's ice cream, and we were all giggly off the sugar and alcohol. I gave him an inviting smile from across the flames, and he came over and flirted. And then we flirted some more the next day. By the third night, we were pretty cozy in my tent.

When Dave left on day four, a day earlier than me, I figured that he was a summer fling I'd never see again . . . until I arrived at the marina the next morning. He'd slept all night in the parking lot in his green Subaru Outback wagon, which was parked next to my white Subaru Outback wagon (I'd traded in my van years earlier), waiting for me. Any romantic fool who'd do that was worth giving a chance.

I fell in love with Dave right away. He was funny and smart and an incredible cook, total bonus. He was also very much like my father and me—gentle, but with an explosive temper—so I felt completely at home with him. Since he lived in Colorado, we began a long-distance romance, with me making the 13-hour drive every other weekend from San Diego to his home in the high-desert town of Grand Junction. I moved in with him the following March, and found Grand Junction to have the friendliest people in the world. I was convinced, as girls in love like to say, that Dave was the man I was going to marry.

In November, though, I met the true love of my life. As soon as I saw Jack in his red collar with little white puppy prints at the animal shelter, it was love at first sight for both of us. Jack was a four-month-old yellow Lab mix, and he reminded me of my old friend Jasper. Jack stood up on his hind legs with his front paws against the door of his cage, as if to say, "Pick me! Pick me! I will be loving and loyal! Okay, maybe for the first two years I'll run away every day when you're not home and make you crazy. But still, you won't be sorry if you pick me!"

Dave and I took Jack to the little play area for a bit, and he was so sweet that we had to take him home with us to join our new family. He even came with us on a skiing vacation to Crested Butte, hanging out in the "Poop Loop"—a flat trail set up for dogs to run free off leash—while Dave and I cross-country skied. At home, he was a bit of a diva and hated mud puddles, but he loved the snow. He had a great time barreling into piles that were twice his height and disappearing, emerging seconds later with a happy-dog face and wagging his tail.

BY THE SPRING OF 2004, I WAS WALKING on a treadmill at the speed of .3 mph for 15 minutes at a time, with no braces. And after talking to a quad at Ned's gym who'd undergone experimental stem-cell injections in China and had some good results, I was ready to take that next step.

I knew it was a controversial procedure on many levels. We didn't allow it in the United States because it often involved using cells from fertilized embryos. My thoughts on that issue is that politicians and pharmaceutical companies use the moral/church stance to deny the research and keep people addicted to their drugs so they can continue to make money and keep people from the truth: that finding a cure and healing is possible.

Dave and I arranged for Jack to stay with neighbors, and boarded a flight to Beijing. This time, I did tell my family—although they were optimistic for me, they were also worried that I would get my hopes up and be unhappy with the results. Dad's way of lovingly showing his worry was to ask, "What stupid shit are you doing now?"

I didn't tell any of my para/quad friends, though. When I'd returned from Mexico previously and showed Lucy a bit of new left-leg movement I was experiencing a few months later, attributing it to Mondo's injections, she laughed. "I'd rather buy a new car with that money," she said, shaking her head. "You should accept being a quad and play wheelchair sports and be done with this."

After we landed in Beijing and dropped our bags off at the hotel, Dave and I hopped in a cab to Tiananmen Square, where soldiers marched along the sidewalk dressed in red and carrying guns. When Dave tried to take a photo of a lion statue, an armed guard chastised him.

One shocking sight was seeing people urinating (or more) on the street, in public, in broad daylight, out in the open. Dave and I were astonished when we saw a little boy squat on the ground in front of us as his mother held a plastic grocery bag under his bum. The little boy pooped into the bag in the middle of Tiananmen Square like a puppy, and then his mother tossed the bag away. Another time, a little girl in front of us stepped off of the sidewalk and went over a few feet in the street, squatted, peed, then got back on the sidewalk and continued walking.

"Remind me to stick to the sidewalks," I mumbled to Dave.

And yet, in a surreal and funny way, it was the ideal setup for a person in a wheelchair who can't always find or get into a bathroom. One afternoon when Dave and I were strolling on a side street and no one was around, I had to pee in the worst way—so bad, in fact, that I was experiencing autonomic dysreflexia, that sudden onset of extremely high blood pressure that can be caused by an overfull bladder. I spotted a drain on the street and made a move to discreetly cath into it.

Dave was indignant. "You can't pee in the street!"

"Why not? Everyone else does!" *When in Rome . . .*

Thankfully, we found an empty water bottle and Dave was spared the embarrassment of having his girlfriend urinate into a Beijing drain.

The doctor came to our hotel with a small staff to check my function and sensation and do other tests. They spoke very little English, though, so Dave and I didn't always know what was going on or what was coming next. Once I was approved for the procedure, I was checked into the hospital, east of the square. Just before they knocked me out with general anesthesia, I said a little prayer to all the unborn babies who may have been involved in this treatment, giving thanks that they were helping me.

For five hours Dr. H cut through muscles, worked around bone, and used fine needles to inject stem cells into my spinal cord at C3 and C6, one level above and one level below my injury. Meanwhile, Dave was flipping out back at my room. While he was waiting for my surgery to be over, he'd watched a cleaning lady mop the entire hospital floor from one end to the other—going in and out of each room along the way—with the same pail of dirty water. After mopping up the communal bathroom, she arrived at my room with her black, putrid water. Dave sent the confused woman away, rushed out to the nearest store to buy cleaning supplies and bleach, then locked himself in my room and didn't let anyone else in.

By the time I returned hours later, he'd scrubbed and sterilized the room and everything in it from top to bottom. (When I left three days later, I was the only patient on the floor without a respiratory infection or stomach bug. God bless Dave.)

During the surgery I'd lost more blood than what's normal, so I was very weak afterward. To add insult to injury, instead of seeing progress right away, I had gotten worse! After feeling a bit of new sensation at the bottom of my feet when I came to, I was suddenly paralyzed again from C3 down. I couldn't roll over, I couldn't transfer, I couldn't do anything! And I was in more pain than I'd ever felt in my life.

"You must eat!" one of the doctors urged me. "You are weak; you need to eat meat!"

I wouldn't eat a bite, though. Not because I wasn't hungry or because I didn't like their food, but because I didn't want to shit myself. I couldn't use their communal bathroom because it was dirty, as well as being a "squat" toilet—a urinal laid flat on the floor that you had to crouch over. The only way that toilet was going to work for me was if I suddenly acquired the superpower to levitate. Every meal they brought me, I shook my head no.

My refusal to eat, and the fact that I was uncooperative in other ways—I had also refused a lumbar puncture—had the staff worried for my mental health, so the hospital psychiatrist paid me a visit.

The very polite shrink sat down next to my bed and began taking notes and asking me questions in English. "So, Dana. Tell me . . . do you have friends back home?"

"Of course I do."

"Are you afraid to go out of your house?"

"No."

I was giving him my usual, non-expansive shrink responses, to be polite.

"Are you afraid to go to the grocery store?"

"No."

"Are you lying?"

"No."

He asked me the same set of questions a second time, and I answered again calmly until he got to the "are you lying" one. I hate being accused of lying.

"Dude!" I said. "I don't live in a communist country, ya know!"

He stopped writing, chuckled, closed his notebook, and left my room with a smile on his face. We got the eating thing sorted out the next day. A nice female doctor came into my room and knew enough English to understand me when I said, "I'm not eating because there's nowhere to poop."

"What do you mean? There's a WC right next door!"

"And how am I supposed to use it?"

"Right . . ."

They had Western-style toilets on the floor below us that were under construction, so we convinced the doctor to let me use them. Dave took me down, and because my function was impaired, he did my digital stimulation. You had to love Dave. He knelt on the ground and put his finger into my sphincter and moved it around in circles . . . and as he was doing it, he looked up and me and said in the most earnest of voices, "With this ring, I thee wed."

We cracked up. "You're a sick man, Dave!"

When we got back to my room, the doctor I'd seen earlier had a surprise for us—she'd ordered the specialty, Beijing ("Peking") Duck, from the restaurant down the street and had it delivered to my room, paying for it herself. The next day, a Western-style porta-potty was delivered as well. By the following day, I was sturdy enough to check out of the hospital and go back to the hotel.

As Dave and I left, we saw two women pulling a teenage boy down the hall, with his legs dragging behind him and his head hanging low. The two women looked as us with big smiles and nodded. I found out later that they had spied through the little window of my hospital room and seen me taking a few steps with Dave's help, so they were copying us. I had been miraculously cured by the stem cells, they thought, and they wanted their boy to be, too.

I actually didn't know what results the procedure would yield for me yet, miraculous or otherwise. As it seemed with so many of these experimental treatments, only time would tell.

AFTER WE LEFT THE HOSPITAL, I WAS STILL WEAK and my neck was in stitches and bandaged up, but we couldn't leave the country without scaling one of the great wonders of the world.

When Dave and I first arrived at the foot of the Great Wall of China, I was in too much post-op pain to lift my head up enough to fully take in the magnificence. We took a gondola up to a high point on the mountain, and when we reached the top, there was a set of stairs going down to get to the actual wall. Five men from Ireland who were standing near us offered to help, and they all carried me down. Then they hoisted me out of my chair and onto the wall.

I knew Dave was itching to walk along the wall, so I told him to go explore on his own for a bit. Even as bandaged and stitched up as I was, I was still able to roll around on the wall a bit and touch the stone with my hands. I could feel the energy of the history underneath me, and I kept thinking, *I'm sitting on the Great Wall of China!*

I took in the view—I was surprised that amid the splendor there was so much pollution in the air above the city—and noticed people nearby taking photos. Not just one family but several were inching closer and closer to me until I was in their camera frames. I'd been told that with the exception of an occasional beggar, the Chinese were not accustomed to seeing people in wheelchairs in public.

I grinned for their cameras; I'm such a ham. Before long, I had entire groups coming up and asking if they could pose with me. I had become my own tourist attraction atop the Great Wall of China! And that was tough competition. Had I thought to charge per photo, I probably could have made a mint in yuan—it could have paid for the surgery. The tab for our trip, which included airfare, hotel, hospital room, pre-op tests, and the surgery, came to $20,000. But it was worth every penny.

About three months after I got home, I reached into the fridge and grabbed a carton of milk and pulled it out.

"Oh my God!"

I put the carton back into the fridge, and pulled it out again.

Ohmygodohmygodohmygod!

It was a seemingly little thing, but it was something I hadn't done since getting hurt, so it was a very, *very* big thing. My fingers had "opened," and I was able to grab the carton! I began to get function back in the fingers of my left hand, and in the following months, the function improved enough to give me a whole new level of freedom. Everything was easier: I could wear pants that fit because I could hook a belt loop with my finger and pull my pants up. Buttons and zippers were easier. One little extra finger movement changed everything I could do.

As for other improvements post-China, I saw them at the gym: I had more endurance in my legs and gradually added more speed to my treadmill workouts until I was walking for half an hour at .5 mph— nearly double the speed and distance I was doing before China.

At the next WSC in March of '05, I had a surprise for Lucy.

She'd always made fun of me when we were out at the pub by grabbing the beer out of my hand. It was a little teasing, playful thing we did together and laughed about. I'd moan and groan, and then she'd give me my beer back. This time I was ready.

We were out one night after a day on the slopes and laughing about something, and she reached over to playfully grab my beer away. She pulled at my beer bottle, but I didn't let go. She looked confused.

"*Aha!*" I yelled out.

She looked up at me, and then understood what was happening and laughed out loud.

"Dana! Oh my God!" She began showing everyone who walked by our table, "Look! Look and see what Dana can do! Watch this!" She kept trying to grab my beer, and I wouldn't let it go. We finally toasted with our beers together, and had a wonderful night.

Lucy was my biggest naysayer, but she was also one of my biggest cheerleaders. I knew that one of the reasons she and others were hesitant to try some of the things I was doing was because they were afraid.

But when you were scaling new heights and climbing on top of great walls, you had to be fearless.

CHAPTER 18

Girls Gone Wild

Lucy and I could barely get through the streets of New Orleans during Mardi Gras in February 2005. They were crammed curb-to-curb with people, and the sidewalks were littered with passed-out bodies (cops checked for a pulse, and if you were alive, they left you there).

At first, Lucy was ahead of me. We figured that as a para, she'd have a better chance at forging a path. "Excuse me . . . excuse me," she said sweetly, in her Southern way, trying to part the red sea of revelers with her *bless yer heart*–isms. It did not work.

"Lucy! Get behind me right now!" I yelled. I got in front and pulled into the crowd, as Lucy pushed me from behind, using one arm to pinch the butts and crotches that were in my face until their owners jumped out of the way.

We bought gloves at a local bike shop because the ground was splattered with every kind of bodily fluid you could imagine. What was on the ground went on our wheels, and what went on our wheels went on our hands. Lucy helped me get my gloves on and off. As we used to say back at the VA hospital, "Every quad needs a good para . . . hands." Heh, heh.

The streets were so out of control that Lucy and I fell out of our chairs a few times. But that might also have been because we were drunk for five days straight.

Our hotel sat between two neon-flashing strip clubs—Dixie Divas and Don Juan's—and a few streets over on Bourbon Street, the Girls

Gone Wild crew had set up camp. One of their guys would ask girls to flash their breasts; in return, they'd get a free Girls Gone Wild T-shirt. I wanted one of those T-shirts, so in my tipsiness I started lifting up my shirt.

Lucy rear-ended me. "Dana! Do you know how many people we know who are gonna *see* that?" she scolded. "We're U.S. military veterans, remember!"

"But I'm wearing my really cute red bra!" I thought that she of all people would appreciate my lacy lingerie, as I had been inspired by her encouragement to stop dressing like a country bumpkin.

Lucy and I looked a bit alike, and people often mistook us for sisters. Now that I was doing my hair and makeup and dressing pretty, people sometimes mistook us for each other. Lucy played that up. In fact, she began to merge our stories together whenever anyone asked us why we were in chairs—a question considered very rude to a disabled person. It's an incredibly personal question, and if we want you to know, we'll tell you. But strangers think it's perfectly fine to ask, "Why are you in that chair?" which happened a lot in New Orleans.

One day in annoyance, Lucy blurted out a response, and it became our friendship folklore. We repeated it several times to unsuspecting listeners.

"We were both fighting at the top of a cliff," she'd begin. "We were arguing over who was better, the Army or the Navy. I tried to throw Dana off the cliff, but she grabbed me and took me down with her."

"Well, I didn't want to die alone," I'd say.

"I landed on top of her. That's why I'm a para and she's a quad."

"Yeah," I'd add, "that's why the Navy is better than the Army. We take the fall for our fellow comrades."

Some people believed this crazy story, and we let them. For us, it was a way to answer the never-ending question about how we got hurt if we didn't want to tell the truth. And I suppose, in a way, it was an attempt to turn our horrific stories of assault and victimization into one about honor and sisterhood—a way to take back some of our power. It was something we both had to constantly fight for, as many women do . . . even and especially, still, among our comrades.

One summer at the Veterans Games, Lucy and I were sharing a hotel room and had been hanging out with a male para who liked her. After we told him it was time to leave, he left our room but didn't close the door all way so that he could get back in. While I was in the bathroom, he returned. When I went back into the room, Lucy was trapped between the wall, the bed, and the nightstand trying to get away from him.

"Get the fuck out of here!" I yelled at him. Lucy's response to the past traumas we'd both endured was usually to crumble; mine was to get mad as hell and want to kill.

The strangest experience we had at Mardi Gras, which neither of us had ever encountered before, was having people repeatedly accuse us of being wheelchair "fakers." Maybe they couldn't believe that two paralyzed women would be so bold (or stupid?) as to come to enjoy the festivities like "normal" people. Maybe we were too young and cute to be paralyzed. Maybe we seemed too happy.

Whatever the reason, I was sick of it. The tenth time it happened, I was really drunk. And you didn't want to mess with a Liesegang when they'd been drinking. A bunch of teenaged boys walked by on the street taunting us: "Hey, you aren't really in those chairs, y'all! C'mon! Fakers!" They were close enough to us that I reached out and grabbed one kid's shirt collar (thanks to my new finger dexterity!), pulling him toward me.

"Do you see these scars?" I pointed to my head. "This is where doctors screwed bolts into me after I broke my neck." I let go of his shirt and pushed him away. "This is *real*," I yelled, as they ran off, "so fuck you!"

MY FEROCITY AND BOLDNESS AT MARDI GRAS was merely the beginning of a two-year period where a strange, wonderful, and fierce momentum gathered.

A month later at the Winter Sports Clinic, Bobby Palm got me skiing downhill on a new piece of equipment he'd invented called "the Slider." Bobby was more than a downhill ski instructor; he was a certifier for adaptive downhill skiing and snowboarding (although he could ski or instruct any discipline). He'd also been inventing gear for adaptive skiing for about 20 years at this point to help people with injuries take part in the sport. I started to get to know him several years earlier in Crested Butte, but much more so around 2000 when he became one of my instructors—along with Molly, who'd invented the ski legs—and we began working more closely together.

Bobby was a creative mastermind, a genius at inventing adaptive equipment, and even had his own construction company. Like me, he was always thinking of new ways for people of *all* levels of ability to play sports more efficiently. Bobby Palm's heart is so big, I'm surprised it fits in his body. We'd become great buddies and were the perfect duo because as I continued to improve, I constantly dreamed up new equipment in my head. I was the perfect muse and guinea pig for his designs, too—always willing to try his inventions and achieve more independence.

I had started off in a bi-ski—where most assumed I'd stay for the rest of my skiing life—but then I went on to the ski legs. And now, Bobby had one-upped the ski legs and made the Slider, which was like ski legs on crack. With ski legs, you are attached to them 100 percent of the time, with a bar going across the front of your skis so you can't cross your tips. You're fixed, rigid. With the Slider, however, the skis are not always fixed; and you can have, if need be, a "bra" made of metal attached to the tips of both skis to keep you in a snowplow and keep your tips from crossing. You have more freedom.

I stood on my skis and used the Slider for balance and stability; I could shift my weight from ski to ski to turn. It felt amazing, and so much closer to able-bodied skiing. Bobby knew me well—like Gary and my old physical therapist Jen, he knew he could push me to rise to the occasion—and I trusted him to know how far my body could go. Except for the time he convinced me to go snowboarding, using the rider bar—a piece of adaptive equipment Bobby had invented with another participant—and I ended up with a massive concussion. I was tired and it was the last run of the day, and it took only a split second for me to lose control and whack my head on the ground.

But we both continued to be fearless and take risks. Now on the slopes with the Slider, we were hauling ass and everyone watching was shocked by how fast we were going. Then we shocked them some more.

Tethered to me from behind, Bobby took me over my first jump with the Slider, and I flew into the air. After we landed, I screamed, "Oh, shit! Let's not do that again!"

A few months later at the Veterans Games in Minnesota, I kicked more ass. The first time I'd played quad rugby 14 years earlier, I had moved like a snail on court. But I'd come a long way since then. It's not that I had that much more muscle function than when I started, but the ones I did have were stronger and my skills had improved.

I'd also begun to take the advice that my buddy Hayes had given me years earlier about resting my shoulders. You see, for a quad or para, our shoulders are the equivalent of the knees and hips of an able-body because we use them so much. Rotator-cuff surgery is common among those with spinal cord injuries who use manual wheelchairs, especially athletes. I always tell myself that when I finally get out of this chair for good, I'll have the knees and hips of a 19-year-old while everyone else will be getting into their wheelchairs and scooters with their bad joints.

I had a memorable rugby game in Minnesota. I'd been the only girl playing rugby at the Games for a long time and had taken a lot of ribbing from the guys along the way—"Who's the girl on the court?!" they'd yell out, "Girls can't play rugby!"—so to win their respect was a beautiful thing.

Before one of the games that summer, my teammate Scotty and I were chatting, when he said, "You know, Dana, you are a total asset to the team." I was so surprised I nearly fell out of my chair.

During the game, Scotty tossed me the ball from a few feet away and I made a triumphant goal by moving backward across the goal line, holding the ball in my lap with my chin. During another play, I tried to block one of the league's top players on the opposing team, a real tank of a guy with arms the size of other people's legs. He barreled his way toward me, and I backed my chair right in front of him as he slammed into me full force, sending me flying. My chair went up on two wheels for a split second then crashed down. Yet I'd stopped the tank for a nanosecond!

One thing about being a quad is that it's a great equalizer. Your ability isn't determined by gender, but by your level of injury and function. By now, at age 34, I'd also learned a thing or two about the power struggle between men and women.

It's no wonder I'd spent so many years dressing in my brother's clothes and beating up boys. I saw as a child and then as a teen that being girly got you in trouble. My sister got yelled at for dressing pretty, and women got blamed for being raped because of how they dressed. It was ironic, then, that I spent the first 19 years of my life acting and dressing like a boy and then fell victim to a crime specifically because I was a woman. I was now, finally, getting to the stage where I was comfortable embracing my very feminine side and putting on some lipstick, while not ignoring the side that had always been me—baseball caps and blue jeans.

Lucy was definitely on the extreme girly end of the spectrum, with her always perfectly coiffed hair and full makeup. She was known to take a curling iron on camping trips. At the '06 Games the following summer in Anchorage, Alaska, I attempted to bring out any tomboy she might have lurking inside her and invited her on a fishing trip. We took a small plane to a river out in the middle of nowhere, and I tomboyed her up as much as her Southern-belle self could handle—she put on a baseball cap, although she was also in full makeup and wearing earrings. After all, there would be men on the boat with us: our young guide as well as another passenger, an older man who'd paid for a day of fishing.

Two disabled women in baseball caps and lipstick arguing over who was a better fisherwoman must have been a freakish sight to these two guys.

"The Army can catch bigger fish than the Navy," Lucy said.

"Are you kidding? The water is home to a seaman. These fish are mine."

No one was getting a bite until Lucy's line tugged and nearly pulled her off her seat. The older guy jumped up to help in that I'm-the-man-and-you're-the-helpless-girl kind of way.

"I wouldn't do that if I were you," I warned.

Lucy shot him a look, and he sat back down. She was girly, but she wasn't helpless. She pulled in a whopper of a salmon about 27 inches long. A little while later, I caught a tiny trout.

Army, big one: Navy, little one.

Girls, two: Guys, zero.

We danced, charmed, and partied our way through the Games that year. The city held a parade to honor the disabled veterans in town and as we got ready to march through the streets, I spotted the local chapter of bearded, able-bodied, leather-jacketed, biker veterans at the front of the line gunning their Harley-Davidsons. Lucy and I sweet-talked them, and a few minutes later they were lifting us right out of our chairs and onto the backs of their bikes, handing us a flag each—the American flag and the Alaskan flag. We left our chairs right there in the street and looped through the town on the back of their Harleys, holding the flags and waving to all our friends from the parade front.

During that trip, I had a very defining moment; I think of it as the moment I got my identity back. I'd been living on Red Bull and Ensure all year, and one morning I woke up, put my ball cap on backward, and headed out the door without makeup on to get my fix and bring one back for Lucy.

"You're going to go out looking like that?" she asked.

"Yep!"

"If you go out looking like that, you are making a statement."

I paused. "I guess I am," I replied. "The statement I'm making is . . . I'm being myself."

Lucy smiled. "Valid point," she said, and off I went.

From that moment on, she never suggested that I wear lipstick for a Red Bull run and I never suggested that she fit her pedicured feet into a pair of wafflestompers. We accepted each other for who we were, and it felt great.

AFTER ALASKA, I KEPT UP MY DIZZYING PACE. A few weeks after returning home to Grand Junction, I went to California to bicycle up Mt. Shasta on what they call "the road to heaven." I rode the 50K around the forested shoulders of the 14,162-foot mountain with my able-bodied new friend, Mike, on a custom-made tandem bike built by my friend Chris, the owner of my local bike shop, Brown Cycles. On the bike the person in front is recumbent and can pedal with their feet or can flip up the pedals and turn it into a handcycle, while the cyclist in back does the steering and gearing. Chris had originally built the bike for my boyfriend, Dave, and me to ride together, but Dave couldn't get the proper balance on it and became frustrated.

I met Mike, an avid cyclist, at the WSC; he helps raise money for vets to come to the Clinic by doing 100-mile bike rides. He was game to scale the extremely steep grades of Shasta with me, even though it was a tough ride that many able-bodied people couldn't tackle. On the day of the ride it was so hot that Mike had to continually throw water on me to cool me off because I couldn't sweat. Near the end of the three-hour ride, with one mile to go, my legs started giving out. I could have switched to the hand cranks, but I was determined to do the ride entirely with my legs. I kept pedaling, using my hands to push and pull my right leg and keep pedaling with my left . . . and we crossed the finish line.

After Mt. Shasta, I went to Lausanne, Switzerland, to handcycle a half marathon and raise funds for Challenge Aspen, an adaptive sports center. It was one of the most scenic rides I've ever done, with a gorgeous lake and mountains and Évian-les-Bains, France, in the distance. I only had one problem: I had been told the course was flat, but it was hills—beautiful but very steep hills.

I may have been the only quad riding; one of the officials rode her bike alongside mine the whole way, and we chatted. "Flat my ass!" I kept repeating as I hand-cranked.

I was the last to cross the finish line, and after I got back to the hotel and showered and changed, I ran into the Challenge Aspen team coach. "Hey, does Dolly Parton look flat to you?" I asked.

"What do you mean?"

"You said that course was flat. Does Dolly Parton look flat to you?"

I HAD TWO MORE DEATH-DEFYING ADVENTURES over the next year or so. In the first one, I died and came back to life. In the second one, I found my life again.

I'd gone boating on the north fork of Colorado's Gunnison River with Dave and my friends Tom and Sean to clean out the trash along the river. The river was flowing fast with the snowmelt running off of Mt. Crested Butte. After nearly drowning in the Grand Canyon, I learned my lesson—instead of duct-taping the paddle to my wrist this time, we used Velcro so I could rip it off "easily" if needed. Fat chance.

I was in the boat with Dave, and the same thing happened as before—water went over my paddle and my hand and dragged me out of the boat. I remember falling over in slow motion, long enough to say to Dave, "I'm goin' out," and take one deep breath before the current devoured me. The pull of the paddle made it impossible for me to roll onto my back in the water, keeping me facedown as I drifted downstream with the current. I tried to roll over but kept struggling—I was freezing cold and so, so tired.

Fuck it. I'm going to die. I've drowned before, and it was easy then.

I felt as though I were leaving my body, and I was in a room with a long table and five people seated in front of me. A familiar-looking man stood to my left and we were talking. He said something that made everyone laugh. Then I said something that made everyone laugh. I felt so happy.

I want to stay here.

Everyone in the room laughed at that thought.

You can't stay . . . you've got to . . . REACH FOR THE BOAT, DANA!

Boom! I was back in my body again, throwing up. Tom was in the water with me and Sean was in the boat, holding on to my life jacket with his teeth and holding on to the boat with his arms, yelling at me to "Reach for the boat!" Dave was still in our boat, farther back.

The guys told me later that when they rolled me over onto my back, I wasn't breathing and they could only see the whites of my eyes. We drifted a mile together in the water as Tom tried to revive me. "I'm surprised you don't have any broken ribs," he said. "To get you breathing again, I was pounding on your chest with my fist. You were dead, Dana. You were dead."

I didn't know what to make of my newest near-death experience or who those people in my "vision" were. I would find out soon enough.

Near the end of 2006, I was driving with Jack from Colorado to Oregon for a camping trip, and I decided to take a detour off the highway so he could take a swim in a nearby reservoir. All day I'd been thinking about Dave and listening to *Manifest Your Destiny* by Wayne Dyer (my go-to guy when my life was in upheaval).

I was confused about our relationship. Dave resented that I couldn't keep up with him athletically . . . and yet during our time together, I had become much more physically able. He dated someone else for a while, then blamed my disability as the problem in our relationship: "You can't ride a bike like I can. You can't ski like I can. You can't hike like I can. You can't camp like I can. You can't raft like I can."

It was like hearing Rick say, "Didn't I compromise by being with someone in a wheelchair?"

The reality was, Dave couldn't adapt to a way of doing things that would include me and be as fun. I knew I had to end it once and for all, but I was afraid I couldn't make it on my own.

I'm stuck, I thought. And then I really was.

I drove 14 miles along a gravel road, crossing a dozen cattle guards, and then down a boat ramp. The reservoir was nearly dried up. I saw tire tracks continuing off the boat ramp, so I kept going. The ass-end of my Subaru started slipping and sliding, so I stopped. It was the kind of mud that sucks you in. *Oh, shit.*

I looked around and honked my horn to see if anyone was in earshot to help me get unstuck, but there wasn't a soul in sight. It was up to me.

I put the car in drive and reverse, and tried to rock it back and forth. I hopped out and crawled on my hands and knees to let air out of the tires, then put a towel under them for traction.

"Jack, go get me a stick!" I grew up watching my father race his truck in the mud for years—I knew how to do this.

When Jack dutifully brought me the stick, I started digging under the tires with it until I noticed the light getting dim.

"Quad," I said out loud, "how far do you think you're going to get digging your car out with the sun setting?"

I saw an outhouse in the distance. "Jack, it's just me and you, buddy. If someone is going to find us, we have to at least make it to that outhouse," I told him. "I did want to camp tonight, but this was not what I had in mind. Anyway, we can take shelter there, and then someone will find us in the morning."

Jack looked worried. He often excelled during emergencies, and saved my life on many occasions. A few months earlier, for instance, he and I were strolling along a bike path in Grand Junction when I started to pass out. I felt so weak I couldn't lift my head, but I had enough energy to attach his leash to him.

"Get me to the car, buddy. I've got a Red Bull there."

That sweet dog of mine pulled me two miles to my Subaru in the parking lot, where I revived myself.

This time, though, he seemed uncertain of what to do.

I hopped back into my car and dragged the body of my wheel-chair over my lap from the passenger seat and put it together next to the car. I could see that the mud was too thick for me to sit in it, though—the chair would sink and get stuck, too.

The route to the outhouse, which would have taken an able-bodied person an easy ten minutes, ended up taking Jack and me two hours. First there was the matter of getting out of the muddy area. I couldn't push myself in the chair because the wheels would sink, so I pushed it from behind, inch by inch, using it as a walker. Once we hit dry ground, I sat and pushed.

Our next obstacle was the boat ramp, the same one I'd driven down. It was like getting up a six-inch curb. I stood up behind my chair and popped it into a wheelie atop the ramp, put my left food on the ramp . . . and then my legs gave out. I fell to the ground with my chair on top of me.

Jack stood over me and pawed at me nervously, knowing very well that I didn't belong on the ground. I transferred myself onto the ramp, then onto my luggage carrier. Now I was high enough to use my legs and arms to push and pull myself into my chair. Victory! I felt ten feet tall!

Using a pile of dirt nearby as little ramp, I managed to push myself onto the boat ramp. Now all I had to do was get up that ramp, then up the gravel road to the outhouse. We were so close.

But the ramp was so steep that I had to go up backward, pushing with my feet while pulling with my arms. I did this inch by inch until I finally reached the top; it took an hour. By this time, it had gotten dark. I saw that the outhouse appeared to be only about 25 feet away.

Jack and I could hear coyotes splashing and howling in the reservoir nearby. *No big deal,* I thought. *Coyotes are afraid of humans.* It didn't occur to me, of course, that to them I was a wounded animal being offered as a meal-on-wheels, with a domestic dog for dessert.

We kept going up the gravel road, and I decided to pass the outhouse and continue going uphill. I figured that in case someone didn't show up the next day, I'd travel better in the cool of the night trying to get the 14 miles to the highway, rather than in the heat of the day, since I didn't sweat. The days in that area reached the 90s at that time, and I'd be risking heatstroke.

Jack suddenly flipped my hand up off my wheel, and I heard the coyotes yipping again, in surround sound this time. I shined my flashlight and at first saw nothing . . . and then there were two eyes glowing back at me.

Oh, shit.

I was terrified; there was no time to say or even think anything. I was in fight-or-flight mode, with flight being the only option. Jack stayed glued to my side as I stuck my flashlight in my mouth, lifted my feet onto the footrest, and hoped that the lights on my wheels, which lit up in red and green as I rolled, would scare the coyotes off—maybe they'd think it was fire.

We raced down the road to the outhouse and made it inside. It was a two-seater, and in the corner on the floor was a dead bird. I locked the latch on the door, hoping it would keep us safe. We heard the coyotes howling for another hour, and heard the sound of a nearby Dumpster lid opening and then smacking down on the other side with a *boom!* I made a move to open the door to see what happened, like those stupid girls in every horror film I'd ever seen (and the audience is yelling "Don't open the door, you idiot!"). Jack gave me a look like, *Bitch. Don't you open that door!*

All night I shivered and whispered and visualized: *Please, let someone in a four-wheel-drive truck come save us. No, wait—please let someone nice in a four-wheel-drive truck come save us.*

At dawn, it was finally quiet. I fed Jack his food and water, while I ate some tuna and drank an Ensure, and we carefully went out the door. My thumbs were bloody, but I pushed up the road that we'd come down and headed back up to the turnoff to the main gravel road, to try to get some help.

As we crested the hill, I noticed a cattle guard. Its purpose was to stop any cows from crossing the road, but it was going to stop me, too. There was no way I had the ability to make it over that.

I looked up to the sky and said, "Okay, God, I'm ready now."

Just then, a huge four-wheel-drive diesel truck appeared to the east of me. I waved my arms in the distress signal, and they turned their truck off and yelled out to me.

I yelled back, "My dumb ass got my car stuck in the mud!"

They immediately started their truck back up and drove over to me. I shed a few tears of relief—the first I had shed the entire time.

My two gentlemen rescuers, Bud and Bob, were out doing some early-morning bow hunting. They said that they weren't sure if they should stop for the crazily dressed woman in a wheelchair with a dog in the middle of nowhere, but when I told them my story, they bundled me up and put Jack and me in the truck.

"I guess there goes bow huntin' for the day," said Bob, as he took a dip of his green-apple-flavored chew. They drove us to Bob's house 20 miles away to get some rope and a shovel.

"You're lucky you didn't come across any of them rattlesnakes out there, warming themselves on the concrete," Bud told me with a chuckle, "or any bears. We had a lot of bear sightings around here these past few weeks."

I leaned my head against the truck window and shut my eyes. Once again, it wasn't my time to go. And if I could survive this, I could handle anything—even being on my own again.

CHAPTER 19

Cry, Burn, Love, Heal

Everything was building up to an eruption; I could feel it.

Early in the summer of 2007, I rented out my house in Grand Junction and moved to Ashland, Oregon, to get some distance from Dave and mend my broken heart. Why Ashland? Well, Jim was still there.

I'd spent those languid days of tea, kisses, and romantic strolls with him nine years earlier, and since then, we'd continued an on-again, off-again romance. Jim was the most emotionally destructive boyfriend I'd had, and the hardest to let go of. He'd pull me in with words of everlasting love and then disappear.

"I'm so in love with you," he'd tell me, and bring me breakfast in the morning before he left for work. "We're so connected."

I rented a room in Jim's house for two months to see one last time if there was a chance for us. All I found was more heartbreak. First of all, he had a girlfriend, which he'd neglected to mention. Yet that didn't stop him from visiting my room one night—no strings attached.

"I'm not into commitment," he explained later. "And I see bigger things in your future than me. I'm afraid I'll hold you back."

My relationships with both Jim and (in the end) Dave had been like part-time, hit-and-run romances that never led to anything real, and I was tired of it. Just like I had to let go of my two additional dads a few years earlier, it was time to fully let go of Jim and Dave. If a man wanted to be with me, whether he was my father or my boyfriend, he needed to show it.

Before I left Ashland, I had the urge to look up Bruce's name on the Internet. To my horror, I found a newspaper report dated a few months earlier about him holding a woman hostage for six days as he read Bible verses to her; she escaped by crawling out a bathroom window. The prospect that he was still out there hurting women shocked and scared me.

What if he finds me and comes back to finish what he started? I can't crawl out of a window.

Out of curiosity, I Googled my own name and saw an article from 1990 for the first time. Soon after I had woken up from my coma, the *Los Angeles Times* had run this brief news item:

Navy Recruit Injured in Fall at Sunset Cliffs
October 27, 1990

A 19-year-old naval recruit who fell 75 feet from Sunset Cliffs was in serious condition at UC San Diego Medical Center Friday, police said.

Dana Liesegang, a [recruit] attached to the submarine tender McKee in San Diego, was walking along the cliffs with a friend in the 4500 block of Ladera Street about 10 P.M. Thursday when she fell and landed on the beach below, police said.

Lifeguards, firefighters, and a police helicopter assisted in rescuing Liesegang from the beach. She was taken to the hospital by Life Flight.

That they'd called Bruce my "friend" made me want to throw up. I tried to comment on the bottom of the article, writing to the editor: *No! This is not correct! It didn't happen this way—you need to change this!* but I had no idea if anyone read my words. Even on the World Wide Web I had no voice.

Why I had to upset myself by looking up this stuff, I don't know. I tried to put the past out of my mind and look to the future—in a few weeks' time, I'd be on my way to the Dominican Republic for another round of stem-cell injections. This time Lucy was coming with me, along with my friend Mack and his friend Chase. Mack was a beefy hunk of a para whom I'd met at the Veterans Games in Minnesota in a very Dana way. I rolled over to him, said "You're handsome!" and kissed him, and then rolled off. We've been friends ever since.

Mack was the first veteran to ask in a positive way about the stem cells I'd received in China, and truly wanted to know more. He'd found an American doctor for us to see in the Dominican Republic who operated a clinic where he'd inject millions of stem cells into his patients. The entire procedure only took a few hours.

Lucy finally decided to join me for a treatment after she realized that I was getting results, and after I gave her a dose of tough love.

We'd gone on a Caribbean cruise together after our Alaskan adventure, and she was in the ship's gym with me as I was working out on the elliptical.

"Quad," she said to me, "you sit down!"

"Para," I shot back, "you stand up!"

She was shocked. Later on, I understood more of what was behind her words.

"Goddamn you for giving me hope, Dana, because now that I have hope, if I don't get up like you, then I fail," she explained. "Then I have to deal with this all over again."

Lucy's thinking surprised me; I'd never in my life thought that way. To me, failure was if you didn't even try.

The doctor in the Dominican Republic had given us a group discount and lowered the price by $5,000 each, so Mack, Chase, Lucy, and I paid $20,000 per person (not including flight and hotel). We stayed at a five-star resort, where we partied it up and had fun while we could (after we'd have the stem cells, alcohol would be off-limits for six months).

On the beach, I met Steve, a blond German who spotted me dragging lawn chairs for Lucy and me across the sand. He was staying at the same resort as we were and came to our rescue in his little Speedo. He was as cute as can be and spent the rest of the afternoon with us, fetching fruit and water.

My friends and I all went in for our injections on the same day—two of us on one floor, two of us on another—and met up afterward. We went back to the resort and pigged out on everything they had. We were ravenous! For the rest of the evening we were bouncing off the walls with energy, as if we were on speed. The next day we sat outside eating breakfast at a restaurant, inspecting our bodies and waiting to see if anything was different. I'd invited cute Steve to meet us, and it was a hot, sunny day. Then, like in the shower in Mexico, I felt a trickle.

What the . . . ?

One perfectly beautiful bead of sweat appeared on my upper lip.

"I'm sweating! Take a picture!" I could have cried. It was the first time in 17 years that I'd sweated. (And it wasn't due to autonomic dysreflexia, the symptoms of which can also include chills, sweating abnormally, and headaches, as well as the blood pressure spikes I've already mentioned.) After cursing my sweat glands for the first half of my life, I never thought I'd treasure one tiny little drop so much.

Steve was there for that historic moment, and also for my first walking "marathon," which I did in Budapest later that summer. He drove over from his home in Germany to support me as I did the 3.5K walk to raise funds for Challenge Aspen. He showed up with team shirts for us: Mine said BUDAPEST MARATHON 2007—CHIEF, and his said BUDAPEST MARATHON 2007—SUPPORT CREW.

It was a difficult walk on cobblestoned streets and through grassy parks, but Steve was with me the whole way, feeding me bananas and Cokes as I focused on putting one foot in front of the other with my walker. Toward the end, my legs started to lose it. I couldn't get them to move forward anymore; they were *done.* But there was no way I wasn't going to finish. I stopped a few times and rested on my walker seat. Sometimes I turned my walker around and pulled it backward.

It took me eight and a half hours to walk just over two miles, and at the finish line I, of course, threw up. But I was triumphant.

AFTER I GOT BACK TO THE U.S., I HEADED FOR the Black Rock Desert in Nevada for my second Burning Man, an arts festival attended by tens of thousands of people who run around naked or in costume. At the end of the week, there is a ritual burning of a large wooden effigy of a man, and everyone cheers. At the festival, you don't buy food and drinks with money because everything is by trade. I once traded some peppermints and a pack of condoms for a grilled-cheese sandwich.

One of the most liberating events for both women and men that I've ever experienced is the "Critical Tits Parade," where thousands of women ride their bikes topless. I put on a pink wig with hair down to my nipples and a cute pair of underwear, and smiled up a storm as I drove my golf cart (most people rode bikes, but I used a golf cart the three years I attended).

During the parade, we didn't get any catcalls from the men. Instead, guys kept coming up to us and saying things like, "Thank you so much for being a woman!" and "Thank you for being able to give birth!" In a crazy way, it was like the opposite of the military or the world I knew back home, where women were whores or bitches or unappreciated.

I'd never been thanked so much for being female. During this festival and especially this parade, men were thanking us for existing, for being women! They were celebrating our femininity, not punishing us for it. And just because we were all parading around topless, it didn't mean that we were asking to be raped or that they wanted to assault us. At the end of the parade line, the women had a little party of their own and burned an effigy of a giant bra. The only men allowed were the ones who served the snow cones and drinks to the women.

On the second-to-last night of the festival, they have fireworks and dancers, and the Burning Man goes up in flames like a big bonfire. Everyone chants, "Burn the man! Burn the man! Wahooo!" It is an incredible experience.

The following night—the last night—is when you let go of things in your life that you don't want anymore at the ritual burning at the temple, which is this huge structure. All week, the revelers pray around it, and people tack up pieces of paper with writing on it or photos of something they want to let go of in their life.

The year before, I'd tacked up three photos on the temple walls:

- A photo of myself in uniform

- A photo of me in the halo

- A photo of Dave and me

In 2007 I burned nothing. Maybe I wasn't sure of what I had left to keep and what I had left to let go of.

My house in Grand Junction was still occupied, so my next stop was Rockwall, Texas. Lucy had been trying to convince me to come live near her there, so right after I got back from my bra-burning tit parading, I headed southeast.

It started out great, with one of the best Halloweens I'd ever had. I scared the little trick-or-treaters by telling them not to get too close to the ten-foot-tall metal doors we had—they looked like castle doors—or they would end up trapped in a chair like me. Then I tried to convince an adorable seven-year-old boy to marry me: "I'm being kept here as a prisoner, but if you marry me they will set me free."

The little boy didn't accept my proposal and didn't save me, so it was downhill after that. The next six months were a living hell. I found that Rockwall was the worst place for someone like me, who likes to ride bikes and be outdoors in a chair. The sidewalks were only on one side of the street, and they ended suddenly without warning. I couldn't find a bike shop in town to look after my cobalt-blue recumbent tricycle—my "trike"—that I had ridden daily for four years now. There were no bike paths near me, and I had to drive 40 minutes to get to a dog park.

Lucy and I had intended for me to do some work for her in her company, but soon decided that being friends and boss-employee didn't mesh very well. So except for my first week there, I saw her only a handful of times during my entire time in Rockwall. I became a loner and stayed in the apartment most of the time, except for when I took Jack to the dog park. After I bought a treadmill, he ran on that. We'd exercise together—me on the elliptical and him on the treadmill. At first I leashed him on it, but as he started to really like it, he'd get on it himself and give me this look, like, *Okay, turn it on! I'm ready!*

One night while Jack and I were exercising together, I had the TV on for us, and we saw Wayne Dyer on PBS talking about Louise Hay's book *You Can Heal Your Life*. Wayne had saved me before and I trusted him implicitly, so I bought the book. My mom and I decided to read it together over the phone, a chapter per night, and then talk about it.

It was an absolute revelation for me. Louise wrote that life was simple—what we give out, we get back—and we're responsible for everything in our lives, the good and the bad. I learned how our body parts hold different emotions—anger can get settled here and depression can get settled there. I started working on my thought process and got myself out of Texas. I went back to Grand Junction, which felt like home to me now. It was where I belonged.

THROUGHOUT THE SPRING AND SUMMER OF 2008, I'd wake up at 3 A.M. to beat the heat and train with Jack for that summer's ride at Mt. Shasta. I had started sweating more since the Dominican Republic, but still not enough to work out in the hot summer sun and be safe.

I rode up and over the 30-mile road that winds through the red-rock Colorado National Monument. I decided that I was going to call this summer's ride my "ride to recovery." As with my other yearly events, the Mt. Shasta ride acted as a benchmark for my progress. This time I rode the 50K by myself on my trike, instead of the tandem with Mike. I used my own legs, and they didn't give out—I was getting stronger. Mike rode alongside me on his own bike to be my buddy and support crew, while his wife and Jack followed behind in the car.

Steve visited from Germany, and the bubbling up to a volcanic eruption continued. It was the Fourth of July, so everyone was proudly displaying American flags on their front porches.

"You guys are too proud of your flag," he said one day, as we drove and passed flag after flag. "There's too many flags up here, all over the place." He went on speaking, doggin' on the military.

"Excuse me, but do you understand who you're with? Also, it's the Fourth of July and *you're in my country!*"

I may have had my own issues with the military, but *no one* puts down my country.

In many ways, Steve was one of the sweetest men I'd ever dated. But some upsetting things began to happen during our visit that summer, apart from the anti-American commentary. Every time he touched me, I exploded with anger and mood swings. He was very lovey-dovey and was expressing a healthy sex drive, but I couldn't

tolerate how touchy-feely he was. He grabbed me like a teenaged boy with his first girlfriend. I remember wishing I'd had a boyfriend do this with me in high school—but now that I had it, I felt like his octopus hands were invading me.

I went to a psychologist in Grand Junction to talk about this, and she explained that I was experiencing post-traumatic stress disorder (PTSD) and that my brain couldn't distinguish between nonthreatening types of touching and threatening ones.

When I discussed the issue with Steve over the phone, he went to see a counselor in Germany. After his session, he told me, "The counselor said it's your problem."

"Yes, but you have to be sensitive about this and change your behavior," I replied, "or we can't be together."

Steve didn't see it that way, so we broke up.

WHEN YOU ARRIVE IN NEW DELHI, the smells of the streets hit you immediately: human, animal, garbage, food, and gasoline. It was January 2009, and I'd come to India for another set of stem cells that I'd heard about. The total cost—which covered airfare, a nurse, the procedure, room and board, leg braces, private yoga classes, antibiotics, additional tests, and physical therapy for two months—came to $60,000. I sold my house to pay for the procedures, and had enough left over to put a down payment on a smaller home.

A taxi picked up Mom and me at the airport in New Delhi, and the journey to our hotel was one of sweat, exotic spices, honking horns, stops for random cows or camels in the street, and driving the wrong way down one-way streets.

The stem-cell center looked more like a modern hotel than a hospital. The daily routine started in the morning with injections from Dr. G and her nurses. She was a former infertility expert, and unlike other doctors, cultured an endless line of stem cells from a single embryo donated by a fertility patient a decade earlier.

The cells she gave me were three to five days old, derived from a cloning method. I got injections every day intramuscularly, plus a three-day procedure in which a catheter was run up my spine and stem cells were injected several times a day as I lay on my side, my stomach, and then on my other side. They were trying to "bathe" my spinal cord in stem cells, they told me. My afternoons were busy with physical therapy and yoga with a very cool, funny, sweet guy named Rawat, who also did some reflexology and acupressure on me that hurt like crazy.

Once a week, all the patients had a mandatory group meeting with the doctors, where we could ask questions and bring up concerns. I was so knowledgeable at this point about spinal cord injuries and stem cells, because I'd been so many places to get them, that I could often answer the questions Dr. G skirted. (I found out later in my stay that because I was so well informed, some staff members thought I was an American spy out to get their stem-cell secrets.)

During my two months in India, I didn't see results like I had in the past. In fact, after some of my early sessions I noticed a backsliding in some of my function. The improvements I did see—improved balance and stronger core—I was certain were coming from my workouts with Rawat. One of my physical-therapy exercises was to climb a wooden ladder that was affixed to the wall. When I arrived there, I couldn't do any rungs; near the end of my stay, I could do four.

During my little time off, Mom and I managed to get in a trip to the Taj Mahal and some temples and the High Court of Karnataka. The main mausoleum at the Taj Mahal had a bunch of steps so I couldn't get in, but Mom went in and enjoyed it for us both.

On Valentine's Day, we dressed up in Indian outfits and went out to a nightclub with the manager from another hospital. My mother and I both felt like animals cooped up in a cage for two months and needed to have some fun! Part of the agreement I signed upon arriving at the facility was that I wouldn't bring or drink alcohol in the hospital. But I wasn't *in* the hospital, we reasoned, so I had one glass of wine. Mom and I were two rule breakers bunking together in one room, so that was inviting anarchy.

At the club we couldn't figure out why there were only men dancing together—the kind of dancing we'd seen in Bollywood movies—and no women.

"Are we in a gay nightclub?" Mom asked the manager.

"Women in India never go out to bars unless they're with their husbands," he explained.

Mom and I weren't going to pass up a night of dancing on my one real night out, so we got out on the floor with all the boys and men and had a great time (and they were happy to dance with women for a change). When we got back to the clinic, we were laughing and still amped up from the fun time we'd had. A night nurse helped me get out of my Indian garb, and Mom and I both went to sleep.

The next morning I went to get my injection as usual, but one of the nurses told me I couldn't have it.

I didn't understand what was going on, so I demanded to see Dr. G. The doctor and some nurses met Mom and me in my room and asked us about our night before. "The clerk on duty said you'd returned to the clinic drunk," one of them said.

"I had one glass of wine! There are other patients here on heavy narcotics and marijuana—and that's what you know about. One glass of wine isn't going to hurt anything." The nurse who'd helped me out of my clothes stood up for me and confirmed that I wasn't drunk.

"And besides, I'm paying you a lot of money to be here," I added.

The doctor nodded and sent a nurse to get my injection. Yes, I'm an American who knows how to have fun. Maybe the male night clerk wasn't used to seeing women express themselves. Maybe it was time more women did.

A few days after that, Mom and I got into a big fight over the wine situation. I was honestly trying to follow the rules for once in my life and told her she couldn't bring wine into the room for herself, as she'd been doing. I told her she had to stop—especially in light of our recent conversation with the staff about my one glass of it—and she got angry.

"Hey, Mom, you know what? This trip is about me getting stem cells and medical treatment, not about you having a good time and drinking wine," I told her. "It's about me. *It's about me.* And, oh yeah . . . *it's about me!*"

Mom came toward me, put her hand over my mouth as I was talking, and pushed me backward into a wheelie and onto the bed—

holding me there as I flailed. I was never so pissed off at my mother my entire life. In that moment, I hated her. She hurt me in a way no one ever should, especially one's mom. It reminded me of Rick pushing me back onto the floor, twice, but it was worse—*she'd put her hand over my mouth.* She didn't hurt me physically, but I was emotionally distraught. She was angry because she couldn't have her wine and tipped me into submission.

Right after she did that, she dropped to the floor on her hands and knees and cried, saying, "Please forgive me, I'm sorry!"

"Get out of my way," I told her. "I need some time to cool off."

The next day, out of nowhere, she began slapping herself in the face very hard. "I'm so bad! I'm such a bad mother!"

"Hey, Mom. I didn't hit you, so you don't get to hit you. So stop the drama."

Something about what my mother did that day was connected to everything I had been dealing with my entire life. It was about violence in families, it was about hurting someone when they're vulnerable, and it was about anger and alcohol. It was about abuse of all kinds that make victims out of people. And then, it was about not speaking out about any of it—her hand on my mouth meant that to me.

What my mother did that day destroyed our relationship for a while, but I forgave her. Sometimes strangers hurt us; sometimes it's the people we love the most.

Everything came to a head in the two years after India.

A few months before that trip, I had started school at Mesa State College (now Colorado Mesa University), majoring in Spanish. The school was a 15-minute "roll" with Jack from my home, and he came to classes with me every day. The school's study-abroad program offered five weeks in Barcelona the summer of 2010, and I went to knock out two classes in a month—and also because I was dating my green-eyed, highly intellectual professor, Ramón, who hailed from Madrid.

The following summer of 2011, the study-abroad program situated the students in Costa Rica, and I shared a hotel room with a fellow student named Audrey. I'd paid half her way, and she was to be my helper in exchange. Yet she was a 20-year-old born-again Southern Baptist virgin who wasted no time telling me I was destined for hell. The truth was, I was already there—we were living two streets away from it.

It only took a day or two before we realized that our hotel was across the street from one of the largest sex- and drug-trafficking areas in the region. Audrey had been warned not to walk alone in our area at any time of day, so we'd stay inside from 2 P.M. when we'd get home from class to 7 A.M. the next day when we'd leave. It also rained like a cow pissing on a flat rock every day, and I couldn't get around in the rain by myself, so that was another reason I stayed locked up inside. In a four-week period, 11 sets of students were robbed at gun- or knifepoint by a well-organized ring of thieves.

At night, we'd hear blood-curdling screams and gunshots outside our window. That was enough to give me nightmares. I'd downloaded Wayne Dyer's seminar *From Ambition to Meaning* a few days after we arrived, and I'd been listening to it for an hour every morning as I drank coffee to give me the emotional strength I needed. By week two, after the nightmares started, I'd be in tears before I put it on, but Wayne's voice mellowed me out and helped me get through the day. By week three, I was listening to him every night, too, to make me feel safe and lull me to sleep. It sounded like hell outside, and it didn't help that my roommate told me I was going to perdition each time I cussed or drank a beer or because I'd had sex out of wedlock.

"I thought about taking the wheels off your chair while you're asleep and hiding them, to punish you," she confessed to me one night.

"If you did that, you'd be dead."

Being punished by a crazy zealot wasn't at the top of my list of how I wanted to spend my 40th birthday, but that is indeed how I spent it.

What pushed me over the edge was a film we saw in class. It was a Spanish film meant to teach some history and culture, as well as help us learn the language. In the film, a woman was raped, and I fell apart in class. After that, I went to bed every night as early as 6 P.M. to try to escape to my surroundings, including my roommate. I'd get my homework done, have a few beers, and then go to bed. But I couldn't escape—I kept waking up in the middle of the night crying from the nightmares. When morning came, I'd put on Wayne's voice to try to save the day ahead.

When I returned to Grand Junction, I felt so vulnerable and raw that I enrolled in a class on self-defense. It didn't occur to me that a hands-on course like that, where people pretend to attack you, would pose a problem—completely forgetting the whole Steve incident and that my brain doesn't discern a fake attack from a real one.

On the first day of class, the teacher asked if there was anyone in the room who'd ever been attacked, and I put up my hand. "It's why I'm in this chair," I explained.

In an effort to be helpful, I assume, the teacher attempted to demonstrate a choke hold on me a few days later, but he didn't get far. When he approached, I started to cry. Sense memories of that night on the cliff began to surface.

You'd think the others in class might have gotten the idea that I was sensitive in this department. Yet one day after class, as I was leaving the room, a classmate thought he'd be funny and test me on the drills we'd been learning. We'd been in the yoga studio, practicing falling grab holds and other moves to escape an attacker. He rushed up to grab me from behind, but I saw his reflection in a mirror. I spun my chair around and headed straight for him, reaching for my keys as a weapon to stick in his eyes.

"I will kill you, you motherfucker," I said, as the professor was stepping between us.

I quit the class and school altogether, and hid in the house for days under my blankets—not talking to anyone, barely eating, not showering. I pretended I was sick, and my ex-boyfriend Dave came and walked Jack.

I was terrified. I couldn't avoid what had happened to me anymore. I had tried for more than half my life to push it down, but it wouldn't stay put. I had to face it.

CHAPTER 20

Letting Go and Letting Goddess

To get to the small, sacred waterfall—the "cachoeira"—in the tropical jungle-like area of Abadiânia, Brazil, you have to walk along a cleared trail and down a steep hill.

The waterfall is atop a quartz-crystal mine and energized by the vibrations of angels, the locals say, and considered so sacred that you are discouraged from taking a photo of it lest you tamper with the holy energies. It is a place you go to wash away anything inside of you that you must let go of. I've known a magical waterfall like this before, the one that Gary and I loved to go to in Three Lynx, my happy place. In my heart I believe that the day I went to this waterfall in Brazil is the day my anger toward Bruce began to wash away.

I had traveled to "the City of Spiritual Cures" in May 2012 to see a "psychic surgeon" by the name of John of God. How I ended up there was another gift from the man who'd helped me through so many difficult times, Dr. Wayne Dyer.

I had signed up for Dr. Dyer's seminar called "Mastering the Art of Manifestation," which was to take place on a cruise around Australia in January 2012. He helped me so much during my trauma in Costa Rica that I wanted to meet him in person and thank him.

The day before the seminar began, I did something bold that I'd never done before. I wanted to signify a new beginning and perspective in my life, one of no fear, so I jumped out of a plane. After the immobilizing terror I'd felt for so much of 2011, I figured that skydiving from 14,000 feet and free-falling at over 125 mph, then floating over the spectacular views of the Wollongong beaches, might be a way to jolt me back to my fearless self.

My friend Leia and I took a train from Sydney to Wollongong, and the skydiving place we'd signed up with drove us to the beach. Each of us was to be strapped to a tandem jumpmaster, and mine was hesitant to take me up.

"It's too windy," he said. He was concerned about a safe landing for me.

"Don't worry, I can stand it!" I assured him. There was no way I was going to take no for an answer, and I told him that. What I didn't realize right away was that our ace jumpmaster had a disability himself, and that was what made him worry. As our little plane ascended the 14,000 feet, he told me his story.

A few years earlier he'd attempted a free jump from the Sydney Harbour Bridge. As he was free-falling, he was so in awe of the architecture of the Sydney Opera House nearby that he didn't throw his chute in time, and he smashed into Sydney Harbour.

"I was a para for a few years," he said, "and then one day I had a spontaneous healing. I gained feeling back in most of my body except for below the knees."

Well, this must be a first, I thought, *an incomplete para taking an incomplete quad skydiving.*

I was terrified, but excited. We jumped, and it was exhilarating, freeing, the best ride I've ever been on—better than rafting and roller coasters. I screamed my head off during the free fall, and I might have screamed more had I known we were in trouble. After my instructor pulled the chute cord, our parachute twisted, and the wind carried us farther than planned. He had to kick us in circles to untwist the lines and steer us back to the park. I was totally oblivious to any danger, so perhaps my jump did what I'd hoped—nudged me toward my fearlessness. It was the perfect prelude to Dr. Dyer's seminar; plus, I was going to need all the courage I could muster for what I was about to face.

The next day in the ship's gym, I was tying my shoes before getting on the elliptical when I heard the voice. It was the comforting, deep voice I'd been listening to for 15 years—the one that pulled me from the suicidal edge in Odem, Texas, the one that kept me sane and alive in Costa Rica. Dr. Dyer and his daughter Serena were checking in at the front desk and walked by me—as they did, I tried to say hi but nothing came out of my mouth, like that time I stood watch at boot camp.

One of the trainers helped me up onto the elliptical, and I told him my whole Wayne-Dyer-saving-my-life-many-times story. The trainer couldn't resist and went to get him.

"You've gotta work harder than that," said Wayne, who was now standing behind me. At least this time I was able to utter a hello, but that was about it.

A few days later I saw him walking by with Serena, and I mustered up the courage to say hello again. I'd come on this cruise to thank him, and now was my chance to do just that.

"I need to thank you," I said, trying to get my words out as fast as possible while I could. "You've helped me so much—I might not be alive today if it wasn't for you. I was raped and thrown off a cliff when I was in the military. I read *Manifest Your Destiny* when I was 25 because I was suicidal, and it help saved my life."

Wayne hugged me tightly and said, "*You* did the work."

At the seminar he was promoting his most recent book, *Wishes Fulfilled,* and I made my own wish after my chat with Wayne: that I'd be sitting at a personal dinner with him during this cruise.

That night there was a beach party on deck, and as the band played "Margaritaville," I was dancing with everyone I could. I spotted Serena on the floor with a few friends, and went over to dance with them for a few songs. We all laughed and danced like crazy and had a great time. Later that night, she asked if I'd join her and her father for dinner the next day so that she could interview me for the book they were working on together, *Don't Die with Your Music Still in You.*

My wish was fulfilled.

Sitting across from Wayne Dyer, I was, of course, quite the chatterbox because I was so excited. The conversation grew serious as Wayne told everyone at the table about the long-distance "remote" healing he'd had from 12,000 miles away by the spiritual leader, medium, and holy man "João de Deus"—John of God—eight months earlier to help heal his own leukemia.

"He can do surgery on a thousand people in a room at one time. He doesn't actually do it; it's the entities who enter his body who do it," Wayne explained. "It changed everything for me. It puts divine love in you." He looked right at me. "You should go to him, Dana."

I was convinced.

Two months later, I had a long-distance "remote healing," like Wayne had his "remote surgery," before even getting to Brazil. This involved sending a photo of myself wearing white to John of God, and he prescribed and blessed a concoction of herbs for me. They arrived in the mail, and after I'd taken them for three days, my arm became one giant blistering mess and I had to stop.

I also had bowel accident after bowel accident—it hadn't been this bad since that period of time after my bladder surgery. Something was going crazy inside of me. Then, about a week before I went to Brazil in May, I noticed my bowels improving drastically each day—by the time I got there, they were better than they'd ever been.

I arrived at the Casa Dom Inácio de Loyola in Abadiânia with Chrissy, who was now a trained nursing assistant, and a friend of hers, Joanne, to see this John of God in person. We followed the instructions given before arriving: abstain from hot spices, pork, and alcohol; and pack a lot of white clothing. After we arrived, our guide took us on a tour of the casa and told us what to expect and what line to wait in the next day (the second-timer's line, since I'd already had the remote healing).

Chrissy and Joanne were set to have a "spiritual surgery" that morning, while I was told to take a crystal bath and return to the main healing room that afternoon for my own spiritual surgery. I was ushered into a space with about 50 people, and we were told to close our eyes and keep them closed until we were told to open them.

João then came into the room, and we all sat quietly in meditation while he did what he does (we couldn't actually *see* what he was doing because our eyes were still shut). When it was over, and only after he'd left the room, we were allowed to open our eyes again. Our instructions were to go straight to bed and sleep as much as possible over the next 24 hours, stay out of the sun for a few days, and keep wearing white—the entities would continue with the surgery while we slept.

When I woke up, I was almost too exhausted to get up and pee, and I had slept 24 hours straight. Chrissy inspected my back and neck and saw red, round dots on my spine the size of a pencil eraser. The second week, I had another surgery, and as I slept I was awakened by the feeling that someone was inside my neck adjusting each vertebra, one at a time, as they held my head and turned it from right to left. I was half-asleep and heard each pop, then was out like a light again.

A week after that, the entities returned and "removed" the sutures as I slept. It's difficult to fully explain in words what I experienced there, or how John of God helps you heal. Faith is a very large part of it—and, as Wayne said, it's about divine love. You open your mind and heart to what is simply inexplicable in scientific terms. Even skeptics and nonbelievers do not leave Abadiânia unchanged.

Before we left Brazil, Chrissy helped me down the hill to the cachoeira and, with a few others, carried me under the falls—immersing me in the purifying waters. I don't know for sure what magical healing powers John of God and his waterfall have, but when we left the clearing, I was able to walk up the hill on my own two feet and, to this day, it's the steepest climb I've ever done.

THE FIRST WEEK AFTER GETTING HOME to Grand Junction, I noticed my bowel function kept improving until I got to the point where I only had an occasional "oops"—this was indeed a major freedom and triumph. Soon after that, I went for my annual "poke and prod" at the SCI unit in Seattle and had my next freeing experience.

I was now 21 years post-injury. During my annual, I had a chat with my former social worker, Marge, who was still there—and still one of the few people in this world who could intimidate me.

She took a look at my records and noticed that I'd been in and out of mental-health appointments a lot. Then she said, point-blank, "You need to tell me what really happened to you."

She'd never believed my story that I didn't know or didn't remember or that I just fell.

I finally told her what happened. I wasn't emotional about it, and Marge was both angry and relieved—angry at what I had to go through and relieved to finally know and get it on my medical records, where it belonged.

"I knew it," she said. "That's why I couldn't get so many things I needed on you."

She had been suspicious the entire time she was trying to get me service-connected because she couldn't get important paperwork from the Navy—when she asked, they always said they didn't have it.

"Dana, we need to put this in your records so you can be treated for PTSD."

I explained to her about my right to remain silent, and the paperwork my father had signed for me.

"That's bullshit. Well, regardless of what he signed back then, you're VA property now. You're not military property at all. They washed their hands of you when you signed onto the VA. They have no authority over you. You don't have to remain silent anymore."

"I don't?"

"No!"

Those words rang in my ears . . . I could hardly wrap my brain around them. I'd been silent for so long that the concept of not remaining that way was dizzying. I'd been talking about it to other women who'd also been sexually abused in the military, of course, and I'd told some family and friends. But Marge's words—*you don't have to remain silent anymore*—had such an effect on me that what happened next was inevitable.

The following month, in September 2012, I went on another cruise during which Wayne Dyer held a seminar aboard the ship. This time we were going across the Mediterranean, to Italy, Greece, and Turkey. I went with my friend Dimitri, whom I'd met on the Australian cruise earlier in the year.

On the first day of his seminar, Wayne talked about "releasing attachment" in one's life. When the chat was over and people were leaving, I made my way up to him. Grabbing hold of the tops of the chairs for balance, I slowly made my way up to the stage. As soon as Wayne saw me, he came over to give me a hug and say hello.

I'd been eyeing his purple cap all morning—it was my favorite color and matched my shirt—and got an inspired idea. "Wayne, how attached to that hat are you?" I knew purple was his favorite color, too.

"Pretty damn attached, thanks," he said with a smile. "It's my favorite."

"Okay, well . . . I'm pretty damn attached to my John of God triangle, but I'll trade you for it if you give me that hat." I showed him the silver necklace I was wearing, which I'd gotten at the Casa de Dom Inácio.

"You went!" Wayne said, excited. "With an offer like that, how can I refuse?"

We made the exchange.

"I think I'll have to change around my talk tomorrow," he said.

I didn't know what he meant by that until the next day at the seminar. Wayne told the crowd about John of God and then began talking about me. He said that I'd been hurt in an accident, but didn't give any specifics. Then he asked me to come up to the front and tell the audience about my experience with John of God.

When I got up there, I was shaky and nervous and didn't know how to begin, so I let my gut lead me: "As Wayne said, I was raped and thrown off a cliff . . ."

But Wayne hadn't said that. I hadn't intended to speak about what happened to me, and it was the first time I'd ever said those words out loud to more than one person at a time, never mind a whole roomful of strangers. *I was raped and thrown off a cliff.* Everyone was shocked by my story.

When I was finished, Wayne told the audience how we'd traded my John of God triangle for his hat, but he wanted to give my triangle back to me.

"Okay, but I'm still not giving you back your hat!" The audience had a good laugh.

I didn't fully realize what I'd done until I was at dinner that night and it hit me: I'd just told an entire crowd of strangers what had happened to me back in 1990, and it was scary but also liberating. I was in shock! I spoke out loud, I had a voice, I was far from silent—this was awesome.

For the rest of the cruise, I kept running into Wayne on land.

When we reached Athens, Dimitri and I went straight to the Acropolis. I wanted to see the ruins and feel the energy of ancient gods and warriors. They'd apparently installed an elevator in 2004 for disabled visitors to use in preparation for the summer Olympics that year. Yet when we arrived, I was told, "I'm sorry, but the elevator is broken. It's impossible for you to get up to the top."

"Impossible? No, *I'm* sorry. I went on this cruise so I could see the Acropolis, and I'm not going to miss it because you don't know how to get my chair up a flight of stairs. I'll figure out a way."

I'd already been teaching Dimitri a good technique on how to get me up and down stairs, and we found some human angels along the way hailing from countries all over the world who helped lift my chair when we needed it.

When we got to the top, I walked up the marble steps to the temple of Athena Nike—she was the Greek goddess of wisdom, victory, war, justice, skill, and righteousness. And I heard, "Hey, that's my hat!"

I looked over and there was Wayne, also admiring Athena's temple. He jokingly grabbed the hat off my head, saying, "I knew I'd catch you with my hat! When are you going to give that back to me?"

"I'll make you another deal," I told him. I could feel the spirit of Athena inspiring me. "I'll give you your hat back when I can walk up to you without any help at all."

"Deal."

In Turkey, I went to the house of Virgin Mary, where many Catholics believe Jesus's mother lived her last days and died, now a shrine and chapel at the top of a hill (why is everything always at a top of a hill?!). I'm not religious, but I believe in the power of unconventional women who have changed history and haven't always been given enough due or their own voice.

When I got home, I put the John of God triangle on Jack's collar to keep him safe and healthy. He'd had cancer lumps on his back leg, and although the vet had removed the tumors, there was a good chance of them coming back. Since wearing the triangle, he's been cancer-free.

Jack was my movie date a few weeks later when I watched the documentary *The Invisible War*. It was horrifying, as it followed the emotional stories of a handful of women in the military who'd been sexually assaulted by their colleagues or superiors and were then shunned, stonewalled, and ignored. Often it led to two choices for the women: either going AWOL or attempting suicide.

One scene showed a father in tears, talking about the time his daughter—a young recruit who had never had sex before—telephoned him and begged him to come rescue her after she'd been raped. Another was an interview with a victim of the 1991 Tailhook scandal, in which she described getting off an elevator and having hundreds of fellow military men ambush her and try to pull her clothes off.

"Well, that's what you get for walking down the hallway full of drunk aviators," she was told.

"Don't wear any makeup," another new recruit was warned, "because the Marines will think you want to sleep with them."

The movie also presented some shocking (but not surprising) statistics: for example, in 2010 the military's annual report showed that 3,158 incidents of sexual assault had been reported. Even more shocking was how few had been followed up on.

The handful of women in the film who took their cases to court found their lawsuit dismissed in 2011; they were essentially punished for being tattletales. The film concluded that the court ruling amounted to be being told that rape is an occupational hazard of military service.

The Invisible War upset me so much that I stayed inside my house for a few days, thinking about it. I realized that I was one story, one woman, of so many thousands forced to keep her mouth shut. The most traumatic piece for so many of these women is that they looked at their fellow military men as comrades and brothers whom they would trust their lives to. Sexual assault in the military, said one therapist interviewed, had the emotional impact "akin to what happens in a family during incest."

After I shook off the sick feeling the movie gave me, I gathered my power and spoke up. It started at home, as they always say.

The uncle who'd grabbed me in my grandmother's kitchen had called, trying to see me, and left messages. I sent him this text in reply: "You're not going to see me anymore because you stuck your tongue in my mouth when I was 17. And Uncle Doug molested me at 14. What you both did was not okay. I forgave Uncle Doug before he died, and I forgive you, too. But I don't want to be around you right now."

When I told my mother later that I refused to be around my uncle anymore, she tried to make me feel guilty about it. "What about your so-called forgiveness?"

"Just because you forgive someone, that doesn't mean you have to see them—even if they're family. Forgiveness is about releasing anger from your own heart," I said. "And I do forgive, Mom."

CHAPTER 21

Forgiveness

A few days before Christmas 2012, I decided that I'd give the gift of forgiveness to another man who'd hurt me: Bruce.

I Googled his name, like I'd done before to try to find him. I knew he'd been sent to prison for holding that woman captive several years previously, and thought he might still be there. My plan was to go see him in person and tell him "I forgive you." I needed to let go of the painful burden of hate and fully get my life back, and perhaps he needed it, too. Not that he was my top priority, but I believed in good energy and karma after so many years of reading Wayne Dyer's books and getting my recent dose of divine love from John of God.

What I found shocked me: His obituary. And the date of his death was even more shocking—it was the day before I'd left for Brazil to see John of God in May.

My feelings were mixed. Along with being shocked, I was relieved and sad. There was a photo with his obituary, and I sat quietly for a moment and stared at it. He was wearing his Navy uniform and cap, with the American flag hanging on the wall behind him. The photo must have been taken right around the time he assaulted me because he looked the same, like a boy . . . a harmless, scared little boy.

On the one hand, I felt an overwhelming fear lift off of me, like I was truly safe and didn't have to look over my shoulder for the rest of my life, worried that he was following me and trying to finish the job on me. My father would have loved to have killed Bruce with his own hands. When I told him the next day that he'd died, Dad laughed—

he was the happiest man alive. "Good," he said. "The son of a bitch deserved to die."

I told him how I'd wanted to forgive Bruce, but Dad was having none of that. "I don't have to forgive him, Dana Leigh, and I don't."

I could understand where my father was coming from, but it also made me sad. I felt sad for Bruce's own parents, and I started crying for them. I couldn't be happy that this kid was dead because someone had now lost their child. I couldn't be happy about this death, even though I'd once dreamed of how I'd torture Bruce and leave him as good as dead.

I Googled his parents' names and got their phone number. I stared at it for half an hour before finally making the most difficult phone call of my life.

His mom answered the phone. I could barely speak.

"I-I knew your son. I'm s-s-sorry for your loss," I stuttered.

She thanked me, and wanted to know how I knew him. Her voice was warm and loving.

"I was in the Navy with him. I'm the one he threw off Sunset Cliffs in 1990."

She paused, then took a deep breath and whispered: "We never knew what happened that night. I don't understand. Why would he throw you off the cliff?"

"Well, ma'am, he raped me first. Then he choked me. And the best I can tell you is he thought I was dead and got scared and tried to cover his tracks, so he threw me off."

"Why didn't you press charges?"

"Because what happened was swept under the rug by the military, and I was forced to take my right to remain silent. That sort of thing is kept quiet: 'It doesn't happen in our military.' I was given the choice to take it to court and lose, or take my right to remain silent and be taken care of for the rest of my life."

"Taken care of?"

"Ma'am, I'm a quadriplegic. At the time they gave me the choice, I had only just begun breathing on my own."

"He raped you."

"Yes, ma'am."

She didn't even try to deny it; she knew I was telling the truth.

I had tried to be strong up to that point, but now we both began to cry. "What I really want you to know, and it's the reason that I'm calling, is that I forgave your son," I said through my tears. "And I'm sorry he died."

"He found God before he passed."

I told her I'd heard about that, but didn't mention the newspaper clipping I'd read years before about him holding a woman hostage and reading Bible verses to her. I asked her how Bruce had died, and she said it was during surgery.

"Is there anything I can do for you?" she asked. "What can I do for you to help?"

"Just forgive yourself, ma'am, because I know how parents blame themselves for what their children do. Again, I'm sorry you lost your son. No parent should lose their child. And know that I'm truly okay, and I live a good life."

PEOPLE ALWAYS SAY THERE IS A CORRELATION between forgiveness and healing, and I found there to be truth in that. Soon after I talked to Bruce's mother, I went to San Diego in January 2013 for a two-month intensive session with a new trainer. We did three hours of hard-core exercising five days a week, with a focus on gait training.

Six weeks later, I put my new skills to good use. I attended a two-day I Can Do It! conference in Denver in April, for which my new friend Wayne Dyer was the keynote speaker. For the occasion, I wore all purple to go with his/my purple hat and sat at the back of the room so I could be near the bathroom. On the first day, before he went onstage, he and I had a few moments together by my seat, and I showed him how much my walking had improved. I got up and walked for a few steps without a cane, without a walker, without braces—just me. I'd never seen a smile so big on Wayne's face.

During his keynote, he spoke about many things: love, forgiveness, manifesting, and the great teachers of this world. I'd listened to his books so many times that I felt like I'd absorbed his thoughts and words. Suddenly, though, everything began to sound more familiar than usual.

"There's someone in the audience . . . she was in the United States Navy . . . she got herself involved in an encounter one evening . . . she was raped and thrown off a cliff . . . she was put into a wheelchair . . . on the last cruise, I gave her the purple hat I was wearing. She said she'd give it back to me when she got out of that chair. I'd like you all to meet her, she's sitting at the back . . ."

Everyone stood up and started clapping and looking back at me, as Wayne began to sing "The Impossible Dream." What else could I do? I stood up and made my way toward him with my walker until I got to his arms, to the cheers of everyone in the room. Wayne gave me a big hug, and then urged me to "tell them what you just did." He was talking about my forgiving Bruce and his mother. I hadn't told him, but he'd heard the story through his assistant Maya. Through tears, I told the story to a ballroom full of people and thousands more on a live stream.

"Now she's walking, and she's one of my heroes," Wayne told the audience. Turning to me, he hugged me again and said, "I'm going to take my hat back when you run your first marathon. Deal?"

That day, one hero taught another about the difference a single person can make. After the night was over, many people approached me to talk, but one in particular stays in my mind: the woman who told me that she'd been raped at age 17, "and I was choked, thrown in a Dumpster, and left to die behind a 7-Eleven."

The woman's family, who were Jehovah's Witnesses, blamed her for the rape. She'd changed her first name because she felt such shame about what happened to her. Now she said, "I want to thank you, because although I haven't been paralyzed physically, I've been paralyzed emotionally for 20 years until today. Now I'm going to change my name back to my real birth name. You helped me."

My injury wasn't about me, I decided that day; it was about the story that millions of women have. I'm only one of so many who have suffered and have the strength to say, "You're a son of a bitch, but I forgive you. And you don't get to win. *I* win, because I forgive myself and I forgive you."

I SPENT THE NEXT YEAR TALKING TO MORE WOMEN, working on healing and forgiveness, and trying to figure out how I could help others. In January 2014, I reached a long-awaited pinnacle in my own healing. I went to the "Healing Power of Forgiveness" seminar in Maui, helmed by Wayne, who was presenting three wonderful speakers: Immaculée Ilibigaza, author of *Left to Tell;* Anita Moorjani, author of *Dying to Be Me;* and Scarlett Lewis, author of *Nurturing Healing Love.*

At the seminar, Immaculée spoke about forgiving the killers who'd murdered her family during the Rwandan genocide, and Scarlett spoke about forgiving the young man who'd murdered her little boy and dozens of others during the massacre at Sandy Hook Elementary School in Newtown, Connecticut. *They know not what they do,* both women realized, and I felt it was the same with the military—they as a collective did not know the damage they did to both women and men, to both victim and assailant, when they perpetuated the rape culture.

For me to fully heal, not only did I have to forgive Bruce, which I'd already done, I had to forgive the military, too. And I had to face, in detail, what had happened that night.

If Immaculée could stand to hear how her beloved brother's body had been chopped up with a machete in the street by people he called friends, and if Scarlett could bear to hold her son's little hand for so long at his wake that she felt it get warm again, then I could find the strength to face what had happened on the cliff that night. It was something I had deftly avoided for almost 24 years.

Wayne set up a session for me with his craniosacral therapist, Kate Mackinnon, to help unlock energy blocks in my body and raise my potential for more healing. I didn't really know what to expect, if anything at all—I'd had a few craniosacral sessions before, and they were nice and cuddly, with energy and happy thoughts flowing.

Kate came up to my hotel room, and we dimmed the lights. I lay in bed, as she assessed my body and what to do. She gently rested her hands on my body, above and below my diaphragm, and I felt the tension I was holding in that area suddenly begin to bubble up.

Slowly, the shoved-down memories and emotions I'd kept from myself for so long came to the surface. It was like that image I'd had in Ireland of the god Poseidon, rising up above my head and over-taking me.

I remembered being so cocky at the beginning of that night with Bruce, thinking that nothing could happen to me. And then being so shocked and full of disbelief when this skinny kid had overtaken me—*I'm so strong! Why can't I fight you off?*

I started crying. "You're safe now," Kate told me. "Remember that you already survived this, and I'm right here."

Even though her words and presence were reassuring, it still felt like it was all happening again, here and now. I began to relive each moment on the cliff, step by step, in horrific detail.

When Bruce started choking me, for instance, it felt like someone was standing on my chest. I cried deeper than I've ever cried in my life, asking *Why? Why?!*

"What's happening now?" Kate asked.

"He's choking me."

"Feel your body on this bed, Dana, and where my hands are. Feel how this energy is now able to move out of your body."

I started shaking and shivering so violently that my teeth chat-tered. "I'm cold," I said. "I'm looking up at the sky, and I can see the top of the cliff . . . *Just breathe, just breathe,* I'm telling myself. I'm so cold. But I'm fighting so hard to live."

"The shaking is your body releasing the energy that got locked up in it," Kate replied soothingly, as she softly placed her hands on my throat. "You are doing an amazing job being present to these intense sensations."

Then came a weird calming. I remembered hearing the sound of a helicopter, and I knew someone was coming to get me and I could let go and slip into a coma.

When it was all over—the entire session took nearly two hours— I was exhausted and light-headed and hungry. I had no idea how much trauma could be locked in the body and buried so deep.

"Be gentle with yourself tonight," Kate said, giving me a hug. "We did a lot, and you did good."

"Had I known it was going to be like that, I wouldn't have done it!" I told her. "But I'm glad I did." You have to wade through the muck and mud in your life to get to the meadow on the other side.

That night, I had the best sleep I'd had in months. When I woke up the next morning at 5:30, I felt like a heavy weight had been lifted. I took a shower and got dressed, put my crutches in my chair, and went outside. I was so excited, I didn't even want to stop and eat breakfast first. There was something important that I had to do.

A hundred feet away from the ocean, as the golden sunrise hit the mountainside ahead, I reached a specific spot that I'd scoped out the night before. I tied my shoes, grabbed my crutches, put my iPhone in my pocket, and set out to do what I intended from the moment I first arrived in Maui—walk through the sand all the way to the edge of the ocean, all alone. I wanted to know that I could have a walk on the beach on my own.

For a moment, the sound of the waves crashing onto the shore made my heart jump in fear. But I reminded myself of my new mantra from Kate: *You are safe, you are safe . . .*

I took my first step on the soft, shifting sand, and then a second. I looked up ahead of me and saw whales breaching and lunging in the ocean. Any fear I might have felt moments before washed away, and strength took over. I stepped again, and again. Strangely, no one asked if they could help me—something that would have normally happened several times by now. This was something I wanted to do completely on my own, so the universe was apparently in agreement. I took another step, and another.

I walked to the edge of the ocean and stopped about a foot from the water, and I took a deep breath of the morning air. About 20 feet away, two little sisters ran up and down the sand, laughing and giggling when they got their toes wet. They reminded me of Chrissy and myself as kids, and my heart filled with joy.

I looked out to the ocean, watched the whales and sunrise, and took another deep breath. *This is absolute freedom,* I thought.

I was hungry. I turned around to go back, and saw my footprints in the sand. They were unique: line, foot, line, foot. The line was my right foot dragging along.

When I turned around, I also saw a man standing by my chair, lingering. He'd been keeping an eye on me, making sure I was safe, but never said a word. He watched me until he felt I was going to be okay, and then with a half-smile and nod, he turned and left. I sent out a message to the stranger: *I'm going to be okay. I just walked on the beach for the first time in 23 years, totally by myself, and I wasn't afraid of falling down.*

I was absolutely going to be okay.

WHEN I GOT HOME, I WAS SO TIRED—but *good* tired—that I slept for most of two days.

On day three, I woke up and went to my computer to write this letter:

> Dear Bruce,
> If you were alive right now, this is what I would say to you.
> First, I want you to know that I forgive you for raping me and then trying to kill me by throwing me from a 75-foot cliff. I was in a coma for 18 hours. I had a severe head injury, a broken neck from cervical 1 to cervical 5. My lungs collapsed, and I had lacerations on my liver and spleen. I woke up terrified and knowing that I was paralyzed from the neck down. My family was told I'd be lucky to live through the night . . . and that if I did live, I'd be on a ventilator and be a vegetable the rest of my life.
> Maybe your intent was to kill me. But you only made me stronger.
> For years I wished I could put you in a wheelchair and make you a quadriplegic for life. I fantasized about how I'd hire people to beat you to a pulp and break your neck and give you the slight chance of living that you gave me.
> And then I went to see John of God, where I found the ability through a spiritual healing to forgive you. I went to Brazil the day after you died. I found that out when I Googled you; I was ready to find you and tell you that I forgive you and move on with my life.
> I saw your obit instead and I was shocked. I called your parents' home and talked to your mother. She had a warm, loving voice. I told her I was the one you threw off a cliff in 1990. She didn't understand, so I explained all the details. I told her I'd forgiven you, and that was why I was calling. And that she should absolve herself of any blame she might be feeling, because parents do that sometimes—blame themselves for their children's mistakes.

We cried together, your mother and me. Can you imagine that?

Bruce, you are no longer in the body that hurt women. You can no longer hurt me.

I am strong and walking.

And forgiving you was the most liberating thing I have ever done.

So now, I thank you for this journey of healing my mind, body, and soul.

You gave me the gift of forgiveness. God rest your soul.

I AM HEALED!

Love,

Engineman Dana Liesegang

I hit "save" on the file and closed my laptop.

It was a beautiful, crisp winter morning with Jack in Grand Junction—our home and happy place together—and I wanted to get out there and take him for a brisk walk to our favorite coffee shop. I put a leash on his collar next to his John of God necklace, packed a few doggy treats into the pocket of my chair, slung my crutches over my neck, and we took the back-door lift down to street level.

Jack and I, we had a lot of walking to do.

EPILOGUE

Onward and Upward

August 2015, Grand Junction, Colorado

I was at a dinner party with a bunch of friends not long ago when the subject of rape in the military came up.

"It doesn't happen," said one guest, a National Guardsman, who was sitting next to me. I'd met this gentleman for the first time that night, and he knew I'd been in the Navy but didn't know the reason why I was in a wheelchair.

His words and dismissive tone made the hairs on the back of my neck stand at attention, like Jack's do when he senses danger. I was about to rattle off a list of horrifying statistics and stories for this guy when I saw my hostess's worried face. So I quietly replied, "You and I, sir, should not have this conversation."

It was shocking to me that after so many tragic stories and so much information had surfaced in the news in recent years about sexual abuse in the military, there were still people—even those inside the military—who denied that it happens or refused to see it. Or they attempted to downplay it or make excuses somehow.

"Marines don't rape one of our own," one member of the Corps said to me a few years ago. "Sure, they'll rape a whore in another country. But not here, and not one of our people." As if being on a foreign land with a stranger makes it okay?

"Rape is not an occupational hazard," I told this Marine. Yet no matter how hard I tried to convince him of how inhumane and irrational his thinking was, he couldn't get it through his thick skull that it's never okay to rape: not if the victim is a prostitute or dressed "sexy," not if you or she are drunk at a party, and not if you are in the military where they make up their own rules . . . *never.*

The mind-set of both of these men—the ignorance, insensitivity, and fear or inability to see the truth—is why the cycle of violence is still in motion. I've talked to hundreds of women in the military about this, and to meet an enlisted woman who has *not* been sexually assaulted in some way is a rarity.

At the end of 2013, a Pentagon summary showed that reports of sexual assault in the military had increased sharply in the previous year: 3,553 sexual complaints were reported to the Department of Defense from October 2012 through June 2013—a nearly 50 percent increase over the same period a year earlier—and the numbers continued to rise after that.

Some thought these statistics meant that incidents of rape had suddenly increased, but I think the stats jumped because more women (and men) are coming forward, and this is good news. The rates of sexual assault were always high, but the military kept us silent; it's impossible for us to ever know the number of rapes in the past that went unreported. But I feel a new awareness brought on by the media, like the 2012 documentary *The Invisible War,* has made an impact. That film helped victims, myself included, feel more comfortable with speaking out. And the only way change is going to happen is if we all talk about it; numbers make change happen.

One change that needs to happen is for the United States Congress to take the power of justice out of the military ranks. We can't expect an entity like the military—where the crimes of war are a normal part of everyday life—to judge a crime like rape (and in my case, attempted murder as well) in a fair way. The nature of the job doesn't allow for a clear and impartial assessment of the crime or the punishment.

This is an issue for every person to worry about, not just those in the service. It's my view that the military is creating rapists who not only harm men and women during their tour of duty, but also after they leave and enter the civilian world. The young man who put me in a wheelchair continued a life of crime until the day he died.

Before these legal changes can come about, however, the victims must continue to speak out and band together. I hope that by my telling my story, more women and men will share their own experiences with someone they trust. It will help them shed the burden of shame, blame, and victimization, and that is the first step for the healing process to begin for everyone involved.

I'VE DONE AN IMMEASURABLE AMOUNT OF HEALING—spiritually, mentally, and physically—over the years, and I will continue to do so. October 2015 marks 25 years since that night on the cliff when my life changed forever. Today, I'm grateful that I'm able to walk. I'm grateful that I can sit by an ocean and not freak out. I'm grateful that I can sit in a café next to a group of young men and not panic.

Only once since my trip to Ireland over a dozen years ago did I experience a bout of PTSD as severe as I did then.

Last year, I planned to temporarily move from Grand Junction to San Diego to do more intensive gait training with a specialist. It didn't occur to me that going back to the city where I'd been hurt would have a negative effect on me now that I had stopped suppressing what had happened to me. But almost immediately after I arrived, the symptoms began.

First, I saw the sign for Sunset Cliffs. Then, as I set up my apartment two miles from Mission Beach—the area Bruce drove to get alcohol that night—I recognized that same cold, damp air from 25 years ago. In the end, I wasn't exactly sure what triggered it, but my anxiety grew until I was bursting into tears several times a day.

I called up my Grand Junction neighbors Bob Noble and Carolyn White, who have become like parents to me (if my addition is correct, that makes eight moms and dads now!). "I need to come home!" I cried. "I can't be here!"

Within a day or two, they arrived to pack me up and take me and Jack back to Grand Junction, where we belonged. *Home.* Healing is an ongoing process, and after all the moving around I've done in my life, I just want to be home.

Bob and Carolyn have been a godsend to me during the last four years we've been neighbors. They dogsat Jack when I had to travel and have swooped in when I had an emergency, like the time I broke my foot this year. They took me for x-rays and made sure I was eating and could get to the toilet and in the shower since I was back to square one again. Thank God for angels on this earth.

I DREAM BIG, AS YOU KNOW BY NOW, and a few months ago, one of my long-held dreams came true.

Ever since I stood up and skied at the Winter Sports Clinic, I hoped one day to be an instructor like the Ponderosa Boys and Bobby Palm. In 2012, after almost 20 years attending the Clinic, I decided this would be my last year as a participant. The Clinic and the people there had given me so much, but I knew it was time for a change. I wanted to give back to the new veterans coming in every year—so many had the frightened, baby face that I had when I first got there.

To symbolize my transition that year, I sang "The Star-Spangled Banner" at opening ceremonies. I rehearsed for months with a voice teacher, and when the day arrived, I had the option of sitting but chose to stand up. I held on to two chairs and stood at attention, singing into the microphone as several military honor guards posted the flags in the auditorium. I felt proud of our country and the people who risked their lives to fight for it.

Bobby Palm had been going to bat for me for years to convince organizers to let me volunteer as an instructor. "She's been teaching the instructors and inventing her own equipment for years!" he'd tell them. After a woman was put in charge, naturally, the door opened for me. In early 2015, I got the call: I'd been accepted to be an instructor for the following year!

I went to the Clinic in March to observe the other instructors, and found I already had a protégé. It never occurred to me that I could be a role model for anyone, but that year one person showed me that I could be, and already was.

"Jersey Jeanne" is a para with multiple sclerosis, and she'd seen me use the Slider a few years earlier. In 2014, she said to herself, *Dana's a quad—if she can do it, so can I!* Which she did, and beautifully. This year, she took her progress even higher and went from the Slider to using SideStix (forearm crutches), which is what I use today. And *then* my protégé one-upped me and used regular ski poles!

After her triumphant lap on the Nordic trail, she handed me a thank-you card that said:

Dana, you are my mentor and inspiration. You are my rockin' warrior goddess!

I had to laugh because I never thought of myself as anyone's mentor . . . and now that she'd one-upped me, I had serious work to do!

"Damn, Jersey Jeanne!" I told her. "Now I've got to learn to use regular poles because you raised the bar!"

It's great to be around others who dream big, too, and want to keep moving onward and upward. And I love the idea that something I did convinced someone else that their possibilities are limitless. A month after the Clinic, I went flying 2,000 feet high as a passenger in an ultralight plane. I felt so free soaring through the sky and defying gravity, with nothing around or under me but air. I thought, *This is what a bird must feel like . . . as if the sky's the limit.*

THIS YEAR, I ALSO SUFFERED THE PLUMMETING depths of agony that a human heart can feel. In August 2015, after 12½ years together, I lost my beloved Jack. He hadn't been well all year, and after x-rays showed he was bleeding internally, the vet said he could not help him.

Bob and Carolyn, my earth angels, came over to help me make the most difficult decision of my life—to take Jack out of his suffering. That afternoon, I hugged him for hours as we lay down in his favorite places: on the floor of my bedroom closet, and on a comfy patch of grass in the side yard.

Finally, I told him, "It's okay to go. I'll be okay, I promise. I love you." The vet gave him a shot, and we all cried—Bob, Carolyn, me, and even the vet.

The love I'd been searching for all my life in people had been given to me unreservedly by this big, yellow dog. He was my child, my best pal, my protector, my teacher, my helper, and my most loyal family member. After he took his last breath, I removed his collar with the John of God triangle and put it around my own neck.

And as I promised Jack, I will continue to climb onward and upward.

NOBODY KNOWS EXACTLY HOW to heal an injury like mine; in fact, most in the medical profession think it's impossible. It doesn't happen, doctors say. And yet, it did. So I've become a pioneer in spinal cord injury recovery, and I hope to bring other believers with me.

I know attitude has a lot to do with healing and that you have to believe your body can actually heal for it to do so. You also have to give your body the tools it needs, be they stem cells, prosthetics, exercise, nutrition, or meditation. There's no quick fix; it's ongoing work for a lifetime. But I won't allow the world to set limits on what I can do, and I don't think you should, either—whether you have a physical handicap or an illness, or even if you're emotionally crippled, because there are plenty of people out there who have that handicap as well.

I hold in mind what Confucius once said: "It does not matter how slowly you go as long as you do not stop."

God blessed me with a broken neck and a way to fall up instead of down.

If my speaking out prevents even one rape, then all of my struggles will have been worth it. In the meantime, I continue to work on leaving the chair behind. But I also enjoy every moment of life in front of me and what I'm able to do in the moment. Even if I don't leave this chair completely, I've reached my goal of walking.

I can walk half a mile by myself with crutches. With a little help, I walked up around the Colosseum and up the Spanish Steps in Rome. I walked up to Athena's temple in Greece. I walked around the Statue of Liberty in New York City and held my crutch up high, like her torch, in liberation and victory.

It's like what I told my father on the phone that day right after I joined up. I was excited about my present and my future, and the Navy slogan said it all:

I am tomorrow. I am the better day.

THANK-YOUS

To everyone at my new Hay House family—beginning with Louise Hay and Reid Tracy—thank you for all your incredible, loving support. Shannon Littrell, you have been an amazing cheerleader and editor; I can't thank you enough for helping me understand the writing process.

To Wayne Dyer and his incredible family—Serena, Skye, Saje, Tracy, Sands, and Marcelene—thank you for seeing more in me than I see in myself. I will never forget the day Serena said, "You have to write a book! Let me call my dad!"

Natasha, my dear co-author, you are a force to reckon with: "Hon, it's just a deadline, nothing to worry about. This isn't the military!" Eating chocolate and our fabulous soups as you so brilliantly helped craft my life from a 30-page manuscript to an amazing book was . . . transcendence.

Thank you to all six of my parents, and the siblings that go with them, for helping to form the person I am today. I learned so much from each and every one of you.

A special thank-you to my mom, Melodie; my brother, Gary; and my sister, Chrissy, for sticking by me no matter what. You never lost faith in me or left me; your loyalty is truly a blessing.

Thank you, Uncle Kent and Aunt Jeanne Morrison, for being the ones to always pick up the broken pieces and help me put them back together. I wouldn't have survived without your strong shoulders.

Thank you to all of my Liesegang and Morrison aunts, uncles, and cousins, for the fantastic support and memories throughout my life.

Thank you to my five grandparents—Grandma Blanche and Grandpa Carl, Grandma Helen, and Grandma and Grandpa Newell—for giving me the love that only a grandparent can give.

And to the Debbie Newell side of the family, thank you.

Thank you to all of my friends along the way:

Jim Eberhard, I don't know life without you in it, and I hope I never do!

Sally, Christopher, and Aunt Phyllis, you are my family.

Amy Sekeres, my dear pal from age 14 to now.

Gene Noreen, for making me smile.

Ronald Mendez, for welcoming me aboard the USS *McKee,* showing me the ropes, and becoming a lifelong friend.

Lena McHone, you stuck by me from ship to shore from the moment we met aboard ship to now.

Mary Callentine-Castillo, my friend from age 19 to present day. I love you and Nathan and my special little guys: Dayne, Lincoln, and Barrette.

Thank you to the Pulford family: Charlie, Michelle, Joey, Kourie, and Kerry.

Sean Gibbs, my fellow paralyzed veteran and friend of 17 years— thank you for saving my life, giving me shit when needed, and sticking by me on my quest to walk. You exemplify the courage and loyalty of a fine Marine.

Thank you to Lynette Riggs, Chili Perez, Patrick McDonald and family, Tricia LaBar, Jeana Perkins, Tim and Caroline Davis, and Peach . . . for so many unforgettable good times, and a few I'll never live down.

Thank you to Shayne and Aaron Schurman, and Terri and Bob Costeldia, for being great family for Jack when he needed a place to stay.

And a heartfelt thank-you to Bob Noble and Carolyn White for being Jack's grand-dog-parents. We would not have made it through these past four years without your love and support. You are there in my greatest times of need, and when I need nothing. And Carolyn, thank you for helping me with my first manuscript.

In San Diego, thank you to the brave souls of Life Flight and to the medical team at UCSD Medical Center for saving my life.

Thank you to Dr. Barry Goldstein and all of my nurses, physical therapists, occupational therapists, recreational therapists, mental-health staff, social workers, and doctors at the Seattle VA SCI unit, San Diego SCI Unit, and San Antonio SCI unit.

And to the wonderful little VA in Grand Junction, Colorado: You don't have an SCI unit, but you are like walking into Cheers, where everybody knows my name.

Thank you to my doctors: Dr. B, Dr. R, Dr. H, and Dr. G.

Thanks to all of the PVA officials, volunteers, and sponsors for the National Veterans Wheelchair Games; and to all of the ski instructors, staff, DAV, sponsors, and entertainers at the National Disabled Veterans Winter Sports Clinic.

A special thank-you to the Nordic team and the Ponderosa Boys at the WSC. Thank you, Bobby Palm, for always being ready and willing to support me in creating and adapting new equipment so I and others can continue to stand up and ski.

A special thank-you to Cathy and Joe Frank for taking Jack and me in at Crested Butte all winter long.

To all the men I have loved before: Rick B., Michael C., Jim M., Michael M., Dave B., Stefan K., Luis S-V. I became a stronger person because of all of you.

Thank you to Karen Auld, Karen McCrocklin, Kate Mackinnon, Anita and Danny Moorjani, Scarlett Lewis, Ibis Caba, Jorge Caba, and Nick Ortner for your support.

Thank you, Malcolm Ness and Dominic Briody—I couldn't have walked up the Spanish Steps and many other places without you.

Thank you to Tom Kay for risking your life to save mine on the Gunnison River. I literally would not be breathing without you.

A special thanks to Debbie Callentine, for being a great nurse and friend to every vet who crossed your path, and for bringing Mary into my life. May you rest in peace.

Thank you to all the trainers who pushed me: Mica, Zack, Ted, Eric, and Dannette.

Thank you, Nelly Garcia and family.

Thank you, Brad Barber, for the plane ride.

And thank you to my loyal and loving pets—Sweetie, TK, Pooka, Runaway, Jasper, Ichabod, Willie, and Gabe—for your unconditional love.

To Bud, Bob, Jack, and two others . . . thank you for helping me get my car unstuck from the mud.

Last but not least, to all the human angels with no name, just a loving helping hand, as I've driven hundreds of thousands of miles. You've pumped my gas, bought me random food, helped with the lift on my van, and many other things. Your help made my life much easier.

And a final thank-you to the love of my life, my little buddy, Jack (RIP).

Love,

Dana

ABOUT THE AUTHORS

Dana Liesegang is an expert in spinal cord injury recovery and a 2014 recipient of the Hero of Forgiveness Award given by the World-wide Forgiveness Alliance. When she's not traveling the world as a motivational speaker, she's taking university classes and hanging out with friends—and until recently, the love of her life, Jack (her yellow Lab who's now in heaven)—in a quaint little town in Colorado. She enjoys every minute of the life she has created in the now.

Please visit: www.danaliesegang.com

Natasha Stoynoff is a *New York Times* best-selling author. She lives in New York City, where she writes books and screenplays, interviews the occasional celebrity, and eats too much chocolate.

We hope you enjoyed this Hay House book. If you'd like to receive
our online catalog featuring additional information on Hay House books
and products, or if you'd like to find out more about the
Hay Foundation, please contact:

Hay House, Inc., P.O. Box 5100, Carlsbad, CA 92018-5100
(760) 431-7695 or (800) 654-5126
(760) 431-6948 (fax) or (800) 650-5115 (fax)
www.hayhouse.com® • www.hayfoundation.org

Published and distributed in Australia by: Hay House Australia Pty. Ltd.
18/36 Ralph St., Alexandria NSW 2015
Phone: 612-9669-4299 • *Fax:* 612-9669-4144 • www.hayhouse.com.au

Published and distributed in the United Kingdom by: Hay House UK, Ltd.
Astley House, 33 Notting Hill Gate, London W11 3JQ
Phone: 44-20-3675-2450 • *Fax:* 44-20-3675-2451 • www.hayhouse.co.uk

Published and distributed in the Republic of South Africa by: Hay House SA (Pty), Ltd.
P.O. Box 990, Witkoppen 2068
info@hayhouse.co.za • www.hayhouse.co.za

Published in India by: Hay House Publishers India
Muskaan Complex, Plot No. 3, B-2, Vasant Kunj, New Delhi 110 070
Phone: 91-11-4176-1620 • *Fax:* 91-11-4176-1630 • www.hayhouse.co.in

Distributed in Canada by: Raincoast Books
2440 Viking Way, Richmond, B.C. V6V 1N2
Phone: 1-800-663-5714 • *Fax:* 1-800-565-3770 • www.raincoast.com

Take Your Soul on a Vacation

Visit www.HealYourLife.com® to regroup, recharge,
and reconnect with your own magnificence.
Featuring blogs, mind-body-spirit news,
and life-changing wisdom from Louise Hay and friends.

Visit www.HealYourLife.com today!

Free e-newsletters from Hay House, the Ultimate Resource for Inspiration

Be the first to know about Hay House's dollar deals, free downloads, special offers, affirmation cards, giveaways, contests, and more!

Get exclusive excerpts from our latest releases and videos from *Hay House Present Moments*.

Enjoy uplifting personal stories, how-to articles, and healing advice, along with videos and empowering quotes, within *Heal Your Life*.

Have an inspirational story to tell and a passion for writing? Sharpen your writing skills with insider tips from *Your Writing Life*.

Sign Up Now!

Get inspired, educate yourself, get a complimentary gift, and share the wisdom!

http://www.hayhouse.com/newsletters.php

Visit www.hayhouse.com to sign up today!

HAY HOUSE

HAYHOUSE RADIO �))
radio for your soul

HealYourLife.com ♥